Acknowledgments

Special thanks to:
Gail Heller (Chancesspot.org / Honoringtheanimals.org) for her invaluable help facilitating the recruitment of a majority of the submitted stories used in this book, as well as for her ongoing promotional efforts; Liz Tufte (Folio Bookworks) for her artful design of the book's interior, wide-ranging marketing tips, and for not popping me in the snoot when Quark went kerflooey and threatened to drive us both insane; Molly McBeath and Rosemary Wallner for their superlative editing/proofreading services; Alicia Schwab for her stunning artwork and Amy Kirkpatrick (Kirkpatrick Design) for her beautiful design of the book's cover; Christopher Mihm (Asterisk * Software) for his fast and fabulous design of the Healy House Books website; Don Rinderknecht (LCRweb.net) for hosting that site and generally looking out for me in my technological ignorance; business consultants Michelle J. Bloom and Linda McDonald for their spot-on marketing advice; and all those around the world who opened their hearts and contributed their stories to this book.

Oh yeah, and most of all, my thanks to my husband, Anthony Kaczor — for keeping the faith.

Good Grief: Finding Peace After Pet Loss could never have happened without you all!

Introduction

When you lose a beloved pet, it's not melodramatic to say you may feel you've lost a major part of your heart, your family, your life. But what are you to do when those fellow humans around you fail to understand the enormity of that loss? It's often tough to handle those emotions when you primarily get responses that range from subtle indicators of others' impatience with your process—such as friends who mysteriously become too busy to take your calls or to visit you while you're in mourning—to direct-dismissal responses like, "Get over it already. It was just a stupid dog. You can get another one just like it at the pound right now."

Grieving the loss of a loved one, whether he or she is human or an animal, is arguably the most difficult task we must all inevitably endure. The pain of that loss is compounded by the withdrawal and/or rejection you may feel from those who value the human-animal bond substantially less than you do. It's no wonder that many of us believe we must either suffer in silence—saving our tears for our pillowcases—or deny the hurtful feelings altogether in order to appease those around us who can't, or won't, understand what we're going through.

Many of us would prefer to stuff away the painful emotions, perpetually distract ourselves from them, or deny them entirely and avoid "feeling" at all costs. This is especially true in our American culture, wherein we spend millions on pain-relieving medications, alcohol, drugs, shopping, gambling, sex, and various other addictive behaviors to achieve that same emotion-avoidance end.

There is, unfortunately, a high price to pay for such stall tactics, not the least of which is missing out on the chance to be fully human, to work through the pain, and get to a place of serenity, acceptance, and a greater understanding of the various stages of "being"—both corporeal and spiritual.

To paraphrase how my dear friend Lisa once tearfully put it after she'd lost her beloved greyhound, Mollie, "It's the pain and the joy and all the other emotions you're forced to feel when someone you love dies that make the experience of grieving so *rich*."

The more I thought about her unusual word choice, the more wholeheartedly I agreed with her. Allowing one's heart to open completely to ALL the myriad emotions tangled up in loss: sadness, anger, resentment, loneliness, fear, dread, relief, guilt, wonderment, pain, and so forth, really is at the crux of human experience.

And as Dr. Wayne W. Dyer quotes in his book, *The Power of Intention*, "We are not human beings having a spiritual experience; we are spiritual beings having a human experience." We owe it to ourselves to broaden and deepen that human experience to its most profound state. Ironically, one way we do that is through our interactions with other spiritual beings that are here on Earth having an animal experience.

I believe there is a divine purpose for our complex humanity, just as there is a divine purpose for our profound connection to animals in general and to our pets in particular. There is something truly unique about these relationships. This may be because of animals' guilelessness, their unconditionally loving natures, and their lack of judgmental or purposefully cruel behaviors—traits seldom applicable to human beings. When such love, adoration, devotion, and faithfulness are showered on us by our pets—with no price tag or strings attached—it allows them to burrow in to the deepest place in our human hearts, the innermost place wherein we actually acknowledge we are worthy of unconditional love and freely accept it, fears of rejection absent, all defenses down.

In short, animals often hold the keys to our emotional vaults, and giving ourselves permission to love them with abandon and subsequently fully grieve their passing can release pent-up emotion and facilitate the souls' healing on an unsurpassed level in even the toughest-to-reach person. Case in point, I have a friend, a doctor, who deals with life-and-death issues continually with a detachment borne of professional necessity. Yet when he talks of losing his cherished hunting companion, a golden retriever he had decades ago, this stoic man has been known to break down in tears.

My own ex-husband, who, in my opinion, mistakenly prided himself on being "a rock" and remaining dry-eyed when several friends and close family members succumbed to illness and died throughout the years, wept freely for the first time when our first-born four-legged child, Tuppence, a West Highland white terrier, died in 2003. Since then, he has credited her passing with opening his heart to all other beings. We both continue to thank and honor her for this accomplishment.

It takes a mighty powerful spiritual entity to effect such change. One might even go so far as to call it an angelic act. I'm reminded of an email I received from a caring friend after my second Westie, Ludwig, passed in 2005 (the original author is unknown to me, but it was supposedly a veterinarian), chronicling a four-year-old child's observations after his own dog dies as to why animals live such abbreviated lives compared to humans. In it, he said: "Everybody is born so that they can learn how to live a good life—like loving everybody and being nice, right? Well, animals already know how to do that, so they don't have to stay as long."

Sad for us, but true. Throughout our lives, numerous pets of various shapes, sizes, and species will touch us. (For instance, I have another friend who, plagued by animal-dander allergies, dearly misses Hermie, his hermit crab. And my brother Dave and his wife, Diana, just became proud grandparents of a baby Russian tortoise.) With rare exception, our life expectancy exceeds theirs considerably, so we know we likely will experience the loss of at least some, perhaps many, of these special friends. We also can know, however, the lessons they teach us, as well as the bonds we share with them, continue to influence us long past their departure to the next realm of existence: the Spirit World.

This book is intended to share stories of the miraculous ways in which that bond remains intact beyond death and the evidence we all can see of it when we open our minds and hearts to our pets' (and even our humans') continued communications of love. Furthermore, it will offer ways by which to honor these much-beloved animal Spirit Guides of ours upon their passing, namely, through the suggestion of many different methods of memorializing your companion's life.

In loving memory of _____.
Mentally insert your own pets' names here.

Semantic Disclaimer

Throughout this book, the word "pet" has been used interchangeably with the term "companion animal." While more expedient to type than the latter and less cutesy than "four-legged child" (however apropos the descriptor may in fact be in many instances), I acknowledge the word "pet" carries with it a loaded connotation for many people. For some, "pet" implies that animals are somehow lesser beings than we humans, or that someone can be said to "own" another sentient creature.

I most certainly would never denigrate the status or worth of any animal with whom we share our homes—or even the Earth for that matter. But logistically speaking, it can at times become cumbersome to change language so as to make it inoffensive to everyone (an impossibility, too, I would assert).

Instead, I beg the pardon of those who wince when I occasionally use "pet" to describe the mammals, reptiles, birds, fish, amphibians, etc. that we take into our homes and/or hearts. I use it in the sense of several of its dictionary definitions: 1) an animal kept as a companion; 2) an object of the affections; and 3) one that is particularly cherished or indulged. Nevertheless, even with this in mind, I agree that "pet" is too narrow a word, in many ways, to describe the human-animal bond in its many forms and facets.

Dedication

To my precious Mortimer, and all my other animal family
members, be they furry, feathered, or finned—from my
past, my present, and my future—who bless my life and
will forever inhabit my heart.

Contents

Part One:
The All-Important Grieving Process

I'd like you to make a list for me. Number down the left-hand side of a piece of paper and write down the names of every human being you've spent nearly twenty-four hours a day with for, say, a dozen years on end. Now, list all the humans you know whose focus in life is seeking you out, wanting to be with you, awaiting your return, never being too busy for you, etc. Tack on the names of those people that never fail to comfort you when you're upset, who make you smile or laugh on a regular basis even from just watching them sleep. Name the humans you continually want to stroke, touch, hold, and massage (in a completely nonsexual way). Make note of all the humans who have never lied to you, could never lie to you. Last, add to that list all the humans who've seen you at your absolute worst and still look adoringly at you.

Pretty short list, huh?

Now, apply those same criteria and list the companion animals you've had throughout your life that fit some or all of them. I would imagine that list has grown considerably.

Is it any wonder when one of these precious creatures dies it devastates us more than almost any other kind of loss?

> "The frequency and magnitude of such nurturing and personal interactions [we have with our companion animals] virtually guarantees that a noticeable psychological and physiological void will appear when we lose our pets.... Only those who have experienced the death of a young child can begin to comprehend what some owners feel when their pet dies."
>
> —Myrna Milani, D.V.M., *Preparing for the Loss of Your Pet*

"The fact that the loss of a pet caused me more anguish than the deaths of certain elderly family members and acquaintances created some feelings of guilt and trauma, and I think that may be more typical than many people would admit."

–Moira Anderson, *Coping with Sorrow on the Loss of Your Pet*

One of the toughest parts of the grieving process is the sense that each of us is alone in how we feel. While it is true that every individual's grief is uniquely his or her own, the belief that there is a certain universality about the roller-coaster ride we call bereavement is necessary for us to successfully process these emotions.

"The problem is that our culture is extremely intolerant of grief," writes Californian animal behaviorist C. Miriam Yarden, as quoted in Moira Anderson's book *Coping with Sorrow on the Loss of Your Pet.* "From childhood, we are taught that crying is a show of weakness, and in the case of boys and men, this attitude is even more rigid.... Most often it is such [emotion-avoiding pet] owners who espouse the attitude of hard determination to never get another pet because 'I can't go through this again.' Of course, they can't go through this 'again' considering that they haven't gone through this in the first place! It is also they who suffer the most."

Four emotions seem to predominate with the loss of a companion animal: anger, guilt, denial, and depression. If you find yourself stuck in any one of those modes, it can become a tremendous obstacle to being able to move on, to heal your heart, and to risk loving again. It is vitally important that you allow yourself to feel all of the dark emotions that accompany grief, just as you experienced all the joyful ones elicited by your shared life with your pet. Light + darkness, bliss + sorrow, love + hate, etc. — each pairing of apparent opposites is part of the balance the Universe brings us all, and no emotion along that continuum of feeling can be ignored forever.

"For many valid reasons, the mourning for a pet can be far more intense than for a human. … [They are our] best friends, lovers, surrogate children, as well as our alter egos. … Western tradition and religion have avoided the subject of pet death, leaving the full responsibility and burden solely up to the confused, lonely, and distraught mourner of a beloved animal."

—Wallace Sife, Ph.D.,
The Loss of a Pet—A Guide to Coping with the Grieving Process When a Pet Dies

Since we are all spiritual beings on Earth to learn what it means to be fully human, the faster and farther we flee from those emotions we find most uncomfortable or terrifying to experience, the sooner another opportunity will surely be brought into our lives to give us another chance to learn the lesson those same feelings have to teach us. Wouldn't it be easier to try and accept what we need to learn the first time out rather than continually have to be given make-up tests? Letting all genuine feelings run their course through you will help you learn your soul's necessary lessons without undue suffering born of endless repetition of that particular "spiritual lesson." In life, as the saying goes, "pain is inevitable, but suffering (i.e., remaining stuck in a negative place) is a choice," and one usually born of fear.

As professional animal communicator Georgina Cyr so eloquently expresses it in a letter she wrote me regarding this book: "Look upon the pain as a gift and a privilege to have the experience of…. The saying 'Nothing worthwhile is ever easy' comes to mind…. I feel the pain gives us power, it touches our soul, and it gives us passion even though we feel torn, spent, vulnerable, crushed, and exposed. Pain is a gift that we find hard to recognize as such. It is like a wound—torn open and bleeding, but when it heals, with scar tissue, it is thicker, tougher, and stronger…. Our finding ourselves is part of the process, and pain starts the process."

It likely will take some time before you're able to say "thank you" to the powers that be for the lessons your grief brings. Make that the goal, but be gentle and patient with yourself as you take baby steps toward it. In the meantime, however, as you open yourself to letting the pain wash through you, be sure to nurture yourself during that process. Take a day or more off from work to cry, scream, swear, pound out your anguish into a pillow, etc. Far from childish, this gives you a necessary release.

> Pets are like our alter egos, they "represent the innocence and grace we feel but cannot express to other human beings. Without a pet, this self-discovery may never be made.... [We often feel] the best part of ourself died with our pet, and we weep for that as well."
>
> —Wallace Sife, Ph.D.,
> *The Loss of a Pet—A Guide to Coping with the Grieving Process When a Pet Dies*

The Price of Pain Avoidance

Repressing, ignoring, or denying your emotions is downright dangerous, as it will undoubtedly cause them to churn inside until they find another outlet—often when you're least prepared for it. Many a longstanding relationship has been irrevocably damaged because of these bottled-up emotions leaking out toward undeserving targets. Statistically speaking, many divorces happen within a few years of the death of one of the spouse's parents, most likely stemming from these intense, buried-then-misdirected emotions. (I know my heretofore mostly quite happy fifteen-year marriage fell into shambles not long after my mother's death from lung cancer.)

In my research, I read of a woman whose husband died of a

lengthy illness. Then she accidentally treated her dog with too much aspirin for its arthritis and it died from the toxicity. She was far more anguished over the death of her dog than that of her husband. Her marriage had long been in a rocky state, and therefore her bond was stronger and more steadfast with her dog. In fact, it was the only stable relationship she'd had in her life, and losing that relationship tore a hole in her heart that led to a flood of pent-up emotions. When someone is totally derailed by the loss of a companion animal, it's good to look at the pet's role in the context of that person's life. Its passing is not an isolated event, and the person's reaction is sure to be colored by all else that's going on in his or her life at the time.

Holding inside bitterness and hurt for years can and does take a toll on your physical health, too. Louise L. Hay, noted author of *You Can Heal Your Life*, attributes many diseases, such as cancer, to repressed emotions like anger and fear. Venting these emotions in the moment can keep you more than just emotionally healthy. Of course, if you know you lack the skills to communicate these heavier emotions in a healthy, nondestructive manner—for instance, if every time you feel angry, the fine China in your cupboard quakes in fear of your smashing it against a wall—speaking to a counselor or joining an anger-management group may help you gain the skills you need.

Moira Anderson explains that denial, another popular pain-avoidance technique, robs you of essential time to prepare for the inevitable loss and may prove physically harmful to your pet, as you may postpone a visit to the vet's office in your refusal to acknowledge the frightening possibility that he or she might be gravely ill. You might just create a self-fulfilling prophecy by your inaction, having your pet suffer unduly or die, leaving you to do battle with overwhelming feelings of guilt afterward. That's quite the price to pay because facing reality might be scary. Heck, facing reality about a loved one's health crisis is almost always scary, but if we love our companion animals we "person up" and do it anyhow.

The most vital step in coping with all stages of a pet's demise is to acknowledge all these emotions and let yourself feel them. "To deny and/or repress that sense of loss would be to devalue the love and affection that the pet brought into your life," said Pat H. of Pennsylvania.

Knowing What to Expect Can Help

One key to successfully navigating the treacherous waters of acute grief is to set up realistic expectations beforehand. If you're blessed with time to prepare for the loss of your companion animal or any other loved one, so much the better. But even if the loss was sudden and you're in the throes of grief now, you can use the technique described near the end of this section to help you through one situation, one obstacle, one day at a time, so your emotions don't have to continuously run your life.

The unfortunate fact is you have to expect to spend time processing each of the well-documented stages of grief: shock, denial, anger, loneliness, self-pity, guilt, and regret. There's no getting around them by sheer force of will, and avoidance has its price, as I have already discussed.

Two of the grieving powerhouses are guilt and anger. We may fixate on any one mistake we've made and feel guilty because, for instance, we failed to seek medical attention sooner for our pet because we hadn't noticed that something was amiss in time; we let our companion animal slip outside unattended to thus encounter a speeding vehicle; we forgot to give him or her a dose of medication; we didn't have the money to spend on the operation that might have saved him or her, etc. It's far too easy to become mired in "If only…" syndrome, focusing on our failings rather than the reality of the situation. In short, we take on responsibility for everything having to do with our pet, even those things entirely out of our control.

SUBMITTED STORY

Basil

by Caroline Garrod of the U.K.

I am beside myself with guilt and sadness about my favourite cat who we found dead yesterday. I am utterly inconsolable.

We moved abroad five months ago (for a fresh start, as went bankrupt after a house renovation). We have six cats and love them so much we paid all our last savings for them to come with us (£6,000).

Anyway, we had a boy cat called Basil—fluffy and affectionate but quite timid. He had had cystitis ever since we had known him and despite regular meds/jabs from vets, it always reoccurred. The vets say it is common in boy cats and is often stress induced.

Over the last month, he started spraying in the house and also on us, which wasn't like him and we sensed he was unsettled. He had also been acting kind of weird, and when we would go downstairs, he would scoot out of the cat flap.

Nine days ago, I caught him weeing on the floor and shooed him out through the cat flap—and we never saw him alive again. I spent days searching, putting posters through doors, notifying the police, everything. Then yesterday I was downstairs cleaning the basement and I smelt a horrid smell like a dead mouse. My husband found Basil dead, well hidden behind some boxes. His jaw was all smashed in. There was also wee on the floor.

I need to know:

1) Could I have done that to him when I shooed him through the plastic cat flap? The vet said (although he did not see Basil) that an injury like that was probably done by a car. (Note: I'm not a cruel person; we adore our animals.)

2) Where had he been for nine days? Was he at home all the time?

3) Why and how did he die? Had he run away, gotten lost, decided to come home, and gotten hit en route?

I just can't handle it. His eyes were half open, and he looked so sad. I did not have time to say goodbye properly as he was decomposing and my husband, Mark, needed to bury him.

I have two small children and just cannot function.

~~ ~~ ~~

Our guilt may also stem from the relief we may feel as part of the misery mix of emotions. Being glad that our loved one is no longer suffering or that our undeniable burden of dealing with their illness—i.e., helplessly watching its progress, stressing over the financial strain, and caring for the pet throughout—can finally be set down, is perfectly normal and doesn't make you a heartless fiend. Relief is a positive reaction, showing that you are aware on some level that things are now better for your companion animal and for you.

We may also be angry with someone else, such as our vet for failing to save our beloved one from his or her disease or injury, the driver of that vehicle that hit him or her, the person who left out that antifreeze that poisoned our pet, etc. When that anger is turned inward, it becomes self-blame, which leads us back to its kissing cousin, guilt. And thus a psyche-damaging vicious circle is born. Like a dog chasing its tail until it makes itself dizzy, anger, guilt, and self-blame chase one another until you can't see straight.

We may also indulge in blaming others—even God or the pet him-/herself—for what happened. But blaming someone else merely distracts us temporarily from these other more painful emotions. It won't change the situation one iota and surreptitiously builds a fortress around the feelings you need to release in order to heal. When you make the effort to forgive another person or institution, you tear down that fortress. Forgiveness, ironically, is not something you do for the other person; it's something you do for yourself to facilitate your broken heart's recovery.

The so-called guilty party need never even know you forgive him or her for the act of forgiving to do you boundless good. And forgiving in no way excuses purposefully bad behavior. All it does is proclaim that you refuse to carry the burden of hate, rage, resentment, etc. toward him or her any longer.

That is not to say you are not justified in holding someone accountable for grossly negligent or intentionally cruel actions toward your animal companion. By all means, press charges against that person who shot your dog, or sue the pharmaceutical company whose new drug turned out to be toxic, but realize that no amount of money you are awarded in court can take the place of your pet. This is particularly true because, in the eyes of the court, pets are mere pieces of property, and you cannot be awarded damages for (your very real) pain and suffering over the loss of your pet any more than if you'd had your cell phone stolen.

Blame that is assigned to someone who was powerless to prevent a random accident or to change the course of disease that could not be altered is really a wasted emotion. In the end, ascribing such blame only postpones our facing our pain and experiencing the subsequent healing that immediately follows.

Regarding the guilt over not noticing a pet's illness, please remind yourself that all animals have hundreds of thousands of years of ingrained, instinctive "masking" behavior, wherein they had to become proficient at keeping their infirmities a secret from others in their pack, pride, flock, or other group, or else risk being ostracized or killed by the other members for being perceived as weak and thus endangering the survival of the entire group. In other words, you may not have noticed something was wrong because your companion animal didn't let you see it until the disease was well advanced. It would be lovely if our pets could reason with themselves like this: "If I tell my human my tummy hurts now, she'll get me medicine and I'll feel better, so I'd better speak up fast." But, sadly, most times that's just not how it works, no matter how we may try to personify them. We can only do our very best to assess his or her quality of life by close observation of our pet's behaviors and actions.

Through the course of their lifetimes, our companion animals surely have forgiven us a multitude of mistakes. And they receive no joy from watching us continue to feel we deserve to suffer after they've moved on to the Other Side. Beyond just forgiving us, they will surely be thankful to us if we put their needs ahead of ours and release them from pain and suffering when there is no possibility of their ever regaining health.

"Primitive or underdeveloped civilizations accept death much more easily and rationally than we do. It's not that they're less sensitive or intelligent. They have not yet been culturally deceived into believing that nature can be controlled so completely."… (Due to veterinary technology and medical advances,) "we're conditioned to feel, illogically, that we've gained such mastery and control over life that death is a mistake or accident and can be constrained.…We need to develop an awareness that we are all part of Nature and its cycles."

—Wallace Sife, Ph.D.,
The Loss of a Pet—A Guide to Coping with the Grieving Process When a Pet Dies

SUBMITTED STORY

The Story of Sam

by Dave Spagenski, San Diego, California

When I first met my "Princess" Diana, my wife now of twenty-five-plus years, she had a darling sheltie named Sam, and after awhile he was able to accept sharing her attentions. (He was very protective, but loving.) He got to trust me enough to ride with me on the gas tank of my motorcycle even though he was irritated by the loud noise of the engine. Many loving years later, a neighborhood dog, a large shepherd/husky, jumped the fence to her yard, and Sam did his utmost to defend our yard from other pets. He, sadly, was so overpowered that we rushed him to the animal hospital, and two hours later, he died from his injuries. The stress was just too much.

We were able to track the other dog's residence and were forced to take them to court when they refused to take responsibility for any of the damages. Sad ending, the court said they weren't responsible because we didn't have solid proof, which only could have been gotten if we'd captured and restrained their dog till the police came. Fat chance, and we knew it wouldn't bring him back, but even the dog catcher (animal control) said they'd had three other reports and complaints on that same dog in the past, and it was even picked up twice by them for running loose. Sad but true. The moral: Be a responsible pet owner.

Sam

In domesticating animals, we upped the ante on how responsible we must be for their lives. They forfeit being able to fend for themselves in the wild to give us love and loyalty, and in exchange, we provide them with love, food, shelter, medical care, and so on. The sad truth is, however, we also often have to intervene and provide them, when it is their time, with the most humane death possible. Our pets can't commit suicide to spare themselves pain or go to the vet on their own to be euthanized. Nor can they create explicit health directives or do-not-resuscitate orders.

The burning question, of course, always is, "When is it time?" The answer is, "When your companion animal can no longer live with dignity and without pain." It's important to weigh the financial and emotional costs to us, as well as the psychological and physical costs to our pet when choosing palliation, or medical/surgical intervention meant to prolong the animal's life in terminal cases.

"It takes the greatest love, devotion, and courage to end a suffering life," writes Eleanor L. Harris in *Pet Loss: A Spiritual Guide*. She calls it "wrongful euthanasia" only when "some cold-hearted individuals view euthanasia as a quick way to dispose of a pet they no longer want."

> "Many vets rank euthanasia as the most difficult task they perform because of its intense emotional demands."
> —Myrna Milani, D.V.M.,
> *Preparing for the Loss of Your Pet*

The Euthanasia Process—
as Described by Veterinarians and as I Have Experienced It with My Companion Animals

Euthanasia is a Greek word, literally meaning "good death." The term "putting to sleep" is an apt descriptor of the process. By design, it is meant to be as quick and peaceful as possible for both you and your pet. First, the animal is sedated so that he or she is relaxed and comfortable if not asleep in seconds. Then a fast-acting sedative is administered via a catheter in his or her leg. In all but the rarest instances, this sedative is strong enough to stop the heart quite quickly. In some instances, you may witness a delayed muscle reflex, the pet's eyes may not fully close, he or she may vocalize (howl, whimper, sigh, etc.) or gasp, or the animal may release his or her bowels or bladder. (None of these has happened with the three dogs at whose passings I've been present, so I cannot personally attest to how common it is. I am thankful to report that my three Westies each appeared to have simply gone to sleep.)

What is definitely true is that holding your pet in your arms, pouring out words of love and farewell, crying, and/or praying for his or her peaceful release is a comfort to your pet and, ultimately, a comfort to you—but only if you're up to it. If you're liable to become hysterical, your pet will surely sense your terror and become anxious him- or herself (and that fear will be his or her final memory).

In that case, the next best thing would be to send in a surrogate, another family member or friend who knew your pet well and cared for him or her. The last option, which is still not cruel in any way, is leaving the animal in the arms of a compassionate veterinarian or technician. (I confess I wasn't courageous enough to be there for the putting to sleep of many of my pets in my youth, but I now really wish I'd been with them at their last moments because the knowledge that I was with them right up until the loving spirits on the Other Side came to carry over their souls meant as much to me as it did to my four-legged family members.)

SUBMITTED STORY

Korppu

by Karin Cooper, Hancock, Michigan

I moved away from Minneapolis (and my family) in 1990, and immediately sought a puppy to be a companion. Within two months I had Korppu (a Finnish word for "cinnamon toast"). She was my buddy. She made me laugh, she loved to socialize with my friends, and, if I was sad, she sat by my side. Everyone loved Korppu—from my young nieces and nephews to my ninety-year-old grandma.

A year after we were married, and two years after I picked up Korppu, we got another puppy to be a companion to her. She was a Lab mix named Kenai, after the city in Alaska where my husband was working during the summer. Our relationships evolved to the point that Korppu was "my" dog and Kenai was "Doug's" dog—not unlike the way parents have an implied responsibility for one child over another through their shared experiences. Kenai went to work every day with Doug, as most of his work involved riding around in a truck, inspecting construction sites, and doing fieldwork.

We lost both dogs to cancer-like growths, and we cared for each of them in their last days until it was clearly time to have them euthanized. Korppu's end was especially amazing to me because she had an uncanny way of telling me that it was her time: She refused to come into the house for dinner, which was enough to tell me she was ready to go. Korppu willingly climbed into the truck when we took her to the vet for the last time. She clearly knew what was going to happen as she laid her head on Doug's lap while he drove away from home.

Korppu, Karin's infant niece Lauren, & Karin's sister Laura, circa 1996

Being present also eliminates any uncertainty you may have that your pet did, indeed, pass away. For some people, not seeing means not believing their pet is dead, and that's a whole different level of anguish to bear. If you were not able to be present when the death occurred—for instance, if it happened during surgery—you may wish to be allowed to visit the body to say your goodbyes afterward. Each of these scenarios is a deeply personal choice you must make.

This doesn't mean we put them down at the first sign of symptoms, of course, because every creature experiences brief bouts of illness that can be cured or from which they simply recover on their own. But when all reasonable measures to restore health have been taken and the things you know your pet most enjoyed can no longer be experienced, such as playing, taking walks, eating, sleeping comfortably, etc., it is time to let him or her go. It takes a keen eye and open heart to pick up on these signs in a pet that has mastered "masking" his or her pain.

Some animals, when sensing their demise is imminent, will go off on their own to allow the natural process to occur. As human beings, it is our own fear of death that we project onto them. Unless the companion animal feels he or she must protect us from experiencing that dread, it is far more likely that he or she would accept death as a normal transition, like walking from one room of your house into another. But because of that sense of responsibility for our feelings

---

Veterinarian Myrna Milani said she felt a "poof" when a pup she was treating died. "It was as if someone or something had blown out a candle, a rush of air that drew a vacuum and instantly took the pup's breath as well as some of my own with it." She said she thought she'd imagined it, "When my technician, who still stood with her back to the pup and me, suddenly cried, 'What was that? Did you feel it?'"

— Myrna Milani, D.V.M., *Preparing for the Loss of Your Pet*

that so many loyal pets appear to have toward their humans, often-times, they need to be given our permission/blessing to let go and make their transition.

Oh, and a word of advice—If you plan to euthanize your pet, if at all possible, don't schedule it on or near a holiday or other special date. Otherwise, the sorrow you feel will always be dredged up when that occasion rolls around.

That being said, prolonging a pet's suffering is selfish, pure and simple. The message you convey to your companion animal is, "I'm too afraid of how much it will hurt me to be without you, so you have to continue to hang on to life, no matter how painful it is for you until I'm ready to let you go." And they love us so much they'll do just that.

> "When she lays her head on my shoulder, I just can't bring myself to let her go. You know what I mean. Sometimes we just hold on too tight to a spirit that needs to be set free, but I'm gonna make her die of old age just like me."
>
> — Our friend Carol Johnson,
> talking facetiously about her cat, Gabby

Make Like a Boy Scout—'Be Prepared'

For Your Pet: "Nothing dissipates fear like knowledge," writes veterinarian Myrna Milani in *Preparing for the Loss of Your Pet*. Because of this she recommends, and I would agree, that you put your pet's Advance Health Directive in writing because it will clarify your thinking, sparing you from making life-and-death decisions in the emotionally charged moment, and will help others to carry out your wishes if your pet is being cared for by someone else when the situation arises. The following has been adapted from her book. Remember, these are just guidelines for you to follow. Think through and record your answers to each prompt. You may change and/or rewrite your responses at any time.

Companion Animal's Advance Health Directive

1) What do you believe your companion animal values most about his or her life? (Examples: food/treats, walks/play time, your presence, etc.)

2) How do you personally feel about death and dying? If you are quite fearful, remember your pet will undoubtedly pick up on that feeling and start to share or mirror it. It may do you both a lot of good to visualize the very worst-case scenario you can imagine having to face with your pet, let the fear well up and dissipate, and come to a place closer to being calm and assured than panicked and hysterical as you imagine handling the situation. (For example: Imagine you witness your pet hit by a car, see yourself administering first aid and transporting him or her to the animal hospital, envision his or her passing on the operating table, then visualize your pet's cremation or burial as bringing him or her peace and freedom from pain.)

3) Do you believe you should do everything within your (or your veterinarian's) power to preserve your pet's life as long as possible?

4) If you don't believe in prolonging your pet's life as long as possible, what physical, behavioral, or other conditions would cause you either not to initiate or to terminate treatment? (Examples might be: When your pet is experiencing pain that is not eased by medication; when your pet becomes disoriented and unaware of his or her surroundings; when your pet can no longer control his or her bladder or bowels; when he or she can no longer stand or walk; or when your pet's behavior changes profoundly and he or she becomes a danger to you or others.)

5) What conditions might cause you to at least temporarily treat the conditions in #4? (Examples here might be if surgery or another procedure/treatment were likely to alleviate the situation—like repair a slipped disk in his or her spine; if a prosthetic device of some kind could restore mobility—such as a wheelchair apparatus that can take the place of your pet's hind legs; if diapers could catch any messes and your pet was otherwise happy, etc.)

6) How much pain and risk would you be willing to put yourself, your pet, and others through if recovery seemed likely?

7) What if the chance of your pet's recovery were poor?

8) Would your pet's age affect your choice to treat or not treat it?

9) Would any religious or personal views affect your treatment of your pet if it developed serious problems? (For example, if you'd lost other family members to cancer and had witnessed the toll chemotherapy had taken on them balanced against what results they'd had, you might opt for or against such treatment accordingly.)

10) Will financial considerations affect if and how you treat your pet? (Would you look into opening a CareCredit account or work out a payment plan with your vet?)

For You: While preparing to face an impending loss, or even if you are currently dealing with the grieving process, considering the following scenarios ahead of time can give you a small measure of control over an otherwise overwhelming situation.

1) "To whom can I confidently turn for understanding and support when _____ passes away?" (If you believe the answer is truly no one, find the number of a pet loss hotline or pet loss/grief support group and post it near your phone. See the Resources section.)

2) "How might I handle this issue when I'm in unavoidable situations, such as dealing with customers, interacting with coworkers, picking up the kids from soccer practice, running into neighbors at the grocery store, etc.?"

3) "What might I be feeling after such a loss?"

4) "Have I ever had to handle such strong feelings before?" and if so, "What coping mechanisms worked for me then? Which failed?"

5) "Where will I allow myself to safely express my strongest feelings?"

6) "Am I aware of any person(s), situations, or settings it would be wise for me to avoid for a while?"

7) "How can I reasonably alter my routine so as to minimize the impact of constant reminders of the loss, at least at first?" (For instance, if you always walked your dog to a certain park, you might now choose to walk somewhere new, say, around a lake in a neighboring town, to avoid the continual reminders until you've reached the point that remembering the happy times again makes you happy.)

8) "How might I tell people to keep their callous, unfeeling comments to themselves without, say, getting fired or winding up kicked out of the condo association, etc.?" (Rehearsing a direct, honest, nonprofane response can help you respond with a cooler head if you find yourself faced with this situation in real life.)

9) "Is there anywhere I can go for a day or two to be alone with my thoughts, a place with which I resonate spiritually?" (Do this only if you are confident you are at no risk of doing yourself harm from overwhelming despondency.)

10) "Is there anyone I can ask to check in with me occasionally during the most acute phases of my grief or help me out with some day-to-day tasks I won't feel up to handling?"

Regarding this last one, we've all probably said it to someone who has experienced a traumatic event: "If there's ever anything I can do for you..." Believe me, people often appreciate being given a concrete, doable assignment that allows them to actually help. I have a friend, Mara, who lost both her parents and a dear aunt in a tragic car accident, and I was grateful to her for asking me to help her by cleaning her house before other relatives would arrive for the memorial proceedings. Another close friend, Michelle, had to have a preemptive double mastectomy, and she was able to ask me to make a couple of casseroles that she and her young child could eat while she recuperated. It eased their minds and lightened their burdens just a smidgen, and I felt much less helpless.

Addressing these issues beforehand helped preserve my sanity when my mother was terminally ill. (Bear with me, as this applies equally to facing a companion animal's imminent demise.) I went into grief counseling for several months before her passing to avoid succumbing to the crippling depression that runs in my family. As fate would have it, I had my last session with the counselor the day after my mom's funeral because it was the counselor's last day at that clinic, too. Fortunately, our work together had prepared me to move on at that point, much stronger than I would have been without that pressure-release valve throughout the process.

Since I'd sought out the support of a professional, I felt relief that I wasn't unduly burdening friends or family—who had their own grief issues to attend to. I felt a small sense of strength amidst a sea of helplessness from seeking to face head-on my emotions throughout the joint processes of my mother's death and my own bereavement. I felt less like I would be judged for telling the counselor of my feelings of anger (at the lung cancer itself, cigarette companies, my mom for ever having smoked, my own and my family's failings as caregivers, etc.) than if I confessed all that to my siblings. I felt no guilt for dominating the sessions because I was paying her—well, the insurance company was anyway—and she had to let me talk and talk and talk. That preemptive venting, though never intended to replace the tears I shed after Mom passed, at least let me feel that my emotions were less conflicted and more expressions of purely loving sorrow, once Mom had crossed over.

You don't necessarily have to pay a counselor for this kind of preventive maintenance for your heart. There are, at no cost, pet loss support groups, grief groups and/or websites, twelve-step-based Emotions Anonymous groups (*www.emotionsanonymous.org)*, and meetings with your clergy person, as well as free counseling clinics where help is available. The way I view these short-term aids is this: Picture yourself swimming the English Channel alongside a small boat. You're doing just fine until, suddenly, your muscles cramp up and you start to sink. The person in the boat (the counselor and/or a fellow support group member) is there for you to grab hold of for a while, just until the spasm (of grief) passes, you've caught your breath, and you're strong enough to resume swimming on your own (i.e., move on with your life). He or she is not meant to be something you cling to so frantically you capsize the boat. If that happens, or you find you simply can't imagine letting him or her go, even after several weeks or months, you're likely seriously stuck in one of the emotional stages of grief and may require more intensive professional intervention or even medication. It takes courage to recognize you might need that additional help, by the way, so don't hesitate to seek it if need be.

Recovering from grief doesn't mean finding a comfy spot in which to perpetually lick your wounds. It means finding the strength and courage to risk life and love again, in spite of inevitably revisiting the pain from time to time.

SUBMITTED STORY

The Mares

by Liz Tufte of Minneapolis, Minnesota

Holly and Nifty contentedly grazed on the dew-covered grass. Their worn-down teeth made little squeaking noises against the fresh green shoots. It was the only sound to be heard in the early-morning misty darkness before the birds awakened.

Erika began to sing softly to Holly. The lyrics were muffled as she buried her face in the little mare's mane, but I knew the tune: "My Favorite Things." She had rewritten the song over the summer months, so for us it will forever be "Holly's Favorite Things." Just thinking of this little piece of music brings a rush of vivid memories to mind.

Over sixteen years of memories. The entire time that Erika and I had been together; our lives had revolved around the horses. Nifty was twenty-six and Holly was twenty-nine. They lived on John and Carolyn's farm in Lakeville, Minnesota, holding their own in a herd of about forty horses.

The morning was warm for October. As the sun slowly rose, everything looked very green through the drizzle, as if it were the Scottish Moors instead of Midwest America.

We kept burying our noses in the horses' manes, taking in their distinctive scent. Anyone who has bonded with a horse will testify that there's a familiar, common horse scent, and then there's a more subtle, individual aroma by which we can identify a particular horse. Erika and I had always appreciated this, as well as a zillion other details about our beloved, strong-willed mares.

We had noticed that the previous two winters had taken a toll on our senior girls.

I was alarmed at how much weight Nifty had lost. And Holly was having a hard time maintaining her weight, too. They couldn't chew their grain very well, and they just didn't feel like eating when their arthritis was bad. We gave them injections for the pain, but that didn't always help. Then I asked the vet to try cortisone shots right into Nifty's bad knee. He wasn't sure that would make much difference, but he was willing to try it. Fortunately, it helped a lot, so she was able to enjoy a relatively pain-free spring and summer.

There were times in the spring that Nifty, and then Holly, seemed to take a turn for the worse, and we would wonder if it was time for them to go yet. One day, Nifty twisted her leg in the deep mud when she whirled around to protect Holly against an aggressive younger horse. The footing was already treacherous in the paddock, and with an injured knee it was downright dangerous.

With every incident like this, we would wonder, "Is it time yet?"

I'm so grateful to be part of a community of open-minded healers, including animal communicators. Instead of guessing, we could just ask the horses directly. I had pretty good skills at communicating with animals by this time, as I'd been learning and practicing for several years. But when we're facing a highly charged emotional issue around our own animals, it's hard to know for sure if we're getting accurate information. So I called Lena Swanson, my main animal communication teacher (I've taken classes from her and other mentors). She checked in with Nifty, who clearly said she wasn't ready to go yet.

It was such a relief to understand what she wanted, without having to guess or figure it out myself.

Another time, Holly was having difficulty eating, and was obviously suffering from acute arthritis. We could provide temporary relief with medication, ointments, massage, and Reiki [energy healing]. But we couldn't take the pain away completely, and we couldn't know how she felt about it without asking her directly. As much as we wanted the horses to be with us forever, it was far more important that they have free choice in the matter. We would never want them to suffer due to our selfish needs.

So we kept checking in with them. It was like they were taking turns; one would feel better while the other one would have a bad day. Fortunately, they didn't act tough and stoic like many animals do; they had no need to hide the pain from us, so they could be honest. If the pain in Nifty's knee was excruciating, she would say so. And she would help us choose the best course of action.

Carolyn, of course, was always at the farm, so she noticed details that Erika and I couldn't see, simply because we drove out only a few times a week. She knew when Nifty's time was imminent, and we discussed the need to schedule euthanasia before the weather started to get cold. We were clear that we couldn't ask Holly to endure another brutal Minnesota winter, but we weren't sure if she was ready to go with Nifty or not.

So we asked her. She was adamant: She would go with Nifty. She had absolutely no desire to hang around without her soul-sister.

Neither of the horses had any fear of death. They had some questions about the procedure — precisely where it would take place, what kinds of shots would be given and what they would feel like, what time of day it was scheduled for, that kind of thing. Once they understood everything, they were fine with it and it was settled.

Once all their questions were answered, they focused on me and Erika. They told us clearly that they had no problem with us having emotions — in fact, they expected complete authenticity. They didn't want us to act upbeat if we weren't feeling that way. It was much easier for them if we would just cry when we felt like it, rather than keep it bottled up, trying to act "normal." They wanted us to talk about memories as they came up — both the good and the bad. And they were totally fine with us leaning on them for support and reassurance. They told us that it's absolutely true about their spirits always being with us. Animals are very connected with God, or Source, or the Higher Power, or whatever we call it. They remember other lifetimes, and they know that we go to a place of pure joy when we leave our bodies. So their biggest concern was for us. They wanted to make sure we would be okay.

They told us to plan a ritual for them by inviting a circle of friends to join us three days after their passing. Their spirits would be staying very close to us for those three days, and they asked for our help to release their souls from this plane of existence so they could continue their journey on to the next level.

I see now that they so strongly insisted on the ritual because Erika and I needed it. We needed the support of community, of friends who had known the horses and understood our deep connection with them.

Magical things happened that summer, as the four of us fell into a rhythm of simply hanging out in the pasture with no agenda other than deep, loving connection. I would give Reiki to the horses while Erika sat on Holly's back, singing quietly. The mares soaked up the healing energy and thoroughly enjoyed every bite of clover and alfalfa. A small bird would sometimes visit — she seemed to be attracted to the Reiki. She would appear and sit on Nifty's back as soon as I started the healing energy. One time she flew straight at me, and I involuntarily ducked — otherwise, I think she would have landed on my head. I was sorry to have missed that opportunity.

The feeling of magic continued that whole summer, especially when Erika would sing. We still make jokes about the "concerts" she performed for a rag-tag audience. Various birds would land on nearby fenceposts and tree branches, watching Erika and apparently listening with enjoyment; they would fly away when she was done. A couple times, she even found herself singing to gophers who popped their heads up out of the ground and gazed at her, transfixed!

We imagined an ancient time when such scenes were common, when people and animals shared an understanding, when communication among species was a normal, everyday occurrence. It felt like we were tapping into a genetic memory, a latent knowingness just waiting to be reawakened. It was like a veil had been lifted and we were reclaiming something precious that had been lost long ago.

A heightened sensitivity to what the horses were feeling and telling us was opening some dormant psychic abilities we'd been previously unaware of. Not only were we tuned into the process of our animal soulmates preparing to leave their bodies, we were also reeling from the experience of traumatically losing Erika's mom only months before. I was also slowly losing my grandmother, with whom I had a very special relationship. Grandma would cross over in September — only seven weeks before the horses would cross the Rainbow Bridge.

Nifty, healthy and content after a nourishing, relaxing summer

So there we were, in the pasture with the mares one last time. It was dawn on October 21, 2007. The birds were awake and greeting the day. The horses were content from a fabulous summer of grazing. They felt good that morning and looked sleek and healthy. It seemed bizarre to euthanize two beings with such a strong life force. The four of us knew exactly what was going to happen in the next hour or so, and it seemed surreal to be acting so calm and normal. In reality, Erika and I felt an undercurrent of many mixed emotions as we waited for Bruce, the vet, to drive up the lane.

When he arrived and parked in front of the barn, we gently took the horses' lead ropes and walked across the pasture. It had been decided that Nifty would be first. Bruce gave them each a tranquilizer shot. After a few minutes, Nifty was relaxed enough to go into the barn, where John and Carolyn helped Bruce expertly move her into position. They gestured for me to go back outside. Erika was singing and crying, and Holly continued to graze. I heard a sound when Nifty's body landed on the earth. It's a foggy memory now; I don't know how it happened that I was back in the barn for a moment, touching Nifty's still-warm neck while tears streamed down my face. I recall going back outside and then escorting Erika and Holly into the barn because I held Erika's hand when she gasped in shock at the sight of Nifty.

Then Carolyn, John, and Bruce expertly moved Holly into place for the euthanizing shot. She was leaning and swaying from the effects of the tranquilizer, but I'm absolutely sure that she was aware of what she was doing because she intentionally fell right next to Nifty, with her nose touching Nifty's tail.

John, Carolyn, and Bruce were astonished at that because they were positioning her to fall the other way, onto her other side. Even in the final detail, Holly was in charge. And just as in life, the two soulmates will always be together.

Nifty & Holly, always together

When Other People Let You Down

Let's face it, life doesn't always hand us Hallmark moments. It's realistic, not cynical, to acknowledge, well before you ever lose a loved one, that there will be people who add to your pain, inadvertently or otherwise. That's why it's all the more vital that you take a "dry run" (before your eyes are filled with tears) to envision how you might handle others' faux pas, or social blunders.

Imagine this scenario: You're at a family reunion just weeks following the death of your nineteen-year-old cat, Pooky. You're talking to some relatives and find yourself choking up over the loss of your dearest animal friend, and your abrasive cousin Larry pipes up, "Get a load of the cry baby—and all over a stupid cat! Cats are only good as road kill anyway."

However tempting it might be to pop this guy one in the snoot, you can recognize in your mental role-playing ahead of time that it won't ease your heartache, won't bring back your pet, and may even wind up with that jerk pressing charges. Launching into a righteously indignant rant about his lack of empathy may feel swell, too, but it is unlikely to teach him anything. Too often, the ignorant and insensitive have their prejudices etched in stone. As difficult as it may seem, for this kind of Neanderthal, leaving the room without even acknowledging his idiocy is your strongest, most dignified option. What's more, it will set him up to look the glaringly insensitive oaf he obviously is in the eyes of any witnesses and just may prompt more compassionate sorts to follow you out and offer their genuine support.

It may also help you set up realistic expectations if, before writing off people who don't understand how you're feeling as being cousin Larry clones, you remember that few people have much experience in dealing with grief, either their own or that of others. The rawness of the emotion can make them very uncomfortable even if they aren't inherently heartless. It's quite possible they do want to help but just don't know how.

I don't mean to imply this is easy to do. I've often failed miserably and taken it totally personally when someone I knew told me that

Characteristics of Bereaved Pet Owners

Population: 71% female/29% male of seventy-six owners studied.

How the pet's death affected their behavior/routines

- 93% experienced some disruption in their daily routine, such as changed waking/sleeping patterns and disrupted eating habits.

- 51% showed significantly reduced social activity. They stayed home, talked little with anyone, and chose to spend time by themselves.

- 45% had job-related difficulties: missed one to three days of work (using sick days or vacation time) or were upset by the insensitivity of work colleagues to their loss.

- Only one of the seventy-six pet owners studied failed to experience at least one of the categories.

–From *New Perspectives on Our Lives with Companion Animals*, edited by Aaron H. Katcher and Alan M. Beck

rather than go home and administer my diabetic dog Tuppence's insulin I should just "shoot it," or when someone who is supposedly very close to me doesn't so much as say, "I'm sorry to hear about your dog's passing" but just prattles on about his own inconsequential interests, pointing out a great sale on snow tires, for instance, right after I'd delivered the news of my Westie Ludwig's death.

It wasn't until much later, in an unguarded moment with that person's spouse, that I learned that years ago when they'd lost their pet poodle, she'd discovered her husband sobbing for twenty minutes in the shower. He did have a heart, after all. It was just too tender to

From the film *Notes on a Scandal,* 2006, starring Cate Blanchett (Sheba) and Judy Dench (Barbara), screenplay by Patrick Marber

Sheba: "You've had a terrible shock." *(Refers to news that her fellow teacher Barbara's cat had not long to live.)* "Can they treat her?"

Barbara: "He says it's just a matter of weeks…. She's only a pet."

Sheba: "Oh no, I cried for weeks when our dog died … weeks."

Barbara: "You get so attached."

Later…

Sheba: *(to her husband)* "Barbara has just had some very bad news about her cat."

Husband: *(coldly)* "My condolences. Poor, poor pussy. Now can I have my wife back, please?"

Sheba: *(to Barbara)* "I'm desperately sorry about Portia [the cat], but as you can see, I have to go."

Barbara: *(pleading)* "Stay with me. I don't know what I'll do!"

let him remember those overwhelming feelings, so he avoided the issue completely. Here I was, feeling in need of consoling myself, yet allowing compassion for his shortcomings to share the stage in my head. I never needed to bring this up with the fellow in question, but I was able to let go of what would have remained for me a lifelong chunk of bitterness toward him. I was grateful to the Universe for urging his wife to inadvertently divulge to me his secret heartache that allowed me to "humanize" his outwardly callous behavior and forgive him.

> "If we could read the secret history of our enemies, we should find in each person's life sorrow and suffering enough to disarm all hostility."
>
> — Henry Wadsworth Longfellow

And, last, as hard as it is for people of our animal-loving ilk to comprehend, a great many people have simply never had a close relationship with an animal of any kind. Reasons for this (that could possibly negate my probably erroneous, tongue-in-cheek hypothesis that these people clearly suffer from "insurmountable character flaws") might include:

1) Being allergic;

2) Having grown up with parents who wouldn't allow pets in the house;

3) Living on farms where animals are necessarily viewed as a commodity;

4) Being involved in a scientific or medical field that views animals as means to test drugs, products, or procedures deemed unsafe for human trials;

5) Having experienced a traumatic attack by an animal, being phobic, or otherwise having cause to fear them; and/or

6) Adhering to their religious or cultural beliefs.*

Realizing from the outset that encountering people who feel no particular connection to animals will be quite commonplace—sadly, more probable than finding animal-centric people like ourselves who will wholeheartedly empathize with us—we can be prepared for their shortcomings when we need support. We also may better be able to put aside our anger and hurt when we get those occasional looks of annoyance or incomprehension during our grieving-for-our-companion-animal process.

While you would be wise to seek out other animal lovers for comfort—be it talking with a close friend or family member who knew your pet, joining a support group for those grieving a pet loss, consulting your vet or veterinarian technician, making a call to a pet loss hot line, etc.—you still must remember that just because they care for critters doesn't mean they necessarily come with a degree in grief counseling.

* Understanding and Respecting Other Points of View

Mursal Osman, a longtime volunteer for the Confederation of Somali Community in Minnesota, says, "In Somalia, dogs are not widely used as pets." Within the Islamic faith, on which the majority of Somali culture is based, Osman said, a dog only may be owned for the following purposes: for hunting (for food only, never for sport); as a guide if the person is blind or needs to keep a dog for essential services; to shepherd cattle and sheep; or to perform police or guard house duties. In any of those instances, the dog must have separate living quarters, and precautions must be taken to avoid human contact with the dog's saliva.

Believe it or not, even other animal aficionados can fall short when handling their fellow human's emotional needs. Their word choices can come across as clumsy or insensitive despite the fact that they share your devotion to pets and, say, their dachshund Daisy means the world to them and they know they'd be lost without her. It may be that your loss is a reminder of their own beloved animal companion's mortality, and that is just too much for them to face at that point. They may have to retreat to protect themselves. That doesn't necessarily mean they intend to hurt you or that they think you're emotionally unstable because of your grief.

Levels of Human Bonding with Animals

Weakly Bonded: Provide physical care and not much else. Tolerate animals but don't love them. Mistreatment, neglect, and/or abuse happen here.

Moderately Bonded: Pet is a pleasing source of entertainment to have around the house but remains an "it" in the owner's mind. Sadness at loss passes quickly.

Profoundly Bonded: Earliest responses are spontaneous and loving and nurturing. Animals cannot speak, so we fine-tune our abilities to read their needs and emotions. Verbalize about pets as nonhuman children, referring to them as "he" or "she," not "it."

Pet responds as would a baby—naturally and with complete innocence and loving trust. The baby-like kinship with animals differs from human relationships because the pet never "grows up and leaves us." They are always dependent while staying loving. Loss of pet is as profound as, if not more so than, losing a human family member.

–Wallace Sife, Ph.D.,
*The Loss of a Pet—A Guide to Coping
with the Grieving Process When a Pet Dies*

I've found this to be a memorable, capital-T Truth: Whatever people choose to do, however they choose to respond to you during your crisis, it generally speaks volumes about them and their issues surrounding death and bereavement and says very little about you. Try your darnedest not to take it personally. (I know. That's a tall order when your emotional world is collapsing around you.) A good rule of thumb—when in doubt as to a person's motives, assume he or she is innocent of malicious intent until proven to be like your cousin Larry.

SUBMITTED STORY

Suffering, A Singular Experience

Lisa Guitierrez, Albuquerque, New Mexico

writing about the loss of Ferocidad,
her miniature pinscher who passed away in 2006

"… My sweet baby boy was gone. My heart is broken. I ache to see him, touch him, smell him just one last time. I have never known this kind of emptiness and pain; it is agonizing. The worst part is that no one seems to understand the depth of my grieving. Even my partner cannot relate to my feelings of guilt and sadness."

Ferocidad

> When an insensitive person strikes, have a planned response ready, such as: "In my opinion, you are not an animal person and have probably never experienced the special bond you can have with a pet. You do not understand the love ... and companionship my pet gave my life. Please do not be so judgmental and intolerant, as I feel deep personal feelings of loss at this time."
>
> —Eleanor L. Harris,
> *Pet Loss—A Spiritual Guide*

While invaluable and something to be cherished and reciprocated, you nevertheless must expect the kindness, empathy, and support of others to have limits. Ultimately, it is you who must take responsibility for your own feelings and do what you need to feel properly supported, even if that means, ironically, being by yourself for a while.

Ms. Yarden makes a good case for being patient with your process, saying, "Grief ... will occur over and over after a loss, and through that repetition comes the slow easing of pain. Each time, one experiences a little more consolation, a little more healing."

Another way of viewing it is that grief is a weight you eventually become accustomed to bearing. You're never fully without it, but through time, you become stronger and more capable of carrying on without it stopping you cold. Just as a twenty-five-pound dumbbell strapped to your back will seem quite heavy at first and you'll struggle under it, one day, you'll find you have adjusted to it and have been strengthened by its mere presence without even knowing it.

Animal Doctor Column, Dr. Michael Fox, *Star Tribune*, Saturday, Oct. 6, 2007. Content reprinted with permission of Dr. Fox and United Media Syndicate.

Grief over pets not 'psychotic,' needs new focus

**ANIMAL DOCTOR
DR. MICHAEL FOX**

Dear Dr. Fox: I had two dogs, both with serious health problems in old age. The husky/wolf mix died at age sixteen. The beagle/shepherd mix died at age seventeen. I had both of them cremated so I could have them with me all the time. I lay the urns by my bed every night.

I used to take them both for walks, and they really enjoyed it. Now I bag up the urns and still take them to the park.

All I do is cry for them. They're the only "children" I ever had. I go to a therapist, and she says I'm "psychotic." What do you say? I still leave food and water for them. I hope you don't think I'm crazy because I just miss and love my dogs so terribly. Please help me.
S.A. Weatherly, R. I.

Dr. Fox says: Shame on your therapist. You are not psychotic. Many people say they have mourned the loss of a devoted, affectionate pet that brought joy and unconditional love into their lives more than that of a close relative. My new book, *Dog Body, Dog Mind* (Lyons Press 2007), will inspire you, especially with the documentation of animals' remarkable awareness of death and the afterlife.

If you are up to the task, adopt another dog (or two) in need of a decent home. You can invite them into your home and help them enjoy a good life.

Or you could volunteer at your local shelter to give to others the love your two dogs gave to you. For your deceased dogs' sakes, it is time for you to express your love and gratitude and say goodbye. To not let them continue their spiritual journey is selfish and unethical, and it's not healthy for you.

Submitted Stories

Madra's Story

by Pat Cumbie of Minneapolis, Minnesota

Madra

My friend (and author of *Where People Like Us Live*) Patricia Cumbie wrote of the passing of Madra (the Gaelic word for dog), the starving stray, calico-coated collie her eventual husband Sean had found when he was living in Ireland more than twenty years ago. Sean believed Madra, his one-blue-eyed/one-brown-eyed girl, was a gift from his Irish ancestors, so he nursed her back to health and had a crate specially built for her trip across the ocean to America.

Pat and Sean met when he was a student at the University of Wisconsin–Madison. He'd had Madra two years by then, she said, and "As I got closer to Sean, we became a threesome: me, man, and dog."

Madra lived another ten years, and on the day before she died, she'd been in their yard tossing a stick around. "Later that day, she had a stroke, and suddenly we were faced with the shocking necessity of having to put her down," Pat wrote.

"In retrospect, we feel grateful for many things after she died. She'd lived a full life and didn't suffer a protracted period of ill health. But, oh, the shock was huge, and we were greatly incapacitated by her death in the year afterward." Two of their best friends, Bret and Ted, dug Madra's grave and led a short service for Pat and Sean, who were too grief-stricken to manage it themselves.

"We feel blessed we have such friends who understood what Madra meant to us … People who knew Madra called us with their condolences, assuring us that Madra was 'the best dog ever.' A few even sent cards," Pat said.

"But not everyone was so kind. We had a few people say, 'You still miss that dog you had?' as if we were some kind of crazy people to be so hurt by the loss. (That's why I'm writing this to you. I think there needs to be more awareness in our culture that pet loss is real and difficult.) We even bought into some of that thinking early on. We'd had a dinner party scheduled a week after Madra died and felt we should go ahead and do it. Canceling because of a dog didn't feel legitimate enough. What a mistake! We got very drunk and ended up crying about our dog to our guests. It made for a bad night and a painful hangover the next day. I still feel sorry for those people that walked into our grief like that. We never should have gone through with it.

"Of course, our fresh grief is gone, but a wistfulness remains. Madra still is the best dog ever. We have another dog now, which is also a very wonderful animal who is beginning to age. We've had a few health scares and are starting to think we should 'be prepared.' We know how deep these animal attachments are and that losing them is so devastating.... [For instance,] my grandfather's last dog was his most beloved. After she'd passed, he said he'd never get another dog; his heart couldn't handle the grief of losing another one. Those were not the words of a man closed off to love, either. I just believe that the grief of losing a special animal is really that hard."

Pat added that, because of what their friends did for them to help with Madra's funeral, "I also think it's really important for those dealing with grieving people to do something to recognize the contributions the dead made while they were alive. It really helped me and Sean when we were going through the aftermath of the loss of Madra.... She was the quintessential immigrant—she left her home country for a better life with Sean.... The ancestors brought us full circle through the cycles of life and death with Madra, and that was a gift indeed."

~~~ ~~~ ~~~
~~~ ~~~ ~~~

SUBMITTED STORY

Iggy

by Christine Marie Henry of Muncie, Indiana

Christmas Eve I was surprised by my parents who walked in the door with a black toy poodle for me. Little did I know, the day that I opened the door to Iggy was the day I opened my heart up to an angel. From that day forward we were inseparable. A year later, I distinctly remember sitting in the school library being read a story from the librarian called "I'll Always Love You." I cannot tell you what an impact this book had on me and would later have on my future. I would eventually become a pet loss researcher.

The book was about the bond between a boy and his dog, who over time became old and died. I realized at that point, at ten years old, "Oh my God, one day Iggy will die." I took to heart the words of wisdom from the book: loved ones will die, so enjoy each moment you have together; and it is important to say "I love you" every night. From then on, and for the next fifteen years, before I went to bed I would turn, kiss Iggy and say I love you.

At sixteen years old, Iggy's kidney's began failing. I was fortunate enough to have a wonderful vet who had him come in for fluid treatments weekly, which extended his life for two years. The day after Thanksgiving, Iggy woke up yelping in pain. It was then that I knew it was time. I was not going to have him suffer. I made the decision and my family was trying to talk me out of it, but I knew. We went to the vet, and I was crying the whole way there. I said my goodbyes in the car and my ex-husband carried him into the vet. I was so glad that he was with Iggy during his final moments because it was too difficult for me to do. Iggy was wrapped in a baby blanket and, before we could put him into the grave, my mother's partner, Anthony, reached under the blanket as if he were going to remove the blanket.

My mother was startled and said, "Don't do that. We want to keep that on him."

Iggy

Anthony looked up and said, "I know," and explained that he had reached under the blanket to pet Iggy one last time.

After burying Iggy, we went to a local garden shop to pick out a tombstone for him. I felt completely numb. As soon as we entered the shop, everyone started to look around and I was left alone wandering around the aisles. Suddenly over the loudspeaker, the song "In the Arms of an Angel" began to play. To me that was a sign from Iggy that he was okay and that he was at last at peace. He was no longer in pain and was reunited with our other dog in Heaven.

I was in my graduate school program for mental health counseling when both of my childhood dogs died. The people in my program were people who were currently or were training to become therapists. When my dog died, I decided to stay home from school to go and bury her. Upon returning to school, I was asked by my fellow therapists, "What's the big deal with your dog dying? You can always go get a new one." A classmate even told me while Iggy was aging that "you need to put that dog down," despite the fact that Iggy was doing well.

I could not believe all these insensitive things counselors were saying to me. I was so puzzled that I went to the academic literature to see if other people have gone through a similar experience of people not caring about the death of a pet. To my surprise, I found that my experience was very common and that most pet owners were greeted with the same cold response. After obtaining this knowledge, I felt that it was my mission to let the world know that losing a pet can be a devastating experience and people need to acknowledge the loss. I did not want people to go through the same experience that I had gone through. I then decided to do my doctoral dissertation on the topic.

To my surprise, even while conducting research in the area of pet loss I was mocked by peers. I had one professor respond to my research by saying that I "need to look at the personality disorder variables that correlate with someone being attached to a pet."

My whole paper was about how healthy being attached to a pet was, and that statement was backed up by quantitative research. However, he still could not accept that and wanted me to figure out what was wrong with "these people" who were attached to pets because it was not healthy. I was completely shocked to have had a similar experience at a grief conference.

While having a conversation with a grief counselor about my research, she responded, "Well, I am all about being empathetic with a loss, but come on, a pet? That's kind of crazy."

I sat there in disbelief. Here is a GRIEF counselor who knows how difficult bereavement can be when a loss is not recognized and there she was doing just that. Luckily, I had a wonderful advisor who saw the importance of the topic and fully supported me through all these trials and tribulations.

I was getting ready to collect data for my dissertation and all I needed was 150 people to respond to my survey for statistical reasons. One committee member stated that he was skeptical that I would be able to get that number. He pointed out that I would have to think hard about all the different ways I could recruit participants, including going door to door to veterinary offices.

One way that I was going to collect data was through online surveys. When I had my site up, I emailed a few people and grief professionals telling them about the study. In half a day I had fifty participants. I saw that number and went to bed feeling comforted. The next morning, I woke up and was told that I had nearly 1,000 responses! I was astonished. By the end of that day, the number rose to 2,000! I could not believe my eyes.

My advisor was skeptical of the numbers and thought that there had to be a data error. There would be no way that I could be obtaining such numbers with such speed. Sure enough, there was no data error. In just one week, I had over 7,000 responses from people who had lost a pet. Nine months later, I now have nearly 9,000 participants. This number clearly shows that people do grieve over the loss of their pets. There are several people from all over the world who have written me their stories about the animal companion they lost. A theme in almost all of them is that they, too, were disenfranchised in their grief. A few people wrote to me that no one knows that they are still grieving because they have been told by several people that it is stupid to be still mourning a dog.

One theory as to why I received such large numbers is that completing a survey online is anonymous. It seems like this is a group of people who feel that they cannot grieve in public, and the Internet could be a safe place for them to express their grief. I believe that society has come a long way since I started pet loss research in 2001. Today, we have the term "pet parents," which is being used more and more. If you go into a card store, you will find several pet loss condolence cards where there used to be none.

Petsmart and other pet stores have also expanded in this area. Stores now offer tombstones for pets in addition to other items that can be used to memorialize a pet. The funeral industry has also begun to make changes to include pets. Pet Angel in Indiana is a complete funeral home for pets. They have a small chapel area where they can hold a formal service for a group of people. If a pet parent wants a more intimate location, they have a private room for the family to gather. The staff prepares the body for viewing and will take a paw and nose print for the owners to have. In addition to the prints, they will take some clippings of the hair to help memorialize the pet.

Animal-human companionship has been an undervalued relationship in our society. People can form strong attachments to pets and, as a result, the death of the pet can be a devastating experience. Society is slowly beginning to understand the intensity of the bond that can exist between a human and an animal. From this new understanding there is hope that, in the future, when someone experiences the death of a pet, they will receive the same support that people receive when a human dies.

~~~ ~~~ ~~~

SUBMITTED STORY

Bruzer

by Elaine Pederson of Andover, Minnesota

Bruzer

My husband Gary and I lost our little precious Bruzer on February 5, 2005, and it was the hardest thing we have ever been through.

The biggest reason that I want to tell our story is to help others who are going through the same thing and let them know that they are not alone, that there are other people who love their pets as much as they do. A lot of people I care about, who love me and my husband, totally did not understand what we were going through and sometimes said very hurtful things like, "You need to get over it, it's been two weeks," "He was just a dog," and "Now maybe you will get a real dog." That comment came from one of my sisters-in-law who had a big dog. Bruzer was a Westie, and she apparently didn't care for the breed.

I cried many, many tears sometimes because of things that people would say to me about our tremendous loss. I also cried because of people who were so special to me but did not even acknowledge his death. Probably the person that hurt me the most was my dad. He doesn't like dogs much, never had a dog, and did not even acknowledge that I had lost my dog.

Months later, I had an opportunity to tell him how much that hurt me, and I cried my eyes out expressing my feelings to him on the phone. It felt good to get it off my chest. He did actually listen and did not interrupt and did not say anything cruel or mean. He just basically said, "I did not know that you had to put him to sleep; I thought he just died," like that really mattered that much. He still never said that he was sorry that I lost my dog. I told him it hurt very much that my parents did not even send me a card even though they knew how much I loved Bruzer and how important he was to me.

I do not know how I would have gotten through that time without my husband and all the wonderful friends that did tell us how sorry they were and sent us many, many cards and notes expressing their thoughts.

(See also Bruzer's story in the Memorializing Methods chapter.)

〜〜 〜〜 〜〜

SUBMITTED STORY

Zoë

by Lila of Athens, Georgia

Zoë was a German shepherd/rottweiler mix; a patient, old soul; and a teacher who taught us balance, unconditional love, and the importance of what is real, here and now.

Zoë

In June of 2005 we discovered she had pneumothorax, or air in the chest cavity caused by a lung leak. After about two weeks in the ICU of University of Georgia Veterinary Teaching Hospital, Zoë was getting depressed. One afternoon, she gave me a pleading look with those soulful brown eyes. I knew without question that she was telling me she was tired of this and could not take much more. With tears in my eyes, I promised her that one way or another it was almost over, that we would take her home very soon.

Despite being financially prepared to do whatever could be done for her, I told the surgeon that at some point this had to stop being about what I want, and it had to start being about her. I was learning that money and love couldn't fix everything. And that goodbyes, while excruciating, can be loving and unselfish.

After this experience, Zoë enjoyed ten months of wonderful health and was back to her old routine. Then, Zoë suddenly developed autoimmune emolytic anemia, a disease in which the immune system attacks the red blood cells, preventing her from moving enough oxygen. In addition, the vet discovered she had a liver tumor.

I looked at my beautiful girl, remembering the promise I had made just ten months earlier. We had to let her go. My husband George and I lay on the floor with our girl [at the vet's office], sang to her, and told her how much we love her and that she did not have to be brave any longer. We thanked her for taking care of us and teaching all of us so many important things. We were both holding her when she died.

Eventually, we picked up the blanket we had brought with us for her and drove home. When we walked into the house, Aly, Collin, and Marcy, our other dogs, ran over. George and I were both crying and we lay the blanket on the floor. Each dog sniffed it, and it was very clear they knew what had happened. They all made their own sad little noises, and that was when I lost it. I screamed and cried for a long time as George held me, sobbing himself.

The first few days were exhausting and I remember very little except aching for Zoë. It was actual physical pain. We walked our other dogs a lot. It was all we could really do. They were grieving, too, and we felt their routine was very important. We were all very, very sad. We told our other dogs over and over that we did not send Zoë away and we would never send them away.

So many people have told me how alone they felt when they lost their pets, that their friends and family members minimized their losses and did not understand. The opposite was true for us. The doctors and nurses at both veterinary clinics were phenomenal. Their kindness and compassion for Zoë and for us was always evident. My friend Stephanie brought us a wonderful homemade dinner that night. George's team at work gave us a gardenia. We received flowers, cards, phone calls, and emails. My boss told me that she was so sorry and to take all the time I needed. We know we have terrific friends, but we were not prepared for the outpouring of sympathy we received. One of the vets that we regularly saw was not working the day Zoë died, but he called us two days later, on a Sunday morning, to tell us what a great dog Zoë was and that he was sorry for our loss. Not one person said to us that Zoë was "just a dog."

Instead, we got cards and letters with the following:

"God created us in His own image and our love for our pets is part of that image. He is caring for your Zoë until you are together again."

"Ask now the beasts and they shall teach thee, and the fowls of the air and they shall teach thee, or speak to the Earth and it shall teach thee, and the fishes of the sea shall declare unto thee, 'Who knoweth not that the hand of God wrought this, in Whose hand is the soul of every living thing?" Job Chapter 12, verses 7–10.

"You were wonderful parents. Zoë was lucky to have you and you were lucky to have her. What a great dog."

"Zoë was the bravest dog I ever knew and a very important part of my clinical training. I will never forget her. I am so sorry."

There are so many emotions and so many ups and downs. Grief has been a bizarre journey, and I have learned that it is all perfectly normal. It is okay to laugh and feel good, and it is also okay to cry and feel like hell. Our pets provide us with the most constant and predictable of relationships. I am so blessed to have shared years of my life with a creature so perfect, a creature who shared the purest love with me. Losing that is completely devastating. Anatole France has told us, "Until one has loved an animal, a part of one's soul remains unawakened." Even though Zoë is not here in a physical sense, the part of me that she awakened remains awakened. My Zoë will always be a part of me, and my grateful heart sings.

Part Two:
Afterlife Connections – Humans

"I do believe in spooks. I do, I do, I do, I DO believe in spooks!"
— Cowardly Lion of *The Wizard of Oz*

What's a statement like that doing in a book on pet loss, you may be thinking. Well, it's precisely my belief, nay, certainty that "spooks" exist that's given me the comfort I've needed to make it through a tsunami of loss in my life, giving me all the concrete evidence I personally need to know that the spirit, or pure energy, of the person or animal who passes over is never really very far away and that the love that binds us together never dies.

Before I go any further, however, let me clarify that I don't literally mean "spooks," as in monstrous apparitions like those being captured in the movie *Ghostbusters*.

"To those who believe, no explanation is needed.
To those who do not believe, no explanation is possible."
— Dunninger,
a mystic and mind reader in the early twentieth century

Beings with threatening or "evil" energy may indeed exist, but I've had no firsthand experience of them, so I'll stick to what I know. Every encounter I've had with beings on the Other Side has been wonderfully loving, reassuring, even playful. I cherish them and rely on their accessible presence in times of darkness in my existence here on the Earthly plane.

While every word I write is the unvarnished truth (ask anyone with whom I've shared these stories, they haven't changed an iota — i.e. not morphed into something bigger or stranger for the sake of good storytelling—over the decades), as with anything I offer, the great English bard said it well: "Take it in what sense thou wilt." And do with these stories whatever you want or need to.

The premise upon which all of the following is predicated is this: I believe we all come from a single Source of light and love (substitute God, Allah, Yahweh, Higher Power, etc., whatever term makes you feel more comfortable—or use quarks and subatomic particles if you're of a more scientific bent), no matter the form we take (in this case, we're each having a human experience, or in our pet's case, an animal experience). Therefore, I believe that when we leave our Earthly "carrying case," or physical body, we simply return to that state of pure energy until it's time to embark on another lesson-learning venture.

If it helps to make this philosophy a bit more concrete, think of it this way: It's kind of like we are all individual glasses of water taken from the same (cosmic) ocean. We may feel we've been temporarily separated from that Source by the confines of the glass (our bodies), but every living thing is and has always been made of the same inherent "stuff" and is inextricably connected. So when we die, we are, in essence, simply returning to the sea from which we originated, intermingling once again with the energies of those we've loved with no more perceived physical barrier, such as that we've experienced during our time spent learning/teaching our soul's valuable lessons on Earth.

According to Christina Donnell, Ph.D., in her book *Transcendent Dreaming—Stepping into Our Human Potential*, there are "different but simultaneous realities—the tangible reality of everyday life and the more primary level of reality that gives birth to all the objects and appearances of the manifest world. The idea of two realities can be found in almost all spiritual traditions." For instance, she says Tibetan Buddhists refer to "the void and the nonvoid," wherein all things in the universe continuously pour out of the void and into the nonvoid, the realm of visible objects. Hindus call it Brahman … "the formless source of all forms which appear out of it and resolve back into it endlessly."

And if that doesn't work for you, there's Albert Einstein's theory of Mass-Energy Equivalence, which says that matter and energy just transform from one to another; therefore nothing is created and nothing is destroyed. He has been quoted as saying he believed in an afterlife for this very reason: energy never dies. If you're the quantum physics type, you might consider that the departed person's vibrational frequency has changed sufficiently for there to be no way for the human eye to perceive the "life force," but that which is commonly called the soul is still in existence on another plane or dimension. (Rather than digress further, I heartily recommend the documentary movie *What the Bleep Do We Know?* for further discussion of such existential topics.)

Some religions, such as Mormonism, describe death as being just on the other side of a thin veil. This belief is part of the nature-based religion known as Wicca, too, wherein it is asserted that there are times of the year, such as All Hallows Eve, when this veil is the thinnest and communication with those on the Other Side is optimal. This thin veil metaphor works for me, too, as people I've known who have passed over have shown they remain nearby, communicating through natural forms of energy, such as fire, water, light, electricity, dreams/mental telepathy, etc. When such communication takes place, it is known as supernormal, or an occurrence that greatly exceeds what is considered "normal" but still obeys natural laws.

Everyone can (and perhaps already does) experience this phenomena in his or her own way, in keeping with his or her beliefs and/or what he or she is emotionally, spiritually, and psychologically prepared to accept. By simply being open to and actively/intuitively observant of the signs, one can receive amazing messages from the Other Side without the aid of a medium or possession of special psychic abilities of one's own. Conversely, if you are afraid, skeptical, or simply not willing or open to welcoming such experiences, chances are you never will have them. What we believe shapes our experience of reality to a tremendous degree.

That being said, my experiences of afterlife connections are mine alone. I present them here only in hopes of either validating others' experiences of similar events or opening a few folks' hearts and minds to seeking their own affirmations of love's never-ending presence in our lives. And please trust me, although these initial stories involve human beings, they will segue into and will prove very relevant to the issue of pet loss and grieving.

Now I will back up what I've asserted with some of the instances I've experienced.

The Key to It All

In 1994, my first husband and I bought a lovely home in the Powderhorn Park neighborhood of South Minneapolis. It was roughly a year after we'd moved in that I had my first supernormal experience there.

One night, after I'd driven home from working out at the local YMCA, I'd parked in front of my house, turned off my car as I always had, and tucked the key in my purse. Shortly thereafter, I went to bed.

In the middle of the night, I awoke, presumably from a dream I no longer recall, sat up in bed, said aloud quizzically, "Uri Geller bending keys?" and went back to sleep.

Note: Uri Geller is a paranormalist who claimed to be able to bend spoons and keys with his mind. The last I'd seen or heard of him had probably been on "The Tonight Show" when I was a teenager in the late 1970s, so there was no reason to imagine I could have subconsciously picked up on something about him I'd heard on TV or read in a magazine that night.

The next morning, when I tried to start my car to go to work, my key wouldn't fit in the ignition. Sometime during the night, it had been bent between thirty and forty-five degrees!

Now, I always try to see if there could be a "normal" explanation for what happens before I start hollering "ghost;" therefore, I tried repeatedly to straighten out the key by hand. Nothing doing. (By the way, later that day, my husband had to use pliers to straighten the transformed key, and he has much greater hand strength than I.) To have caused this myself, I'd have had to have pulled out the key in the car's ignition a little more than half way and strained to bend it as if it were in a vice, and even then it's more likely it would have just broken off in the ignition. I promise you, I did nothing of the sort.

Anyway, back to the story. I used a spare key to head out for work. No sooner had I driven one block than I heard the thwump, thwump, thwump that indicated I had a flat tire!

Someone or something either wanted to let me know something would soon be wrong with my car or was telling me to play hooky. I don't know the intent or the identity of the messenger. I simply report the facts of the story. Draw whatever conclusion you like.

A certain amount of skepticism is healthy. As I've said, I always try to rule out any mundane explanations for unusual things that happen before I ascribe to them supernatural sources. I find it helps me own my credibility in a way I could not if I were to gullibly accept everything anyone asserted—on this or any topic, actually—as gospel.

I think I learned this best from my half-sister Sandi. She is seventeen years my senior, and for a while after our father died in 1975, she and her daughter moved in with me and my mother (her step-mother) to help settle his affairs. I was thirteen at the time.

Sandi loved to go on about her belief in all things mystical, and I didn't necessarily disagree with her, but I did notice that she, in her devotion to the idea of spirits inhabiting our house, tended to more or less ignore obvious logical explanations for things. She was a bit like a charter member of the group of ladies in the 1960s Don Knotts comedy *The Ghost and Mr. Chicken*, whose shared hobby was zealously attributing supernatural explanations to everything that happened around them.

Well, doing what any annoying little sister would do, I started messing with Sandi's head. She'd once told me of a book that had fallen off a shelf in a room in her South Carolina home in which no one had been; this, according to her, was evidence of communication from the Other Side. (And in that case, it may well have been; I cannot say. But this particular meddling kid couldn't resist pulling a pseudo-paranormal prank.)

One night, I knocked one of my father's Readers Digest Condensed Books off the bookshelf in our family room downstairs and opened it to a random page. I then ran upstairs, feigning breathlessness from hysteria, and told Sandi that I'd found a book mysteriously de-shelved. Her eyes glowed with enthusiasm and anticipation. I don't remember what the story was, or what the text on that open page said, but she eagerly ran with the suggestion, pronouncing that we obviously had a ghost in our midst.

I nearly burst from held-in laughter. (It's a wonder bratty little sisters ever survive to adulthood.)

I repeated this about three times at random intervals over that summer. No harm, no foul, right? My sister was ecstatic to have her own personal ghost "advising her" through a super-abridged version of Peter Benchley's *Jaws* or some such thing, and I get to laugh about it to this day.

My outlook on such things became similar to that of comedian Bill Murray's character Dr. Peter Venkman in *Ghostbusters* when he sees a large stack of books in an allegedly haunted library, the presence of which his cohorts instantly ascribe to paranormal activity. Knowing he is himself a charlatan in his field of parapsychology, he wryly notes, "You're right. No human being could stack books like that."

You may remember, however, that Dr. Venkman is made a true believer not much later thanks to firsthand experience of the super-natural. I guess you could say I followed in Venkman's footsteps, just without the slime and other special effects.

Or, if I may strain to use another pop culture reference, this time from "The X-Files," as the incidence of uncanny occurrences I'd experienced grew in number over the years, my internal Agent Dana Scully, the skeptical needer of empirical proof before accepting the possibility of anything inexplicable, has come to inch far closer to my inner Agent Fox Mulder, the poster child for wanting to believe everything paranormal is the unequivocal Truth.

Generally speaking, I still start out on the Scully end of the continuum and only gravitate toward Mulder's when rational explanations are ruled out to the best of my ability. That way, I can defend my inner Mulder that much more convincingly because, after awhile, I have to admit, the evidence for the validity of these experiences piles up, and now I only have to give Scully a passing nod before "I believe."

Frances the Friendly Ghost

When we bought our house, the previous owner, an elderly woman named Frances, who was apparently much loved by the neighbors but whom we'd never had the opportunity to meet in person as her son handled the sale, was in a nursing home. We were never formally notified when she died. She found a way to let us know herself.

It all started when, one day, I'd called my Westie, Tuppence, to come upstairs with me, and I noticed she'd abruptly stopped two steps from the top of the stairs and barked. It took a long while of coaxing and cajoling her, before she would come up the rest of the way. This happened repeatedly after that, but I thought nothing of it, assuming she was a little goofy in the head or too lazy to climb the rest of the way. Why do it herself if she could annoy her human mama into carrying her, right?

Then, one night when I was in my office on the second floor, alone in the house with just Tuppence and my two Siamese cats, Dudley and Genevieve, I heard someone turn on the water in the bathroom just across the landing, roughly twenty feet away from where I sat. At first, I called out to my husband, thinking he might have forgotten something and returned unexpectedly from work. No answer.

The water continued running full force.

> "Local people tell me they would have felt [the spirit that dwelled in our new house].... We didn't. They can't understand why we didn't know what it meant when our dog wouldn't go up those stairs. Animals see the blasted things, it appears."
>
> —*The Uninvited,* 1944, starring Ray Miland, written by Dodie Smith and Frank Partos

You might expect me to have been afraid of an intruder. After all, there had been a tremendous increase in crime around that time, specifically gang activity from the Detroit Boys establishing territory in our neighborhood and earning our fair city the moniker "Murderapolis—Land of 10,000 Wakes." But somehow, I didn't leap to the conclusion that we'd had a break-in by a criminal with dirty hands in need of washing in my bathroom sink.

No, I, like any normal person would, thought the cats had somehow, for the first time in fourteen years, learned to turn on the water faucet.

As per usual, I ran through my pseudo-scientific tests to rule out that theory. My first clue that it couldn't have been the cats was they were both fast asleep, curled up on one of our radiators downstairs. But still, I turned off the water and tried to casually bat it on again, as one of the kitties would have had to do. My second clue pointing to their innocence was that it was an old house, built in 1926, with old plumbing. If I did manage to get the faucet to move just a little—and it was so tight and hard to turn that the cats would have needed to have been on steroid-laden catnip to manage it—the pipes would start loudly bam, bam, bamming in protest. Whoever turned on the water had to swiftly turn the faucet a good two or more inches to get the water flowing that hard without that particular serenade preceding it.

Not even a thirsty, sleepwalking Siamese could have done that. And Tuppence simply couldn't get up there. It appeared I had my evidence of yet another supernormal encounter.

A couple of weeks later, in another of those too-weird-to-predict events that dominate my life, an old friend of mine, Char T., with whom I'd taken improvisation classes through Dudley Riggs' Brave New Workshop and whom I hadn't seen in years, called. She was opening a new coffee shop called The Laughing Cup—Home of the Brew Ha-ha and wanted to treat her business partner to a reflexology session with my husband. She and I sat downstairs in the living room chatting, while her partner received his therapeutic treatment in my husband's office upstairs.

We yakked of this and that, until she suddenly halted and said, "Excuse me. I'm sorry to interrupt, but she's really insistent and has something to tell you."

I looked around at the otherwise empty room and asked, "She who?"

"I'm guessing she's the previous owner, an elderly woman. She's at the top of the stairs right now, and she wants to tell you she loves what you guys are doing with the house."

My eyebrows rose. That was the extent of my shock and awe. What I actually first thought was, yes, we were perpetually in a state of remodeling, and it was nice to know she didn't resent our removing the robin's-egg-blue-and-gold shag carpeting from the living room.

"She says the wood has a life of its own."

I nodded my earnest agreement, once again grateful she'd never opted to paint over all the natural wood trim and built-ins. The hardwood floors had recently been refinished after the aforementioned hideous carpet (no offense, Frances; I'm sure it was stunning in the '70s) had been disposed of.

More dumbfounded that my old pal possessed such a psychic gift and I'd never known it than unable to believe Frances was there for a visit, I stammered, "Did she turn on the water in the bathroom the other day?"

Char nodded, "She says she's sorry if she frightened you," which, of course, she hadn't. "She just wanted to see what kind of physical effect she could still have in this world before she moves on. And she has always loved that room."

Char added straightforwardly, speaking for herself this time, "I think she's not quite used to being dead yet."

Suddenly, it dawned on me, "Was Tuppence seeing her when she stopped near the top of the stairs all those times?"

Confirmed.

I told Char to tell Frances she was perfectly welcome to visit anytime; then Char said the spirit had exited. Please note that Char had never before been to my house, and she knew nothing beforehand of my experiences of the now-infamous Water Faucet Mystery.

I told Char she had "some 'splainin' to do," á la Ricky Ricardo, and I learned that when she was much younger she had died in a drowning accident and had been resuscitated. Since then, she discovered she could communicate with those on the Other Side. Something inside her on an energetic level had changed, too. For instance, she couldn't wear a watch. Put one on her, she said, and it invariably stopped cold.

She also told me fascinating stories of her work with local law enforcement officials to help them find missing persons who were supposed to have been murdered. Okay, I confess, I was pretty impressed.

But her credibility was further enhanced the next week, when my husband stopped by The Laughing Cup to drop off a script I'd written for her — it was for a commercial for her coffee shop.

He'd just approached the counter when Char launched, unbidden, into an eerily accurate description of the client from whose house he'd just come. She knew her age, hair color and style, and that this woman was angling to make him more than just her reflexologist, if you know what I mean. (And, no, there was no hanky panky between them.) This was just something that happened upon occasion in his work with particularly needy people; maybe reflexologists' clients experience emotional transference, too, just like psychotherapists.

Char warned him to keep strong boundaries around this client. He told me she'd only confirmed what he was already perceiving from this woman, but he was astounded that Char could get all that off of him and without his having said a single word.

It goes to show how much energy people give off and how certain people's energies can cling to and (often-negatively) affect us. World-famous medium James Van Praagh calls those people "energy vampires." I think I dated one of those after my divorce…

But I digress. Back to the story of Frances.

After Char's impromptu visit, I put her reading to the test. When Tuppence was traipsing up the stairs with me and stopped again near the top, I said, "Frances, if you're here, would you mind please moving back a bit so Tuppy can come up the stairs?"

No sooner had I said that than Tuppence bounded up the remaining steps.

"Thank you, Frances. You're always welcome here," I reiterated.

Tuppence, by the way, never hesitated at the steps again.

Communication: A Dying Art

Almost a year later, Frances helped facilitate one of the most important long-distance messages I ever sent.

My five elder siblings are actually all half-siblings. My sister Sandi and I shared the same father. The father of my sister Diane and brothers Dave, Don, and Doug was my mom's first husband, Art. He'd lived a hard-drinking, heavy-smoking life and, suffice it to say, certain of his behaviors caused many a rift in his own family.

But everyone, regardless of the mistakes he or she has made, has some redemptive quality, and Art had an enormous heart for his St. Bernards, Romeo and Juliet, his giant goldfish, and his rescued cockatiel, Samantha, not to mention myriad stray animals he'd cared for over the years. At any given time, he was feeding dozens of feral cats and keeping them sheltered in his rickety garage. He also bore one of the greenest thumbs I've ever seen, growing a palm tree from a seed in his Mounds View, Minnesota, greenhouse until it became so tall it had to be pruned, and those pieces propagated into still more trees, before it could burst through the ceiling. And he loved cooking Thanksgiving meals and made-from-scratch German potato pancake dinners for his extended family, of which I'd always been included as a part. Such was his contradictory nature.

It was an early summer morning in 1996. Art had been hospitalized with advanced-stage cancer and various respiratory ailments, and his prognosis was not good. My brother Dave, Art's eldest son, had flown in that day from San Diego.

Our mother called me to say that Dave was at Art's bedside. I was alone in the house, except for my pets, of course. I was gazing out the back door off the kitchen at the row of canna lilies along my picket fence. Art had given me twenty or so bulbs to plant each spring. (Mine didn't get enough light to reach the magnificent heights both he and my sister Diane could effortlessly achieve with theirs, but at least I tried and managed not to outright kill them.)

I said a quiet prayer for his passing to be peaceful and as pain-free as possible. Then a thought came to me and I enlisted the aid of my resident spirit, saying, "Frances, if you're still here and can hear me, could you please take this message to Art for me? Tell him it's okay to go now. His kids are with him, and they love him and forgive him. He doesn't need to keep suffering. It's okay to let go."

I'd shed a tear or two and turned around to cross through the kitchen when I saw it, the stove's right rear gas burner was burning with a high blue flame, and I had not even gone near the stove at all that morning!

I must explain that our kitchen had two doors through which one could enter it. Come in the one that was right across from the front foyer and you passed the stove on your left and a center island on your right. Come in through the other one near the rear of the house, just off the dining room, the way I had that morning, and you passed a small bathroom on the way to the back door. By that route, you're nowhere near the stove.

Nevertheless, again, I ran through my series of tests, such as walking unsteadily past the stove, arms swinging, to see if I could have accidentally hit the knob. Nope, it was the second one in, anyway, so I'd have turned on the front burner if I'd done it that way. I tried to catch the correct knob with the pocket on my skirt. No go again.

I'd just completed my last failed experiment when the phone rang. It was my mother, telling me Art had just passed away a couple minutes previously — approximately the same time the burner mysteriously lit itself.

The search for "logical" explanations exhausted, I had no choice but to tearfully thank Frances for relaying my message and perhaps even helping to guide Art's spirit to his next destination.

That was the last I ever heard, saw, or felt from Frances the Friendly Ghost. Perhaps the greater intelligence of the Universe knew she had this last important deed to do before moving on herself. Wherever she may be, I hope she still feels my gratitude.

Art made his own appearance when the grandfather clock Diane had inherited from him and had shipped to San Diego, where she was living at the time, mysteriously stopped. Not only that, but she says, "The pendulum fell off on Thanksgiving and the clock was not jarred or tipped upside down, nor was there even an earthquake to explain it." The weighted pendulum had had to have been physically lifted off its hook, she said, as none of the parts in question had been broken or damaged in any way.

My Good Buddy Bruce

Bruce Olson was a talented tie-dye artist I'd met when I was selling my handmade jewelry on the arts-and-crafts show circuit in the mid-'90s. We admired each other's work so much we frequently did trades. I'd make him a mismatched pair of earrings, say, a dog and a hydrant or Sherlock Holmes and his magnifying glass, to use as gifts, and he'd give me some of his brightly spattered sundresses or tank tops. He used a spray bottle to apply his dyes to the rubber banded fabrics so the saturation of color wasn't complete; the effect was singularly groovy and one I've never known anyone else to replicate.

He was only in his forties when he had to have a liver transplant. He survived that only to be struck down by cancer shortly thereafter, just a couple of years into his marriage to his lovely wife, Linda. His passage was tragically swift-moving, at least as seen by an outsider such as myself. For him and Linda, I'm sure it was too soon to be leaving and too long to keep suffering, all blended together.

Bruce was determined to follow through before it was too late on some promises he'd made in the past. For instance, he'd said he'd show me someday how to tie dye, but I figured it was one of those "We simply have to do lunch sometime" kinds of things said in passing. It was that pledge that led him to my basement with several bottles of fabric dye and a box full of rubber bands.

He was emaciated from the chemotherapy and had lost feeling in his hands, rendering them almost useless, but still he guided my husband, Anthony, and me through the steps to creating our own colorful, wearable works of art. We could never approach Bruce's earlier expertise, but I was pretty pleased with the outcome of our fledgling effort. Now, every time Anthony dons his tie-dyed boxer shorts or I put on one of my '70s-flashback T-shirts, we think of our friend.

It was an evening in mid-October 2005, almost 10 p.m., when Linda's call came. She explained that Bruce was at the U of M hospital and wasn't expected to live much longer. We hurried over, grateful of the chance to say goodbye.

Bruce was comatose but we talked freely to him anyway. I sang him a Finnish lullaby my father always sang to me. And before we left, I gave him specific instructions to let me know when he'd passed. I kissed his forehead and left.

Bruce

The next morning I wasn't in a big rush to get up to go to work, so I sort of lounged around in bed, my eyes closed to the morning but my brain busy organizing my day. Suddenly, I saw a flash of brilliant white light against the backs of my eyelids. My eyes flew open to see nothing but the soft morning light filtering through the venetian blinds. I said out loud to my ever-present pets, "I think Bruce just died." I looked over at the clock. It read 9:03 a.m.

Early afternoon that same day, Linda called to say Bruce had passed over peacefully that morning. I cautiously asked her if she knew the exact time of his death.

"Ooh, that's hard to say," she said. "I think it was around nine."

"Linda," I said, "I've got a little something to tell you …"

〰️ 〰️ 〰️

Just days after he died, Bruce made some interesting visits to me and to Linda. Twice, he knocked my purple clock off the back of the toilet tank in my bathroom. Repeated testing with jostling the tank, banging the seat, sitting down roughly while having the clock too close to the edge, etc. still didn't result in what had happened when I repeatedly heard those crashes. Even if I could manage to nudge the clock far enough toward the edge, it simply fell straight down to the floor beside the toilet tank. When Bruce was responsible, however, the clock managed to fly three feet in front of the toilet seat to the opposite wall!

I acknowledged the honor that he was bestowing on me by visiting —I think he chose me because I'd made it clear I was open to and expecting his presence and so he wouldn't be wasting his efforts on someone who would be too afraid or just oblivious to the messages he was sending. But, I added, "I love ya, buddy, but could you lay off that clock? You might break it, and it's my favorite one."

Ever agreeable, he moved on ... to the grandfather clock on our third floor. I was sitting there alone, reading, when I heard a single loud bong. This clock was in perfect working order and chimed fully and melodiously, but only on each quarter hour. The single-note chime Bruce sent me was at 7:21 p.m. Never before and never since has that clock made a noise like that between quarter hours.

I just smiled and said, "Hi there, Bruce. I love you, too."

You know, despite how much you miss their physical presence, I personally find it's a lot easier to accept someone's death when he or she hangs around briefly afterward like this to let you know all is well and he or she is never farther away than your thoughts.

Linda was more than a little freaked when I told her of the white light that signaled her husband's passing, but I think hearing it from me, someone she trusted not to be pulling her chain, allowed her to be a bit more ready when Bruce made his presence known at their house.

The first time, she told me, she smelled his cigar smoke as fresh as if he were sitting in his favorite chair, puffing away. No one had smoked in the house for months.

The next time, she was alone in her house upstairs when, suddenly, up from the basement came the blaring sounds of a stereo that had been unused for years. It had been tuned to a spot between stations and filled the house with cacophonous white noise. Linda was more upset than pleased by the visits, however, and asked me to have him cool it. I explained to Bruce that the visits were making it harder for Linda to cope with her loss and asked him to just pop in at our place if he felt the need because we found it comforting to know he was nearby.

To the best of my knowledge, no repeat performances have been made at his house or, I'm kind of sad to say, even at ours.

Editor's Note: I may have spoken too soon! Bruce's wife Linda explains in an email what she experienced after having had to put Bruce's German shepherd mix, Wilma, to sleep on May 2, 2009, a few years after her husband's passing: "I was sitting here on my couch yesterday after I got home from the vet. I was sobbing with my face in the arm of the couch, and I saw Bruce. He was walking quickly through a field, grinning. I clearly heard him joyously yell, "Willie!" Then I saw them together, Bruce laughing and petting her, and Wilma grinning up at him. I felt much better after that. It's so great to have friends to share these moments with who respect the magic."

~~~ ~~~ ~~~

We All Love Lucy

My mother, Lu Korpi, née Lucia Cacciapalle, was plunked in front of a microphone in sound technician Mark B.'s home studio in Minneapolis. He was told to start recording and "just let it keep running." It was October 20, 1997, and she'd just undergone her first chemotherapy treatment for inoperable lung cancer. To her chest was strapped a much smaller accordion than the 100-base version she'd first played sixty-plus years previously when she began working as a self-taught professional musician during the Depression, posing as her own mother's twenty-one-year-old sister when she was only fifteen so the two of them could work six nights per week playing gigs in taverns to support her grandmother and two siblings.

That day, the cancer had made her contralto voice a little raspier than usual, but the Source of All Kindness was with her and gave her one last opportunity to play and sing her favorite songs, leaving her children with a shining memorial of her phenomenal talent. Her voice carried much of her former power and energy, belying her frail frame.

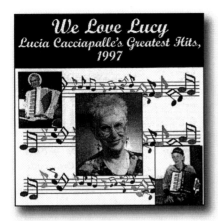

Among the thirty-plus songs Lucy recorded that day —including polkas like "Just Because," early classic rags like "Chattanooga Shoeshine Boy," and foreign-language ballads like "Celito Lindo"—was a beautiful rendering of "Red Sails in the Sunset" she performed on the house piano.

A couple of years after her death, I happened to have had the privilege to join my first husband's early-jazz band as the "canary," or vocalist. Risking the fact that I always want to burst into tears when I hear it, we decided to add "Red Sails in the Sunset" to our repertoire. The eight members of the Freight House Jazz Band were rehearsing in our sax player's basement the first time we tried out this song.

No sooner had I begun singing it than the light bulb over my head went out.

That could have been a simple coincidence; that bulb might have been at the end of its life, right?

Could have been a coincidence, but it wasn't.

As soon as the song was over, the same light bulb lit up again and stayed lit until we ran through "Red Sails" again later in the evening, when it pulled the same off/on stunt because my nephew, Dean, had dropped by for a listen. We all knew it was my mom making her presence known, no doubt glad to hear her musical legacy being carried on in some small way. Evidently, she was digging being an unencumbered spirit, capable of being with us whenever she liked, wherever we happened to be.

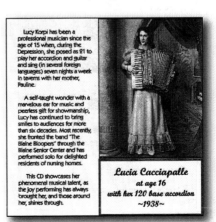

Lucy Korpi has been a professional musician since the age of 15 when, during the Depression, she posed as 21 to play her accordion and guitar and sing (in several foreign languages) seven nights a week in taverns with her mother, Pauline.

A self-taught wonder with a marvelous ear for music and peerless gift for showmanship, Lucy has continued to bring smiles to audiences for more than six decades. Most recently, she fronted the band "The Blaine Bloopers" through the Blaine Senior Center and has performed solo for delighted residents of nursing homes.

This CD showcases her phenomenal musical talent, as the joy performing has always brought her, and those around her, shines through.

Lucia Cacciapalle
at age 16
with her 120 base accordion
~1938~

The Bag Lady

Wonderful, generous, loving, and goofy-as-all-get-out most of the time, Mom was plagued her whole life through with terrible insecurities, leading her to be a bit of a green-eyed monster when it came to her hubbies. Her first husband, the aforementioned Art, unfortunately, had lent credence to many of her jealous suspicions, so she fostered that mistrusting mindset throughout her adult life. She often assumed she was somehow being betrayed, with or without substantive proof, and usually to her own emotional and relational detriment. One of her last lingering resentments had been directed toward an unhappy, middle-aged neighbor lady who, according to Mom, had once inappropriately rubbed the shoulders of her third husband/my stepfather, Lenny. Whether this was actually a big deal or not is irrelevant, as she sadly took that suspicion with her to the Other Side.

A few days after our mother had died in 1998, my brother Dave, who was staying at her house in Blaine, Minnesota, answered the doorbell. On the stoop stood said next-door neighbor, Julie B., her arms loaded with two grocery bags filled with homemade foods she'd made for our family. He opened the door and started to thank her for her thoughtfulness when, suddenly, both bags flew out of the woman's arms and onto the concrete steps between them.

Her eyes grew wide and she exclaimed, "I don't know how that happened! I was just standing here. It was almost as if something pushed them out of my arms!"

Dave helped pick up the dropped items — luckily, none of the Tupperware containers spilled, thanked Julie again, and then took the bags inside. Once the door was closed, he smiled knowingly and said out loud in mock chastisement, "Mom! Shame on you!"

Waterworks

For my mother's memorial service, we pulled out all the stops. We had a four-piece Dixieland jazz band (Fidgety Feet, my ex's first such band) playing New Orleans-style hymns.

We had a huge banner that had been put together for her surprise seventy-fifth birthday party two years before, featuring photos and reminiscences and wacky stories of her goofier exploits, such as the time in the '70s when she initiated a "pancake fight" with me at the kitchen table, just for fun.

More recently, two more panels had been added from her hospice bedroom, where all her visitors wrote on colored slips of paper an adjective to complete the sentence: "Lucy Korpi is…" I wanted her to be able to look up and constantly see what wonderful things people thought of her and how loved she was.

We had a stereo that played a few of her own songs from the recently recorded CD. Believe me, she was such an extrovert and ham, I know she was tickled pink to sing at her own service.

We danced a symbolic four-person schottische with me holding her invisible hand as my partner. She never missed a step … I think.

And last, but not least, we gave her a twenty-one-squirt-gun salute! This, of course, degenerated into a water fight, which kind of freaked out the Morningside Memorial Gardens staff but was absolutely perfect for the celebration of our zany mother.

The day had been beautiful and sunny throughout the service. Then we went to her favorite restaurant, Old Country Buffet, for the reception, where we played more of her music on a portable cassette player. When it came time to leave, however, the skies suddenly turned dark, and it started raining … but only over the parking lot in which we stood and a few adjacent blocks! Two minutes of driving, and we were back to sunny skies.

My sister Diane was just starting to drive home her then-boyfriend Mike K. and his granddaughters when the youngest one, age five, suddenly rolled down her window and began shooting water outside with her squirt gun. When asked what she was doing, she simply stated, "Grandma Lu was spraying us with water, so I'm just squirting her back."

All I Have to Do Is Dream

During my divorce process, I felt very sad, afraid, and unsure that I could make it on my own. A man I was seeing at the time, Joe, who shared my strong connection to the spiritual world, listened to my tales of woe, then wrote something he wouldn't show me on the back of a small card. He placed it, written side down, on his kitchen table. Then we went for a walk, and that was the last I thought about it.

That night, I had an intensely real-feeling dream that my dead father and mother were alive again and with me. I seldom dreamed of my parents, and when I did, the dreams were rather nightmarish, wherein it was understood they were dying of cancer all over again and about to leave me. This dream was markedly different.

My dad was in the uniform he'd worn when he worked as a deputy sheriff in the 1950s. He sat on the front steps of the house I'd grown up in and put his arm around me. My mom was watching us through the front door screen. I was telling them of how terrified I was—apparently there was a giant snake out there in the yard threatening me; I can't clearly remember more about that part. They both told me they loved me and were very proud of who I'd become. They assured me they were around and not leaving me to face things alone. Then the dream ended, and I awoke with tears of relief, happiness, and gratitude making a salty, soggy puddle on my pillowcase.

That afternoon, I hurried over to Joe's house and tearfully told him the wonderful dream I'd had. After I had finished, he silently walked over to the table, where he picked up the card on which he'd written that significant something the day before.

My knees nearly buckled when I read it: "I asked Lu and Elmer (my parents) to send Sid a dream of love and support." It was dated the day before.

There is no doubt in my mind that our most-beloved ones can and do receive our hearts' messages and give us theirs in return.

And this was no fluke. Even when this gentleman and I hadn't spoken for a long while, if I were thinking of him and asked my mother to send him a dream, he'd invariably call or email me the next day and say he'd dreamed of my mother, whom he'd never met while she was alive.

66

Home for the Holidays

Apparently, our loved ones often like to conserve energy, showing signs of their presence when groups of family members are gathered.

SUBMITTED STORY

Lucy's Hello

My mother loves to make her visits known to us in interesting ways. The first Thanksgiving we celebrated after her death, she waited until all of her kids, who were in Minnesota at the time, were gathered together in my living room. As the day wore on, we all started to feel a little chilly, then downright

Samantha

cold. We checked and discovered the furnace's pilot light had blown out. We didn't associate it necessarily with our mother until the very same thing happened on Christmas Eve, when we were all again gathered in my living room opening gifts.

Though, of course, we were glad of her presence around us, I had to ask her not to use that particular method of reaching us because the drop in temperature was bad for our cockatiel Samantha's health. Mom readily complied.

Here's little background on this dear bird: Samantha was born with a defect called bumble feet and would have been killed by the breeder if my sibling's father, Art, hadn't rescued her. After Art died, I dreamed of Samantha for the first time ever. Then next morning, my sister called and asked me out of the blue: "Would you be interested in taking my dad's bird?"

Though I'd never had a bird before, I said, "Well, she came to me in a dream last night, so I guess I'm supposed to." Luckily, my husband didn't "squawk" about it. Sweet Samantha was a delightful addition to our home for more than six years. I still miss her bliss over having a spray-bottle shower bath.

~~~ ~~~ ~~~

Chuck's Passover Visit

by Cindy Sue Benzaquen of St. Louis Park, Minnesota

Chuck was my stepfather since I was thirteen. He was more of a father to me than my own father, who disappeared to Europe after he was divorced from my mother when I was eleven.

Chuck was a kind and gentle soul, but he was also very firm and commanded respect. He was deeply passionate about Israel and very proud to be Jewish.

He did not like all the hubbub associated with family gatherings but was always present at any Sabbath meal or Jewish holiday.

He was always bragging that Momy, my husband, was his son-in-law and was an ex-Israeli soldier. Chuck died two years ago this Father's Day (in 2007). It was so strange and coincidental that right during the Passover meal at my mother's house, when my brother was cutting up the turkey, which was normally Chuck's job for the last thirty-four years, all of a sudden, the phone rang. Momy had just been commenting that he was thinking about Chuck at that very moment, and the voice on the other end of the phone asked for Chuck!

Goosebumps went up and down our arms as all of us heard the voice and remembered Chuck's voice just then.

It was so amazing we couldn't get over it! We all just sat there with our jaws dropped open and said, "WOW!" He was trying to make a connection with all of us. His spirit was all around that house then at that very moment.

Talk Through the Animals

I've shared instances when folks on the Other Side have communicated through natural elements and other energetic means. They also can utilize our animal friends to send their symbolic messages.

Cardinal Knowledge

As you've probably inferred, my mother was quite a colorful gal. Red was her lifelong favorite color, so when she passed over, I asked her to send me beautiful red cardinals to indicate her presence. Now, of course, I know she has not sent me every cardinal I encounter—although every time I see one or hear one singing, I do think of her and send her my love. But the timing of several key appearances—such as every single time my siblings come over for a holiday dinner—leave me little doubt that these gorgeous birds carry her loving message on their wings.

There have been too many to note here, but I'll list a few of the highlights.

#1) After my divorce, I was trying to end a painful relationship with a chronically depressed man I was trying desperately, wrongly, futilely to "fix." We'd just had our 175th argument, and I literally prayed we were finally over.

His fiftieth birthday was coming up soon, and I awoke one morning and somehow *knew* I was supposed to throw him a surprise party, even though we weren't a couple anymore, in a last-ditch effort to show him how much he mattered to a great many people, so I could feel I'd at least done him some good despite the failure of our private relationship.

The so-called "responsibility" fell to me, I felt, because I had a long history of creative party planning/catering and was, frankly, the only one who could (or would bother trying to) pull it off. I knew even then it was not going to be an effort to win him back; I shuddered at giving him that mixed message. I even planned to deliver the food to the church basement site, leave, and return to clean up after he was gone. Despite my misgivings, the intuitive feeling was very clear; I had to do this as part of my own soul's purpose and to practice unconditional love for someone whose behavior often made that quite difficult. I had to strengthen my own best self in completing this task.

I knew this in a very deep part of me, but still the first thing I said to my Guides that had "inspired" me with the idea: "Oh man, you have got to be kidding me! No way. No f***ing way. That's nuts!"

I don't mince words with my Guides.

To confirm that this was truly a message from beyond and not a co-dependent relapse, I went to Springbrook Nature Center in Fridley, Minnesota. I would often go there on long meditative walks to process my painful emotions as my mother's illness grew worse years earlier. Few people were there and I had the chance to commune with Nature in solitude, feel grounded, de-stress, and talk to my Guides freely, without a passerby assuming I was schizophrenic for talking out loud to myself.

This time, I was deeply conflicted. I didn't want to go through this much effort and expense if I were simply prolonging a painful situation. But if I could accept that this was truly coming from the Divine Source, I knew I would do it. The problem was, how could I be sure I wasn't just acting out of some strange version of post-traumatic stress syndrome induced by the past five years in which I'd lost three beloved family members, four cherished pets, my marriage, etc. I was desperate for confirmation that this was not a wacky idea of my own making, rather, that it was what I was really supposed to do for my spiritual growth—my own Ark that needed building, or some such thing—in order to heal myself.

Well, I was fretfully walking through those beautiful early-fall woods, asking my Guides, my mother, and/or whatever Higher Power was looking out for me to "Give me a sign, please, that this is really what You want me to do." No sooner had I uttered that request than I rounded a sharp corner along the wood-chipped path and came face-to-face with a brilliant red male cardinal perched at eye level in a bush. I froze, not quite three feet away from him, and stared at the beautiful bird that made no effort to fly away, and my heart nearly burst with gratitude. I began shaking and tears flowed freely, as I mouthed my thanks to the Universe. It had to be a couple full minutes before the bird finally took flight. I had my answer, presented in unambiguous terms.

By the way, the party was tremendous if I do say so myself. I decorated the Walker Community Church's party room and hung a banner I'd made with scanned pictures from throughout the man's life, emphasizing his talents and other various good points for all to see. I made fourteen entrées that fed the thirty+ folks who all managed to conspire with me to get him to a fake band rehearsal at the Minneapolis church. I wasn't able to leave, per se, but I stayed busy in the kitchen the whole time so as not to detract from the party's proper focus, the birthday boy. I was grateful to notice that several mutual friends who knew what had been happening between us looked at me with respect and what I believe was some measure of understanding that I was doing this with a pure heart for someone I had truly loved and wished the best for.

What he ever felt about the experience and whether it made any discernable difference in his life, I cannot say. By my efforts, I provided him with the *opportunity* to heal his damaged heart just a little; I am not responsible for the results. I came away from the experience stronger, more open-hearted, and more courageous than before. At the very least, I owe him my thanks for being the impetus for that growth in me.

#2) The day of my step-uncle Benjamin's funeral, I'd taken a walk along the Heritage Trail near St. Anthony Main in Minneapolis to get centered for yet another funeral service at which I'd be delivering a eulogy. I stopped on a wooden bridge overlooking a stream near the main body of the Mississippi River, rehearsing what I'd written, when a cardinal swooped down from a tree, missing my head by only a couple of feet. That certainly got my attention. I knew my mother had been there to greet Ben, and I smiled.

As an aside, Ben sent his own animal emissary to his memorial service that day. When people first arrived to get things set up, they saw a duck had waddled up to the twin glass doors of the church and was pecking at the glass, trying to get in. They had a heck of a time trying to dissuade it from coming inside.

My mother had frequently taken Ben, who was mentally retarded, on outings to Roseville's Central Park to feed the ducks. It seemed fitting that he should choose that particular critter to represent him. How does that song go again? "Be kind to your web-footed friends, for a duck may be somebody's brother"?

#3) In 2005, the ancient 1988 Toyota I'd inherited from my mother was on its last legs, so, sadly, I donated it to Auto Technical Institute (ATI) in St. Paul, where I knew it would be repaired and made available to a low-income family or given free of charge to a women's shelter. As much as I enjoyed riding my 1950s replica Schwinn Cruiser bicycle to work through the early summer, I knew I would eventually need to get another car.

Anthony and I had just gone to a Toyota dealership, and I looked at other older cars, knowing that they just had to be reliable, not fancy, for my purposes. Just before they were about to close, I got behind the wheel of a 2004 Corolla for a test drive. I never imagined myself in so new a car, but something about it felt astoundingly *right*. That really surprised me, but the thought that popped into my head and wouldn't leave was, "I'll know my next car by its license plate. It'll have Mom's initials on it." There it was, that certainty that comes from thoughts I don't think I personally generate, ones that were inspired by my Spirit Guides and/or my mother and just sort of pop out of my mouth so I'll be sure to hear them.

The next day, Anthony called up a young couple who'd advertised in the Minneapolis *Star Tribune* a 2004 Toyota Corolla for sale in my price range due to its having fairly high freeway miles. I made arrangements to see the car, and that afternoon I walked outside to greet the owner as he drove up.

Before I made it to the sand-colored Corolla, however, I stopped in my tracks. Right there in the street, I started jumping up and down and screaming with glee. The license plate was LKB 819, and

Lucy Korpi was my mother's name! I had zero doubt that this was going to be my car. I almost didn't bother test driving it.

To his credit, the young man took my histrionics in stride and thought it a very positive omen that my mother's initials were on the car as I'd predicted the night before. He and his wife—he was from Alabama and she from China—were both musicians with the Duluth Symphony Orchestra, thus the high highway commute miles from Minneapolis, and they had been invited to move to Beijing and join that city's orchestra. We chatted a good long while, and I explained all about the messages my mother sent me. I liked them both very well, especially when his lovely wife told me that the appearance of a cardinal is considered very good luck in China.

I said to them, "Don't be a bit surprised if my mother sends you a cardinal because of this." They grinned. I cast over my shoulder as I left, "I'm serious, you know. She'll do it."

That very evening, the young man called me, excitedly telling me that he and his wife had just been out barbecuing, and when they sat down to eat, a bright red cardinal flew down to rest on a pine tree bough just a couple of feet from their picnic table and stayed throughout their entire meal.

He said, "You should have seen my wife's face! She looked, um..."

"Like she'd seen a ghost?" I offered.

"Exactly," he laughed.

"I told you so. My mom's got great follow-through."

#4) After I'd accepted Anthony's wedding proposal and we were planning our wedding (see Pennies from Heaven, page 75, for more magical details of our shared afterlife connections), he and I were on the phone, talking mush and confirming our mutual certainty that this was the right move for both of us, and I abruptly stopped speaking, my voice now choked with tears. I was looking out my picture window and saw not one, not two, but SIX CARDINALS at my bird feeder!! I'd never seen more than a single male-female pair together before in my entire life. This was a stunning endorsement of the next step we were taking with our lives.

Kamikaze Sparrows

Some months after my mother had died, I met our close mutual friend Loraine for lunch. We hadn't seen each other in quite a while, so this was like a reunion. On our way to the restaurant, as I drove down a quiet backstreet in South Minneapolis, a cluster of maybe ten sparrows landed in front of my car, forcing me to put on the brakes. Seconds later, they flew into the air, only to land in the same grouping in front of my car maybe twenty feet further down the road. Again, I had to brake for them. This happened no fewer than four times on the same street when a pickup truck that had been behind us pulled alongside my car and the driver rolled down his window.

Expecting to be the victim of this stranger's road rage, I immediately launched into an explanation about why I kept stopping in the middle of the street. "I HAD to stop, sir. All these birds keep landing together right in front of my car, and I'm NOT going to run them over!"

Instead of being angry, though, the gentleman said, "No, I just wanted to let you know your brake lights are both out."

I'd have never known and might have gotten in a serious rear-end collision if my mother hadn't used those birds to reveal the car's defect that way. As soon as I'd expressed my thanks to this kind stranger, I drove on, with nary a sparrow to block my passage. Her message had been received.

As we proceeded to our lunch date, we talked nonstop about the goofiness of my mom in the car (with the radio off so we could focus solely on the conversation). Loraine and I then went into the restaurant and later, upon returning to the car and starting the engine, discovered my mother had evidently wanted to say hello again, or confirm my sparrows-as-messengers hypothesis. This time she did it by turning on the previously silent radio full blast. We both jumped in our seats when the high-decibel greeting accosted our ears. The doors had been locked, the windows rolled up, and nothing else had been disturbed in the car; and neither Loraine nor I had touched that radio before leaving the vehicle. Anyone with another explanation for this is welcome to share it with me.

Pennies from Heaven

We had a "Pennies from Heaven" theme at our wedding. This is an excerpt from the text for Anthony's and my wedding program.

… Sid and Anthony knew their rightness for one another in a short amount of time, this is true, but when a pairing is apparently arranged, blessed (and beautifully meddled with) by one's dearly departed parents, who's gonna argue?

What? Didn't they tell you that part? Well, that's where the "Pennies from Heaven" theme comes in.

Sid and Anthony came to realize their mothers (Lucy and Maggie, respectively) had probably actually met when they were alive. They had each had a child at St. Mary's hospital in Minneapolis, just two days apart, in January 1962 — namely, Sid (January 27) and Anthony's brother George (January 25). Who knows? Maybe "baby girl Korpi" and "baby boy Kaczor" were nestled in beds next to each other and complained to the nurses of each other's snoring!

More than four decades later, the two mothers clearly reconnected on the Other Side, compared their Earthbound children's heartfelt wish lists, discovered by them via prayers overheard (Sid's for someone with healthy self-esteem who would truly appreciate her and Anthony's simply for happiness) and said simultaneously, "Hey, that sounds like my kid! Maybe we should get them together!"

Among other things, Lucy loves to leave pennies for Sid to find as a reminder that she's around. She then started to include Anthony in this, leaving pennies in odd places, such as on his bedspread (after the bed has been made, untouched by anyone else, and heretofore penny-free), for instance.

Maggie, on the other hand, stops clocks to say hello, including stopping Sid's battery-powered kitchen clock for three hours and then restarting it.

But continuing in the copper-currency vein …

Anthony proposed marriage in Sid's kitchen on September 10th and presented her with a tin ring he'd won six years earlier at a church festival at some kids' game. This beautifully tacky "place-saver" held an actual penny that spun around. Something had told him to keep it all those years.

That same evening, at friends Joe and Mary Ann O.'s invitation to hear Joe's brother's band, Sid and Anthony went swing dancing to celebrate their betrothal at yet another church festival, this one at St. Odilia's. There, the Jerry O'Hagan Big Band was playing, and vocalist Charmin Michelle just happened to start crooning "Pennies from Heaven" as if just for them as they arrived.

The following week, the lovebirds were led to their engagement/wedding rings by the Mom Squad, who helped them pick them out in just five minutes — as the store was closing no less — and even scored a fifteen percent discount from the woman in the credit department. The store in question: JCPenneys.

(Like, pennies, get it? And, what's more, Sid bought her wedding dress and Anthony his wedding suit at Penneys, too, over the next few weeks — both as effortlessly found as their rings.)

After buying the rings that night, Sid and Anthony went to let the momentousness of the day's events sink in while gazing at the Minneapolis skyline along Lake Calhoun. The night was temperate but totally overcast. No stars, no moon were to be seen ... save for one conjoined pair of stars directly situated before them. They both stared in astonishment at what could not have been physically possible to see, for there was no break in the cloud cover, and no stars could be closer to Earth than those clouds, yet there they were ... two more glistening pennies from Heaven.

Lucy and Maggie thank you all for joining in celebrating the magical union of their two adorable children.

Blessed be.

Mavis' Ladybug

I was blessed to know a phenomenal woman named Mavis Vitums for more than a decade. There were more times than I could count when I saw evidence of her doing the work of angels in people's lives, my own included. She was the most giving person I think I've ever known. In her sixty-eight years on Earth, she had fostered dozens upon dozens of children and later gave homes to adults in need of foster care, including my stepfather Leonard and his mentally retarded brother Benjamin, who both lived quite happily in Mavis' home until their deaths in 2001 and 2003, respectively.

After years of battling numerous forms of cancer and heart disease —after even having died twice in the ER and been resuscitated—she finally chose to let herself stop fighting and truly transform into the celestial being I knew she always was on the inside.

However, while she was in hospice care in her nursing home room, a few days before she died, I had said to her, "Mavis, we have to work out an important detail. What are you going to send me as a sign that you're around and doing all right once you pass? I want to be able to recognize it."

She thought a moment and then said with a grin, "A ladybug. Red with black spots. I think they're classy."

Well, she died on September 19, 2007, and I was to perform a wedding ceremony on September 21. I'd gone into the ladies' restroom at the golf course clubhouse in Shakopee, Minnesota, for a final freshening up before the ceremony was to begin, and when I reached into a basket of paper towels to dry my hands, I stopped short because there, atop the stack of towels was a red ladybug with black spots!

The members of the bridal party who'd been gathered there waiting for the big moment said they'd seen it earlier and just thought, "Oh that's nice. It's good luck."

I told them of Mavis' promise to send me a ladybug, and they promptly cursed me out for making them all cry before the ceremony. I put the bug on my left palm and ran around the party room, showing as many of the 250 guests and/or wedding party members as I could find. The ladybug just contentedly sat on my hand, occasionally stretching its legs and preening but otherwise never budging. I picked up my note cards and decided I would perform the ceremony with a bug on my hand. The wedding went off without a hitch; I can't imagine where my newfound confidence could have come from!

My husband took a Polaroid picture of this as untampered-with photographic evidence.

After about an hour of holding my palm turned upward, though, my hand started to cramp. I said to the ladybug, "I'm going to have to have you climb up on my dress, okay?"

As if it understood me, it began crawling toward my chest when I held my hand next to me and wound up positioning itself on my dress approximately where a brooch would go. It sat there for nearly another half-hour then

Mavis' "Ladybug" 9/21/07

got a little bit "antsy," pardon the pun, and crawled along my collar.

I said to it, "Oh, I get it. You have to go now, right? I'll take you outside."

I placed the bug back on my left palm, where it sat, pouting, legs tucked in and unmoving. My husband, Anthony, and I went outside to near the waterfall beside which I'd just performed the ceremony. The ladybug remained motionless until I said, "I see some impatiens in the rocks over there. I'll put you there, okay?"

The instant I'd said that, the bug began crawling up my palm to the tip of my index finger, just like a trained flea circus performer. I placed my finger next to a leaf on the purple impatiens plant, and the ladybug readily climbed onto it. I turned for just a second to hug my husband and say tearfully to the heavens, "Mavis, you rock!"

When I turned back, the ladybug had disappeared.

Later on, as we were leaving, I saw Stacy, a.k.a. the new Mrs. Jake Adelmann, racing across the parking lot like a runaway bride, only she was running toward us. She called out, "Tell your friend how grateful we are she came to our wedding!"

In honor of Mavis, for Halloween, I dressed up my two Westies, Mortimer and Blanche, as, you guessed it — ladybugs.

Our Geezer Gala Gals

On March 20, 2009, my husband Anthony turned fifty. He wanted a big shindig to celebrate, but I said teasingly, knowing his tendency to develop grandiose ideas and trust me to make them happen, "There's no way we're going to that much effort and expense just for you!"

We wound up planning a party that was specifically aimed at anyone who would be turning fifty that year, their friends, and the general public. Then we decided to try and have some lasting good come of the event, and thus was born the "Geezer Gala—'50s Sock Hop & Alzheimer's Fundraiser." We decorated St. Clement's Catholic Church auditorium in Northeast Minneapolis like a malt shop; had a great band, Rich & the Resistors, playing terrific oldies music; provided genuine 1959-based "vintage" birthday presents for those fellow half-centurions and gave prizes for the best '50s costumes/dancers; had a magician perform; and served chili dogs, popcorn, and root beer floats, as well as birthday cake. We managed to get some publicity about the event and wound up with 165 people filling the place to comfortable capacity and keeping the dance floor jumping. At only five dollars per donation, we still managed to collect just over $1,000 for the Alzheimer's Association. We'd also set up a Memory Board for people to post pictures and/or write messages to people they knew who were afflicted by this "Disease of the Living Lost," as I call it.

Several things indicated the time was right for us to do this. For one, I had just officiated a wedding in Anoka and was passing out Geezer Gala invitations to the parents and stepparents when one of the women read the invitation and sighed, "You know, my uncle is Verne Gagne." (He is a world-famous retired wrestler from Minnesota who had been in all the local headlines for having attacked a fellow nursing home resident during an argument, breaking the ninety-seven-year-old man's hip and causing his death due to complications two weeks later. Both men suffered from dementia, and Gagne was later judged not responsible for his actions.)

We dedicated the Geezer Gala to these individuals and their families, as well as Anthony's Aunt Deloris, my former father-in-law's mother Wilhelmina, and our dear friend Evelyn, who had just passed away the month before at age ninety-six and had suffered from Alzheimer's for about five years.

We received unmistakable blessings from the Other Side the weekend of the party. From my mom — I had a cardinal waiting on a tree branch directly overhead, singing his heart out, every time I stepped out of my house (this was the first cardinal I'd seen in several months); from Anthony's mom Maggie — I found a penny as I was buying the last of the dance contest prizes, a hula hoop for the Twist-Off; and from Mavis — while I was sweeping up the church floor, I discovered a dead ladybug in the debris! The day we were taking down the decorations, however, I discovered a *living* ladybug crawling under the checkerboard "Scene Setters" (temporary wainscoting) cloth! This is Minnesota, and we were barely out of one of our harshest winters on record. Live ladybugs are not common this time of year, I assure you!

The fourth such message came when my husband carried in the keg of root beer just before the party. I saw the unusual brand,

Anthony & Sid at their wedding with gal pal Evelyn Huffman, center. December 21, 2004.

Frostop, and I said to him, "I was wondering what Evelyn would be sending us to let us know she's around! It's this root beer." I hadn't had this brand in more than forty years, since I was a small child and my mother took me to the Frostop drive-in restaurant in Fridley, Minnesota, after our trips to Moore Lake beach. That is, until I had some bottles of it served to me just a few years ago by Evelyn before she'd had to move into a nursing home. She was the only person I'd known who bought that brand. I didn't even know where I could find it if I'd wanted to, and yet here it was at the sock hop we were dedicating to her memory.

With that high-powered spiritual support team behind us it's no wonder the evening was such a success and had people clamoring for us to make the Geezer Gala an annual event!

Part Three:
Animals and the Afterlife

As promised earlier, I am about to tie into the subject of pet loss all the aforementioned examples of afterlife connections. It is my fondest desire to have what I have seen, personally experienced, and/or discovered about our beloved animals' so-called "exit" from this form of reality we as finite humans are able to comprehend give you a measure of comfort when facing a companion animal's impending death or when dealing with your own grief after the fact.

> When your companion passes, there's a "new spiritual relationship you have; it's the love and communication that is possible between you in the physical world and your pet in the spirit world."
>
> —Eleanor L. Harris, *Pet Loss: A Spiritual Guide*

As dark and painful as the grieving process can be and often is, we never need feel we are completely alone in times of trial. For a great many, a religious faith assures them of this. For others, the assurance comes as more an open communication from a spiritual realm. I truly believe there exists a loving energy beyond what we can readily perceive on our Earthly plane. Whether this is derived directly from the spirits of our loved ones or from ancestors who have passed on, our lost companion animals themselves, angels, Spirit Guides, the collective unconscious of the Universe, Nature, God, Jesus, Mary, gods/goddesses, Buddha, Allah, the Divine Source, Light, etc., etc., etc.—however you choose to view it, using whatever form or image best resonates with you—it is there and readily accessible to anyone who is open to its signs and messages.

Can scientists necessarily re-create these experiences under controlled circumstances for the sake of amassing empirical evidence?

Probably not. Does that mean the events never took place, never brought comfort, never soothed a breaking heart? Definitely not. I once read of a famous magician who was asked to explain the secrets of his magic. He said, "To those who believe, no explanation is necessary. To those who do not, no explanation is possible."

Those of you who wish to have faith in the shared experience of love these stories hold will doubtless find healing here. Thankfully, those who would write us all off as getting "scary scores" on the MMPI (Minnesota Multiphasic Personality Inventory) — meaning we're being fitted for our straitjackets now — probably won't have picked up this book in the first place. Most people who have loved their companion animals as much as we do, and who have held them in as high esteem as we have, will feel an essential truth underlying every story.

But good journalism is balanced, so I'll play my own devil's advocate. Perhaps these people (myself included) were just so desperate to continue their connection with their lost loved ones that they imagined these sightings/events. Could be, Doubting Thomas. But, even so I say, "So what if they did?" Maybe that was their own inner wisdom stepping up to help them cope in a crisis, kind of like the many defense mechanisms, such as denial or sublimation, we humans employ when a stressor is just too great to adapt to. They serve a purpose, namely to

> "Many humans view the body as a structure that contains the soul. But the body is created by the soul, the same way an idea exists before we manifest it into physical form." The term soul means "the highest divine energy of who we are that creates our physical form." Spirit means "the life force within the body that lifts out after death, rises into the light, and rejoins with the soul. The soul creates whatever physical form it desires for each lifetime in order to learn the lessons it wants to learn."
>
> –Jacquelin Smith,
> *Animal Communication: Our Sacred Connection*

protect a fragile psyche, when used for the short-term. It only gets dicey when the defense mechanism becomes the natural default on a day-to-day basis.

I cannot speak for the dozens upon dozens of wonderful folks who opened their wounded hearts to tell their extraordinary stories for this book—although I strongly suspect they're all being completely honest in what they've shared—but I can and do swear on my dearly departed and even still-living pets' souls everything I share with you that I myself experienced is the absolute, unvarnished truth. It's these experiences that prompted me to write this book in the first place, and they're wondrous enough for me to let them stand on their own merits.

As always, I advise you to use what you can to help you lessen your pain or gain a broader perspective of the cycle of life, discard whatever does not work for you, and know the intention of each writer was doubtless to help as many other bereaved animal-loving people as she or he could.

Genevieve– A Story of Guilt and Forgiveness

It was the mid-1990s, and shortly after her fraternal Siamese twin brother, Dudley, died, that my gorgeous chocolate-/seal-point Siamese cat Genevieve (pronounced in the French way, like the actress Genevieve Bujold, star of the movie *Coma*) became ill as well. We'd had her in to the vet's office on an almost daily basis, until one day, she appeared to be at death's door, weak and listless, and we made that always-impossible decision to have her euthanized. In the car on the way to her doctor's office for that final visit, however, Genevieve became energetic and agitated. I, of course, was sobbing and confused the whole way there. I would have sworn she'd been ready to pass over.

Noting her renewed vim and vigor, even the vet said, "This is NOT the cat I've been seeing these last several days!"

Hoping against hope that she'd spontaneously healed, we took home our darling girl and spent the day petting, kissing, and loving her up.

Needing a short break from all the stress and heartache, and seeing a window of opportunity to unwind while Genevieve appeared to be better, we accepted my mother's invitation to come over for dinner and play pinochle that evening. It was a warm summer night, so I left the small windows open between our living room and the enclosed porch, and as always, I locked the front porch door with a latch hook. I kissed her goodbye and we left Genevieve comfortably asleep on the couch on the porch, which she loved.

My mom lived twenty-five miles away from us, and we decided to spend the night at her house in the guest room rather than drive home because it was very late when we finished our last game. Please note, this was highly unusual for us. I can count on one hand the number of times we chose to stay over. Even at the time, I wondered at our decision. It seemed something we were supposed to do.

When we returned the next morning, we found out why we'd been mysteriously compelled to stay away: Genevieve was gone.

Genevieve at the threshold

The front porch, front door, and back door of the house were all still locked. Though we called and searched and tore apart the house for an hour, there was no sign of our beloved feline child. A neighbor said he'd seen her briefly standing on the back stoop the evening before. Though it was physically impossible, my soul itself knew it was true. Something otherworldly must have assisted her in her escape.

My husband searched the neighborhood as thoroughly as he could, but I just looked at him through my tears and said, "Don't bother; she's gone" and went inside to bawl my eyes out.

A part of me knew we'd purposely been distracted (i.e., sent to my mother's place) so she could slip away unnoticed to die naturally. Genevieve so didn't want to be put to sleep at the vet's, she'd mustered all her remaining strength to fake us all out that she was well enough to return home.

I knew this in my heart to be true, she'd done it to make things easier on us all; but I was absolutely tormented by the image of my poor baby getting out and then being on the back stoop, trying in vain to get back into the house while I, the worst cat-mother on Earth, was off enjoying myself! Each time the forlorn mental picture formed, I'd collapse in another puddle of guilt-ridden sobs.

That night, I slept quite fitfully, intermittently soaking my pillowcase with still more tears.

Then a most poignant thing happened. I'd heard somewhere — on a "Batman" cartoon episode, I think — that when you dream, you cannot read actual words. Now, as much faith as I put in the reliability of animated characters' psychological theory, I beg to differ. I'm a professional proofreader and editor, and I can and do often dream with words and puns, literally.

I'd had a very brief dream just before waking the next morning in which I was proofreading a newspaper with a giant headline that simply read: "The End." Using my pun-based method of dream interpretation, I knew this meant I was needing the bad "news," the "proof" that this was indeed "the end" of Genevieve's fifteen-year life.

Shortly thereafter, I received a call out of the blue from a friend named Alison who makes her living as a psychic medium. She asked how I was doing. I told her, "Not well," and explained what had happened.

Alison responded, "So that's why they told me I had to call you this morning!" She was referring to her Spirit Guides, who gave her uncanny information from the Other Side.

She insisted on coming right over to help. When she arrived, she suggested we take one more walk around the block. My neighbor and friend, Lorraine, joined us. Alison said, "Does the address 3737 Emerson Avenue mean anything to you? Could Genevieve have gone there?"

I thought about it and said, "No, she'd never have been strong enough to make it there. Besides, she was an indoor cat." We were on the 3700 block of Elliot Avenue in Minneapolis, and Emerson was roughly a mile and a half due west of our Powderhorn Park neighborhood, past a freeway, in Uptown.

We made it to the end of the block, passing a garbage can in the alley across from our house that had the house number 3737 painted on it. At the very end of the block, we encountered a neighbor's beautiful German shepherd/wolf named Mullock* in his yard. Alison said, "He knows why you're hurting. I think he saw her come this way. Maybe that's where I got the '3737' from. It might have been something Genevieve had seen as she passed by."

Mullock was usually enthused and excited to see me because I'd always reach over the fence and give him a massage for his arthritic hips and a rawhide chew toy to enjoy. This time, though, he approached the fence very slowly, head down. Then he looked up into my eyes, and I swear that mystically beautiful dog wore a somber expression of deep sympathy and compassion as he looked right into me. I sobbed again.

Alison, Lorraine, and I turned back to go to my home when Alison said, "No. That's not all of it. Sorry, but they keep sending me 3737 Emerson. Let's take a ride."

We all piled into Alison's car and I directed her to the street she'd never before been on. We traveled west on East 38th Street, over Interstate 35W, past Nicollet Avenue, and on to King's Highway, which was a bit of a misnomer because it was more of a "mall," a two-way street with a tree-lined median dividing them. Next up would have been the 3700 block of Emerson Avenue. I say that because we could go no further. We were facing the enormous Lakewood Cemetery, where that 3737 address, if such a one existed, would have been! There was my "proof" that it was "the end" of Genevieve's life!

Genevieve

We drove through the beautiful, fenced-in cemetery, past the mausoleum and glorious headstones and other monuments, and we all cried, with equal parts sorrow and joy, because we knew this was the comforting message from Genevieve and/or those who'd greeted her on the Other Side to let me know I'd been right to stop looking for her, that she'd peacefully passed on just as she'd wanted to, and that she loved me enough to release me from my guilt over having left her alone that fateful night. My heart was able to heal much faster than normal because of the enormity of this evidence of her/their presence on the Other Side and their ability to get messages to us by whatever means necessary. My sweet girl was no longer sick; she was reunited with her wonderful sibling Dudley, and all was well with them.

Thank you, Genevieve, for arranging this loving "goodbye" letter.

* Months later, my husband awoke from a powerful dream that Mullock had come to greet him at the fence again, but the shepherd/wolf was floating several inches off the ground as he did so. We knew it was his goodbye to us because we never saw our dear friend alive again.

Tuppence and "The Arby's Effect"

Tuppence at eight weeks old

When my thirteen-year-old diabetic West Highland white terrier, Tuppence —named after the Agatha Christie character Tuppence Beresford of the "Tommy and Tuppence" detective series—was about to pass over, she was blind and her kidneys were failing despite my administering her insulin shots every several hours, every day for more than two years. My soon-to-be-ex-husband had moved out of our house, but we were still trying to support each other through the loss of our firstborn "child," and as brutal as it was on me, I know his

At thirteen, Tuppence was mostly blind but still happy

being physically separated from her presented its own kind of hell for him.

Animal communicator Jacquelin Smith posits in her book *Animal Communication: Our Sacred Connection* that many animals will choose to leave this realm following a great upheaval or change in their family's life, such as after a death, divorce, birth of a child, or a move to a new home. I doubt it's coincidental Tuppy passed so shortly after my ex's and my separation.

During her last week with us, I had taken to sleeping on the living room floor on an inflated mattress so as to be near my baby, who no longer had the strength to bark to alert me that she needed to go outside to go potty. Each night, I would pray that she would go gently in her sleep so that I wouldn't be forced to make that most terrible of decisions for her. No such luck, of course.

She had finally stopped eating and had little or no control over her bladder, and we knew it was time. When we'd made up our minds that Tuppence would have to be brought in to be put to sleep the following day, we invited over some human friends who'd loved her dearly for years so that they could say goodbye, too. We shared memories of her antics, pored through album after album of photos of our sweet girl, stroked and held her, and cried and cried. We slathered her with love, as was her due.

That night, though, a friend of mine came over with a bag of Arby's roast beef sandwiches and Tuppence became a dog transformed! Her energy returned and she eagerly begged for several pieces of the tender meat. Of course, she was given all she wanted. With her apparently renewed well-being, which I would henceforth call "The Arby's Effect,"* I called my estranged husband and said we would be waiting a little longer before taking her into the vet.

Within a day or two, of course, the Arby's Effect was but a memory and we brought in our darling Tuppence. Two vets at Alta Veterinary in Minneapolis greeted us tearfully, for they'd loved this brave, always-sunny little girl, too. Dr. Kimber Schnepf, a Westie owner herself, even came in on her day off to be with us.

Friends & former neighbors Shannon & Kirby bid Tuppence goodbye

Dr. Cathy Sinning made sure a candle was lit in the room and saw to it that Tuppy was very relaxed when the vet finally administered the injection that released Tuppence from her tired, old body, as her daddy and I held her. They followed up by sending us a sweet card signed by all the technicians and doctors, as well as a cute little stuffed Westie in Tuppence's honor, along with her ashes, which we later scattered at Loch Ness Park, in Blaine, Minnesota, the last place she'd taken a walk with me.

Shortly after her departure, I was sent the "inspiration" (from the words "in spirit") to draw a portrait of Tuppence. Now I confess I do draw well enough to generally win at Pictionary with my hastily scrawled descriptions of things like "broom" and "cactus," but I'm not what anyone would call an actual artist, and I've had no training whatsoever. But when I sat down with colored pencils and drawing pad before me, I could feel that what poured through my hand was not coming solely from me. I drew three sketches of my little girl within a few minutes and with better accuracy than anything else I'd drawn in the past. What's more astounding was that I never had to erase! If I'd struggled on my own, I might do a reasonable job at the likeness, but the paper would have holes in it from my having had to erase until the table showed through. I know that some artistic Spirit Guide from the Other Side had led my hand and given me this lasting gift to commemorate my precious girl.

Tuppence followed up with a visit to me in a dream, showing me that she was at last restored to health and enjoying lying in a sunny

Tuppence's divinely inspired portrait

patch in the verdant grass. It's not that I imagine the Other Side is an exact replica of our environment here on Earth; I'm fairly certain she was simply returned to that loving energy that unites us all. But for the sake of providing me with comfort,

she sent me images I would best understand and relate to from our time here together. I awoke with tears of gratitude for her kind assurance, and I thanked my Guides again for their assistance with Tuppence's portrait. Though it didn't lessen for me how deeply I missed my baby, I was comforted by knowing she was fine and not far away, with loving beings like her "Gamma Lu," my mom, to take up the task of spoiling her rotten.

Tuppence & her Gamma Lu

* I've seen evidence of the so-called Arby's Effect, or sudden rallying of strength in the terminally ill, in one of my Siamese cats (see the story about Genevieve) and several human beings, too, through the years. This included my father, Carl Korpi, who died of stomach

cancer in 1975, when I was thirteen. The last time I'd seen him in the hospital, he'd been hallucinating (about having a steak and onions and requesting a Coke) from the morphine and unable to "see" any of us in the room. The following afternoon, he was lucid and talking coherently with my mother and my half-sister Sandi. He died at 3 a.m. the next morning. My only explanation for this is I think we're often given a last gift of coherence before we die, so we can say final goodbyes, express our love for others, and be clear about our choice to leave our Earthly bodies.

> "An animal's spirit uses their most recent personality to communicate through so as to be recognized by their person.... They may have had spiritual ties to their person through many lifetimes."
>
> –Jacquelin Smith,
> *Animal Communication: Our Sacred Connection*

Giles' Story:
A Supernormal Experience from a Still-Living Cat

More than a decade ago, months after I had lost my two beloved Siamese cats, Dudley and Genevieve, I knew my home was in dire need of more kitty energy to complement the doggy energy provided by my two Westies, Tuppence and Ludwig. As is so often the case with me, I knew what my upcoming pet's name would be before I met the actual animal in the flesh. I knew I was on the lookout for two cats named Giles and Xander (after characters on "Buffy the Vampire Slayer," one of my all-time favorite TV series).

I'd been casually visiting places like Petco during their adoption days and seeing many beautiful, sweet cats, but I sensed that none of them was to be mine. I went home empty-handed time and again. And this is unusual for me, being someone who'd like to adopt every needy animal on the planet.

Finally, my husband at that time and I had gone to a Holiday Boutique sale at the Golden Valley Animal Humane Society and decided to stroll through the cat section just to say hello. Again, I petted darling kitties through their cages, visited several that were free to roam in a special interaction room, and still, my heart told me to wait, these weren't meant for me.

Just before we were about to leave, however, my husband pointed to a charcoal-and-gray-striped tabby in the last cage in a long row. He said, "What about this one?"

My eyes met luminous green ones, my heart skipped a beat, and I exclaimed embarrassingly loudly. "Oh my God, it's Giles!" No deliberation was necessary. I literally "recognized" him. I knew as certainly as I knew my own name this was Giles, not Xander. We took him from his cage and he climbed into my arms, stretching his front legs around my neck like a desperate hug. Several people came by as I held him and noted his incredible handsomeness, expressing interest in adopting him. I flatly pronounced to them and my husband, "We're getting this cat."

While he went along with the purchase at first, quite to my surprise, once we'd gotten home, my then-husband got angrier with me than I'd ever seen him in our (at that point) ten years of marriage. It wasn't that he didn't like the cat; he pointed him out to me in the first place. It was just that, to him, I was apparently making a unilateral choice and somehow disrespecting him by doing so; I can understand his perceiving it that way because, outwardly, I'm sure it seemed I was a little nutty. But I couldn't walk away from what I knew was the Universe's gift to us, our Giles, just to say I'd taken time to properly deliberate. When I know something is right to do, I do it. Simple as that. Consequences be damned.

I think, too, my soon-to-become ex was correctly noting that my love more readily flowed toward our pets than toward him (and the same likely was true for him). I won't say we divorced years later because of Giles, per se, but my desire to expand my furry critter family, and my obvious adoration of them all, and my husband's subsequent resentment of all that surely exacerbated our growing distance and difficulties. I believe part of the reason Giles was brought into our lives was to help bring to light what was seething beneath the surface of our relationship. Sometimes what we need to see isn't always pleasant.

Giles

This is not to say my first husband didn't come to love Giles; he most certainly did, and he never mistreated him. It was just me he came to love less and less — a sad fact that had to happen to move us both along our respective, separate paths to where we were supposed to be years later. Though not something we would consciously wish, it is understandable that we might transfer our affection to our unconditionally loving companion animals when we feel the people to whom we were closest are withdrawing from us.

But not all times with this newly expanded family unit were unhappy or strained, of course, and one in particular was downright phenomenal.

It was early December 1997, and I had drawn up some Santa-themed flyers for my husband, who was a reflexologist (therapeutic foot massage therapist and teacher of same), to send to his clients to color in and enter into a drawing for prizes. We'd received dozens of entries and wanted to be truly random in choosing the winners. Folks had been told it wasn't important that they colored well, just that they made some small attempt and at least mailed in their entries on time.

I got the goofy idea to have Giles choose this year's winners. So, I made a large circle (about seven feet in diameter) on the living room floor, evenly spacing the 8.5x11-inch papers along the edge. I then placed Giles in the center of the circle and said, "Giles, would you please help us choose the winners for this year's contest? Show us who should win third prize, the foot-care basket."

Giles looked at me for a moment, then walked very deliberately to a colorful entry at the 7:00 spot on the circle. He placed a paw on it, looked at me again, then returned to the center of the circle and sat down! My husband and I gaped at each other. I noticed my hands had begun shaking a little, and I forced myself not to jump up and down screaming, not wanting to spook Giles.

I thanked our cat profusely and took away that entry. I then repeated, "Giles, would you please choose who wins second prize? Who wins

Another of Giles' talents

a copy of our book, kitty?" (That was *Reflexology: Therapeutic Foot Massage... and other matters concerning the soles,* ©1996, which we'd co-written and I'd edited and designed for him to use in his classes.)

Again, that handsome cat looked knowingly at me, then went to a colored entry sheet at the 1:00 spot, put his paw on it, and returned to the center of the circle and sat down!! "Fluke" was no longer a term we could apply to what was happening. My voice cracked a bit as I thanked Giles and retrieved the second-prize winner's sheet. I silently whispered to my husband, "Did you see that?" He nodded, stunned, from his post on the sofa nearby.

One last time, I asked Giles if he would kindly choose the first-prize winner, the one that would receive a free reflexology session. The third time was still charmed, for he went to the 5:00 spot, placed his paw on it, and returned once more to the center of the circle!! I finally couldn't stand it, and I scooped him up and gushed praise on this remarkable creature. I kept saying to my husband, "Oh my God, you saw that, right? I didn't just dream this, did I? Giles actually understood and chose those winners, right?" He just kept nodding his head, eyebrows raised impossibly high.

I pointed out to my husband that not only had Giles chosen

entries when we asked him to, but he'd also chosen the three that had been colored in the most artfully!

I immediately got on the phone to my brother Dave in San Diego, practically screaming into the phone, "You are never going to believe what our cat Giles just did!!!"

I spent another hour on the phone, calling everyone in our phone book and telling him or her what happened.

The rest of the evening, as we drove around town delivering the prizes and Christmas cookies I'd baked for friends and family, I periodically checked in with my husband, "You saw it, too, right? It really happened?" He reaffirmed my perceptions about twenty times before I finally shut up and accepted that either our cat is a genius or someone from the Other Side was working with him to blow our minds.

Giles is still a wonderful cat, but he's never re-enacted such a supernaturally miraculous feat since then. He actually appeared chagrined from all my gushing. I posited the theory that he wasn't supposed to actually reveal his full animal brilliance to us because pretending to be "dumb animals" is the natural kingdom's greatest defense against humans discovering these creatures' inherent superiority. I'm sure he felt he'd shown us too much and now might have to kill us to keep the secret safe. Tee hee.

> "Outside of a dog, a book is [wo]man's best friend.
> Inside of a dog, it's too dark to read."–Groucho Marx

Ludwig's Saga

I had received a gift certificate to the Animal Humane Society (AHS) from my first husband for Christmas in 1996. For months, we'd call or drop in, searching for a Westie or similar-sized mix breed to be compatible with Tuppence, our firstborn West Highland white terrier. We weren't equipped to adopt one of the large black Lab-rottweiler-German shepherd mixes so readily found there (pardon me as I digress into a Soapbox Moment), the maddening result of people who so thoughtlessly fail to neuter or spay their dogs who, in turn, have litter after litter of unwanted offspring that perpetually wind up in shelters or euthanized.

Every call I made to the AHS received the same negative answer, no smaller dogs at all, much less a West Highland white terrier. (At the time, we'd not heard of particular breeds having rescue associations.)

One day, when placing what I figured would be another fruitless call to the AHS, the girl who answered said, "Well, we do have one three-year-old male Westie being shown on-site at the Petco in Eden Prairie."

Once I was resuscitated from the effects of the shock, I called the Petco in question and inquired as to whether the Westie was still there. The employee said, "Yes, but there's a lady looking at him right now."

I brazenly told her, "Tell her to go away. I'll be right there!"

My husband and I raced over to the store, ran down the aisles to the pet adoption site, and watched with sinking hearts as a middle-aged woman signed her name to adopt a beautiful purebred male West Highland white terrier.

I was dumbfounded. I had felt with such cosmic certainty that this was supposed to be my next dog, I walked up to him and petted him while she did her paperwork. My heart was breaking despite my never having seen this dog before in my life. I truly am not the spoiled-brat-who-wants-what-she-wants-when-she-wants-it type and, normally, I would simply be overjoyed any animal in need was going to get a loving home. But something was amiss here. I could most definitely feel it, and my fears were played out as we stood there.

I read on the dog's intake form the following information indicating why he had been surrendered to the shelter: "Family was allergic" and "Doesn't do well alone for long periods."

What was the first thing out of this adoptive woman's mouth? "Well, we're all allergic, too, but we'll see how it goes."

My breath caught and I stared at her, heedless of how rude I'm sure I appeared. Did she think this dog was like some sweater she'd bought and decided once she got it home that it had looked better in the store? You can't treat a living being like this! I began to quietly seethe, knowing what being shuffled into another home would do to this poor dog's already surely high level of insecurity.

Then this bastion of denial said, "We're all at work all day, but he'll be fine, right?"

My Minnesota Nice teeth were grinding. It was, frankly, surreal, this veil of ignorance surrounding both the woman and the screening employee in this little play. I couldn't believe this transaction could actually be taking place.

Trying to maintain at least an outward semblance of calm, I mentioned the length of the dog's fur and said, "He'll be due for a grooming soon, I see."

Her response: "Oh, you don't *have to* do that, do you?"

My blood pressure rose as I couldn't believe the employee was choosing to ignore these obvious red flags. My husband knew I was turning all "mama bear protecting her cub" and stepped back to a safe distance.

"Do you even know what kind of dog this is?" I asked her incredulously.

She blinked at me in wide-eyed innocence, as though my question were utterly irrelevant. Her expression seemed to say: "I think he's cute. Isn't that enough?"

Finally, I had had it. I threw out all sense of my polite Midwestern upbringing and asserted myself like an East Coaster.

"Listen, lady, my husband and I already have one Westie at home, I run a home-based business just so I can be a good dog-mom, and we elevate animals to godlike status in our household. So when ... and (begrudgingly) if ... this doesn't work out, here's my card. Call me immediately!"

I then pet the dog once more, heartbroken for what I knew he was going to have to go through, turned on my heel, and stormed out to the relative privacy of our car where I could safely rant and rave in my righteous indignation, spew profanity befitting a proverbial sailor, and weep helplessly over what had just happened.

That was on Sunday afternoon. By Thursday of that week, the woman had called to say the dog was available if we still wanted him.

I met her in the parking lot of the Humane Society and

Ludwig & Tuppence meet

introduced the new fella to our seven-year-old Tuppence. They were peaceful around each other if not outright playful, so I knew it was worth taking him in. The lady said she'd paid for her vet to check him and get him whatever shots he'd needed, but they just didn't want him because when they were gone all day at work, he'd peed on their pillow. (Poetic justice, I say.)

I know she and her adult daughter who had ridden with her had inherently kind hearts because the pooch's head bore the pink stains of lipstick from the daughter's having kissed him several times in the car. I assured the woman she'd made the best decision possible for this dog, thanked her for her efforts, and took him off her hands, paying her back only what she'd spent on the original purchase. Call me petty, but I felt letting her foot the vet bill could serve as part of her lesson.

The dog's name had been Rudy, and we figured out we were at least his fourth home, counting the breeder's. We decided that neither his name nor his past had worked too well for him, so we renamed him right away. With his long hair hanging into his eyes, he looked a bit like a scowling German composer, so Ludwig (á la von Beethoven) he became. Maybe it sounded similar enough to Rudy to him, or maybe he was just happy to shed his former identity and start fresh, but he immediately responded to his new name.

Now, Ludwig was not without "issues." You try being shuffled around that much and find a sense of security. He was enormously territorial and tended to nip people from time to time if they were perceived as interlopers. But he was also loving and cuddly, so we assured him he was in his forever home now, part of our "pack." We also put in the money, time, and effort, utilizing tools taught to us by an animal behaviorist to help him get control of his less-desirable traits. He became a phenomenal pet who was so well respected and loved that, upon his passing in 2005, he'd had thirty adult human beings attend his memorial service. (More about this in the chapter on Memorializing Methods.)

As I mentioned in the story about Tuppence, I have read and concur that it is quite common for pets to pass away around the time of huge, family-life-altering events such as a death, birth, or divorce. For instance, I know of numerous instances wherein beloved animal companions became suddenly ill or began behaving in ways completely contrary to their regular nature, such as becoming vicious — thus resulting in their being given away or euthanized — when they sensed a baby was on its way and they'd be losing their status in the pack or no longer be needed by their people.

So it only made sense that Tuppence died shortly after her human father and I separated and Ludwig had a brush with death just months later, once our divorce was final.

I'd noticed that when we were taking walks in the park, Ludwig would stop dead a short way into the walk and just look at me pleadingly. He was usually filled with boundless terrier energy. I know dogs are often accustomed to masking pain, so fearing something was wrong, I took him to his vet.

I think that loving Spirit Guides/angels/whatever you choose to call them gather near to us when we are facing traumatic situations. They do their best to communicate with us what we need to know at those times and miraculously shield us from what we do not need to know. Such was the case with my much-adored Ludwig.

His doctor had run the normal tests and come up with no diagnosis. She then ran some not-so-common tests, whereupon she came to me wearing a tightly controlled expression.

"I think you'd better get Ludwig to the U of M Veterinary Hospital. I'll call ahead for you. Go today," she'd said, explaining nothing further.

> "Our dog is not a child substitute. At least, that's what his pediatrician tells us."
>
> —comedienne Rita Rudner

Obediently, I raced Ludwig to the university, where we met Dr. Love. (Great name, huh?) She looked over his charts, ran more tests of her own and then told me he'd contracted leptospirosis, at the time a rare form of bacterial infection that can affect humans as well as animals. (Now, unfortunately, it's becoming increasingly common.) Most likely Ludwig caught it from taking dips in and/or drinking water from nearby lakes that had been urinated in by ducks and other wildlife. Most vets weren't accustomed to looking for it, so it could frequently be missed in diagnosis. Among its symptoms were lethargy and severe muscle pain, which Ludwig probably was experiencing on his walks.

Dr. Love immediately put Ludwig on powerful antibiotics and had me leave him at the hospital overnight for observation. I hated leaving him alone at all, but I knew he was in the best of hands. And, to tell the truth, I think I was too emotionally numb to argue.

A couple of thousand dollars later, my sweetheart was home, feeling mostly hale and hardy. When I brought him in to the U of M for his periodic recheck a couple of weeks later, Dr. Love and her staff seemed inordinately happy to see him.

"We're so glad to see Ludwig because only ten percent of dogs that contract leptospirosis survive," she said. The leptospirosis bacterium settles in the kidneys and causes permanent damage and/or death if left untreated.

Fortunately, for my sanity's sake, that news flash had been withheld from me previously. (Thank you, Spirit Guides, for urging me to bring him in to this hospital and for later sparing me the undue terror of knowing how near death he was since I was already doing all I could to help him. In my ignorance, I just assumed the antibiotic would take care of everything, which, thank the Universe, it did.)

For many months afterward, Ludwig's regular vet monitored his kidney function, which had shown signs of permanent damage from the infection. However, through nutritional supplements, a proper low-protein diet, and some Reiki sessions (an alternative medicine technique in which energy is channeled from the practitioner to the recipient to promote healing and reduce pain, etc.), he surprised all the doctors when he eventually regained full kidney function. They said they almost never see a reversal in kidney damage.

Looking back, I now see he had to miraculously get well because Ludwig had another very important job to do during his time on this Earth: keep his mama's heart in one piece as she hit emotional bottom. In just a few short years, I'd lost my mother, stepfather, and step uncle to various forms of cancer; my two Siamese cats, Dudley and Genevieve; my dog Tuppence and my cockatiel Samantha; my fifteen-year marriage; and a subsequent significant relationship that was tumultuous and incredibly painful.

My stalwart friend, Ludwig, almost single-handedly kept me anchored here and circumvented the increasingly appealing thought of my joining the multitudinous forces on the Other Side, where, it seemed, anyone and everyone who loved me now resided. This wonderful dog did so until he could feel secure that I was once again loved and supported and safe. He waited until I'd met, fallen in love

**Ludwig,
our ring bearer**

with, and married Anthony Kaczor. Ludwig was our ring bearer in the wedding ceremony.

My sister Diane had led him in on a leash during the processional, with him looking dapper in a little doggy tuxedo and with the rings in a silken bag tied to his leash. During the ceremony itself, he took a nap on Diane's lap. I began my vows, explaining how I'd been doing all right on my own, happy to be with my "four-legged children..." when, as if on cue, Ludwig awoke, lifted his head, and looked right at me! Many a wedding guest noticed and was taken aback by his understanding.

His new daddy adored him unconditionally, which was, of course, a requirement of anyone being with me. Shortly after our Winter Solstice wedding, on tax day, April 15, 2005, we'd all moved into a fantastic 1886 Victorian home built by master builder T.P. Healy and listed on the National Register of Historic Places.

That fall, I had just gotten together Ludwig's Halloween costume for the big bash we would be hosting soon. He was going to wear a pink bikini with "peace," flowers, and "Sock It to Me" signs made to look painted on his midriff and yellow hair spray on top of his head. He was, of course, "Laugh-In's Goldie Hound." He loved being the center of attention and played it up for all it was worth, a real party animal.

A couple of weeks after the party, I noticed Ludwig straining to pass stools in the backyard. Apropos of nothing, as though whispered to me by my Spirit Guides, I said aloud, "It's prostate cancer." It had never even occurred to me that dogs had prostates, and I would have thought it would affect urination, not defecation anyway, so I had no rational reason for thinking this on my own. It was just one of those "certainties" given me by those on the Other Side who watch over me.

I didn't panic because I knew many human males who have prostate cancer who went on to live long lives, with and/or often without surgery. Right?

I brought him in to a new vet at the clinic, who told me straight-forwardly, "Ludwig has prostate cancer, and it's inoperable. He may only have a few months left. I'm sorry."

Through the years of a tsunami's worth of loss, I'd gotten pretty good at driving while seeing through torrents of tears. I went home and continued to sob over my keyboard, enlisting for Ludwig the prayers and healing thoughts of all our friends and family.

My only personal prayer was this: "Either cure him completely so he can have a full, happy, pain-free life, or please take him quickly and without fear or pain." My prayer was, indeed, answered.

To look at him, to see him rest peacefully in his slumber and run circles around the house with his daddy, you'd never know he was sick, much less that he'd be gone in two short weeks.

I'd noticed our cat Giles had taken to hanging around Ludwig much more than usual. He sat beside him on our living room couch, taking note, evidently, of how Ludwig would perch on the pillow on the couch's arm and bark out the window to protect his home.

It was the night before Thanksgiving, around 6:30 p.m., when Ludwig gave me the clearest sign that he wished to be freed of his fail-ing body. My sweet darling had come to me while I was standing at my bathroom mirror and he suddenly raised his leg as if to pee on me! I shouted, "Ludwig, no!!" and he put down his leg, but the desperate look in his eyes told me what he needed from me.

I struggled not to upset him as I cried quietly and told him, "I know, baby boy. It's time for you to go. Mama will help you, I promise. I love you so much."

I wrapped him in a blanket and frantically tried calling all vets in the area to find one who would come to our home to perform the euthanasia. I wanted Ludwig as peaceful and comfortable as possible. I'm sure I sounded a bit unhinged as I broke down crying to every vet or tech I reached. No one was available, thanks to the holiday. But I knew I couldn't make Ludwig suffer for another night, no matter what.

A wonderful friend who often does the work of angels, Ludwig's vet tech and Reiki master, Tai Salisbury, happened to be home when I called for help. She offered to come over and help to confirm what I already knew, that Ludwig was ready to go.

We lit candles, bundled him up, and held him tight until she arrived. Using what is called Muscle Testing or Applied Kinesiology to tap into the unspoken messages the body wishes to tell, Tai placed one hand on our sweet dog, extended her other arm, and asked him one question: "Ludwig, are you ready to go to Heaven now?"

She had me press down on her extended arm. Had I been able to push it down easily with moderate pressure applied from me, that is, if there were weakness resulting in no resistance, it would have indicated his body transmitting a message of "No" to her. Her arm stayed strong and immovable, indicating an unambiguous "Yes."

Any remnants of doubt and/or guilt were eliminated for me at that moment.

She made a call to an emergency vet she knew well and accompanied us to his clinic. I held and cuddled my baby the whole way there, as Anthony drove and the three of us bade Ludwig a tearful but peaceful farewell. He died quietly in my husband's and my arms, and we said our goodbyes for several long minutes. Tai generously offered to transport Ludwig's body to her vet clinic for cremation after Thanksgiving.

Two days later, we went to pick up Ludwig's remains and Tai presented us with a beautiful clay paw print on which she'd etched our boy's name.

In the days after his passing, we noticed a phenomenal change in Giles. He took to standing perched on the pillow that rested on the arm of the living room couch, looking vigilantly out the window. (He never barked, of course.) He and Ludwig had clearly made a deal that Giles was to take over the task of "watch cat" in his absence. My wonderful kitty did this with gusto for weeks, until the job pressure got to him and he started yanking out his fur in tufts. We knew he needed his replacement to come soon, but first we had to have proper closure for Ludwig's passing.

The first week in December, we sent out invitations to all our friends and family to join us for Ludwig's All-Pets Memorial Service. Even my former father-in-law Jim came, and he was one of the unfortunate souls Ludwig had bitten years earlier. Ludwig had been a perfect gentleman before and after that, though, and, not to excuse his behavior but to explain it, as I'm convinced it was because of all the turmoil in the house during the pending divorce that made him lash out. His Grandpa Jim apparently forgave him, too; and his presence at Ludwig's memorial meant the world to me, the grieving mom.

(For full details on this service, please see the chapter on Memorializing Methods.)

We kept up the All-Pet Memorial display throughout the holidays, until January 1, 2006, when Anthony and I built a fire in our wood stove and sent out individual prayers of thanks to each and every animal listed on those slips of paper. It took us more than an hour. This action had magical effects, but to learn of those, you'll have to read the following section about Mortimer.

> "I think God will have prepared everything for our perfect happiness (in Heaven). If it takes my dog being there, I believe he'll be there."
>
> –Reverend Billy Graham, evangelist

Mortimer – The Chosen One

Any one of us who has ever lost a beloved pet can relate to the pain and sorrow of bereavement, but what of the feelings of guilt at "betraying" our pet when we try to move on and invite another animal to share our lives? My husband, Anthony, and I found a way around that when we lost our West Highland white terrier/child, Ludwig, just before Thanksgiving 2005. Instead of "replacing" him with another dog, we asked him (and Tuppence, his sort-of sibling Westie lost a couple years before) to find for us the exact dog they knew would be right for us. Not only were we getting permission to heal our hearts, we were honoring our departed pets' love for us and resting assured our new companion would be "paw picked" just for us. We knew there would be cause for celebration and gratitude when we found this dog, not guilt and anguish, as might have been the case.

New Year's Day, 2006, we wrote an extensive list of traits and attributes we wanted in our next Westie—we surely do show brand loyalty—and put the list in our fireplace, so as to let the smoke symbolically reach the heavens and our two faithful scouts. By January 3rd, we'd received our answer. Anthony had searched Petfinder.com and found a three-year-old male Westie stray had been rescued and was currently cared for at the James River Humane Society (JRHS) in Jamestown, North Dakota. He contacted them from our home in Minneapolis, explaining that ours was a "Westie-wise household," which is very important with these strong-willed, spirited terriers.

It would be some weeks before we could pick up our boy because of a trip to San Diego we'd scheduled long before. We didn't want to bring him into our home just to up and leave him for another week in strange environs. There was ample evidence that he was being lovingly cared for at the JRHS and, in the meantime, we sent him clothes with our and Giles' and Xander's, our two cats', scent on them; toys; photos to be put in his kennel there; and a letter to be read to him, telling him how much we already loved him and that we'd be there as soon as we could to bring him to his forever home.

We'd been inspired to give him the name Mortimer, after Cary Grant's character, Mortimer Brewster, in *Arsenic and Old Lace*. We

chose that name because the
character was overjoyed to
discover he'd been "adopted."

The first weekend in
February, we drove to be
united with our precious
pooch. Naturally, it was love
even before first sight. When
we got there, I scooped up
Mortimer (who is the largest
Westie I've ever met) and
hugged him to pieces. Our
camera had been in the car
trunk overnight and the lens
was a little fogged up, which
only made the photo look
more appropriately ethereal.

**Mortimer, freshly "sprung" from the
Jamestown Humane Society**

I held and sang to Mortimer the whole way home as Anthony
drove, solidifying our bonding. He had adorable "Horatio
Hornblower" hair on his ears, not having been groomed in quite a
while. We absolutely lost our hearts to him.

We knew, too, that Ludwig and Tuppence had chosen him for us
because the moment he was in our home, our two cats walked right
up to him, sniffed him and were at ease. (That is NOT Giles' normal
response to anyone coming into our house, much less a new dog—
he freaks out and hides for hours or even days.) Because they all
seemed to "recognize" one
another, we were certain there'd
been communication among
them all on some level that served
to ease all their transitions. There
was no doubting this was the dog
we were supposed to have.

Westie coin purse

A quick side note: When we
were in San Diego, shortly before
picking up Mortimer, we'd

bought at a flea market (pardon the pun) his personalized dog tag ID with his name and permanent home address on it. Shortly thereafter, at a craft fair, we bought a zippered coin purse with the picture of a large Westie sitting next to a little Westie puppy. Little did we know that that photo would become reality when we adopted Blanche, a ten-month-old female Westie, from the Southwest Metro Humane Society in Chaska, Minnesota, in early April. She never grew past twelve

Giles & Mortimer were instantly relaxed together. Shown here on my husband Anthony Kaczor's lap.

pounds, just a peanut, and the proportions between her and Mortimer, at twenty-two pounds, remain perfectly matched to that coin purse picture! By the way, Blanche (née Zoey, the name she came with but to which she simply wouldn't answer) was named after Blanche DuBois of Tennessee Williams' *Streetcar Named Desire,* whose signature line was "I've always relied on the kindness of strangers." These kinds of names happen when the adoptive mom used to be an English/film studies teacher. We also have two finches named Atticus and Scout. (Bonus points if you catch the literary allusion there. See the end of this story.*)

Since our loss of Ludwig, our home has practically exploded with new furry and/or feathered sources of love and joy. So much so, in fact, I was inspired to change the lyrics of the folk song "The Water Is Wide" to the following:

The doggies are white
And the cats are dark
And I live in
A Noah's Ark.

With two of each,
Including birds
And all I do
Is pick up turds.

Believe me, it helps to keep a warped sense of humor as you try to housetrain a headstrong Westie youngster like Blanche.

Blanche

The only bittersweet aspect to our newfound happiness was that on our list of attributes we'd submitted to Ludwig and Tuppence, we'd specified "young adult," hoping to buy as much time with our new baby as possible. As it turned out, Mortimer has been rapidly "aged" since we adopted him, with one vet saying, "I don't think he's quite ten … but he's much older than three." That's almost seven years of our lives together stolen from us in a millisecond! We wondered how Ludwig, Tuppence, and/or the Universe itself could have played such a terrible trick on us while we were still so raw from having lost two dogs within a few years' time.

After a bit of preemptive mourning, my husband and I determined that sometimes there's a greater knowledge out there for what is right for us. We can't see it from our earthly vantage point. We believe now that we had to be "nonmaliciously misinformed" about Mortimer's age, because, had we known, we wouldn't have considered adopting him, being so afraid of facing another loss of a geriatric dog too soon. Now, however, we couldn't be more grateful that we'd had sort of "spiritually placed blinders" on and that the adoption went through because this boy is an absolute angel in our lives. We also needed a reminder / lesson that we must live in the moment, cherishing every valuable second with our beloved companion animals, no matter how long that is supposed

Sid, Blanche, & Mortimer

to last, and that age is irrelevant when compared to the amount of love the right pet can and does bring to our lives.

Besides, despite degenerative arthritis in his knees, Mortimer, who's given daily doses of glucosamine and other nutritional supplements, occasionally plays like he's a pup with his little sister, Blanche. So we know we've greatly increased his quality of life … just as he and Blanche have ours.

* Bonus Points Answer: Atticus Finch was Gregory Peck's character in the film version of Harper Lee's famed novel, *To Kill a Mockingbird*; Scout was his daughter's name in the movie and book.

Mr. Moto's Musical Message

Always liking names to have some kind of quirky historic or literary link, I helped my mother name her new pug puppy when she brought him home in 1990. To me, the adorable little critter looked a bit like Peter Lorre, who portrayed a Japanese detective named Mr. Moto in several films throughout the 1930s–40s. Not to be politically incorrect, but I figured a Chinese pug was at least closer to Japanese than the bug-eyed Hungarian actor.

When our mother died in 1998, my sister Diane inherited Mr. Moto. She took phenomenal care of him and he was a blissfully happy, pampered pooch, munching impatiens in her vast garden during his last summer with us, despite being deaf for years, nearly blind, and having heart problems and breathing difficulties, among other ailments. Because of those mixed signals he sent, saying, in essence, "I'm still really enjoying my life here with you although everything in my physical body seems to be giving out," it was heart-rending for Diane to have to make the decision to put him to sleep at age sixteen and a half before he was showing obvious signs of pain.

She'd set the date for a Tuesday when our brother Dave would be in town visiting from San Diego, so he and another close friend, also a Dave, could help her carry out this benevolent plan.

Meanwhile, in what seems a ridiculously off-topic event, the Saturday before this, I was ordering a CD by a trio of female vocalists

Mr. Moto

from England called the Puppini Sisters because a review of their concert in Minneapolis had caught my eye in the *Downtown Journal,* one of the many publications for which I worked as proofreader. When things like that jump out at me, I've learned to follow up on them. There's inevitably a reason they're beckoning me. I just figured it was because my husband and I teach beginning social dance and East Coast Swing is a real favorite of ours, so the Puppini Sisters, who sing both old-time and newer music arranged to sound like 1940s Andrew Sisters-style songs (e.g., "Boogie Woogie Bugle Boy") would be a good group to add to our collection of danceable music. I ordered the CD from Amazon.com and was stunned to see it arrive first thing on Monday, the next deliverable day, when it usually takes five to seven business days for such orders to be filled.

Point is, I had the CD playing in my car the afternoon that Mr. Moto passed away. I was heading out to Blaine, Minnesota, to be with my sister — and to take my two Westies, Blanche and Mortimer, and her schnauzer, Pebbles, and poodle, Corky — for a walk in a nature center. Toe-tapping tune after toe-tapping tune went by when the song "Java Jive" came on. At one point, I almost drove off the road when I heard this lyric: "I love coffee sweet and hot/Oops, Mr. Moto, I'm a coffee pot."

I believe you can probably count on one finger how many songs use the name Mr. Moto in them. I knew with absolute certainty this was a message of comfort being sent to us from loved ones on the Other Side, saying they had greeted this beloved dog and that he was doing fine.

I turned down the volume on the music completely once I arrived at Diane's house, wanting to be able to really be present for her as we spoke of her ordeal and reminisced about Moto. I told her about the phenomenal song incident as we made our way to the park and said, "I've just let the disk keep running, so I have no idea where we are on it, but I'll find the song so you can hear what I'm talking about." I turned up the volume on my car stereo and what was the first thing we heard? You guessed it: "Oops, Mr. Moto, I'm a coffee pot." It was at that exact spot in that exact song the instant I turned up the volume!

My sister and I smiled, wept, and smiled some more. That divine message went a long way to easing any feelings of guilt or uncertainty that she'd done the right thing for Mr. Moto and at precisely the right time.

> Sandy Shawn and her three daughters would have died in a fire if her pet angelfish hadn't leaped out of the bedside tank and landed on her face to wake her. She found the room filled with smoke and flames. Her fish was safely placed back in the aquarium and the fire was extinguished.
>
> —Paul C. Dahm, *Rainbow Bridge*

Misty, Chester, and Schatze– Sudden Losses

Losing our dearest friends to old age or a protracted illness is hard enough. Sudden deaths due to accidents or senseless acts of violence amplify our grief by not allowing us to prepare ourselves emotionally and/or opening the door to impotent rage at the perpetrator. Unfortunately, my sister Diane knows of this firsthand, having lost several dogs suddenly.

One, Misty, a bubbly blonde-coated terrier mix, actually jumped out of Diane's car window while it was parked at the side of the road, presumably needing to chase a squirrel or something. Sadly, a speeding car interfered with her rodent-chasing quest and left all of us who loved Misty in stunned agony.

Chester

Another was her delightful jogging companion of many years, Chester, a schnauzer-terrier mix who sang a great tenor with our mother's two dogs — Chihuahua-terrier mix, Misty (the second), and white German shepherd, Major (á la Three Dog Night) — whenever you got them started with a howly command to "Si-i-i-i-ing!!"

One night, Diane had let Chester out into her backyard to do his before-bed business. Quite unusually, he didn't come in when she called. Not much later, however, tears sprang unbidden to her eyes and she had a heart-crushing feeling that somehow compelled her to walk over to his food bowl and leash and throw them away. She simply knew in an instant that her darling boy was gone. She later found out that, because he'd very uncharacteristically run out of her quiet suburban cul-de-sac, he'd been instantly killed by a passing car; but it was her sensation of his spirit saying goodbye that first brought her the sad news.

More recently, Diane opened her heart again to another schnauzer, Schatze, who'd come along as a puppy to help her overcome her grief over losing Chester. One day, she discovered he had become violently ill. The vet told her he was experiencing liver failure, and she strongly suspected he had been poisoned by a drug-addled, emotionally unbalanced next-door neighbor who'd threatened him in the past. He remained ill for two days, and nothing the vet gave him helped. She was virtually inconsolable when a phenomenal communication from the Other Side came to give her strength and courage. Our mother, Lucy, who had passed away in 1998, made sure Diane knew she was there, ready to collect Schatze, as he would pass over just hours later.

Diane had been in her bedroom when she noticed a single piece of foliage in the center of a dried floral arrangement she had in a large vase had begun to move, very deliberately, side to side several inches, as

Schatze

if someone had reached in amidst the bouquet to move just that piece. It seemed so strange, she checked around to see if any windows were open to provide a draft or breeze that could be moving it. They were all closed. She checked the floor register to see if the air conditioner had blasted it with some air. It was not running. Yet still the leaf kept moving left to right, while everything else in the vase stood stock still.

Feeling our mother's presence, she excitedly called out to her then-boyfriend Mike, who'd been in another part of the house, to come and see what was happening. The moment he answered her call, she saw the leaf stop moving. When she hollered back to him, "Never mind," and started to question her own perceptions, the leaf suddenly resumed its uncanny movement.

Shortly thereafter, she had to bring her baby to be euthanized. Though her heart still shattered at the loss, accompanied by the impotent rage at the neighbor she could never "prove" had killed her dog, at least she had the comforting reassurance that her beloved Schatze was going to be in the best of hands on the Other Side — namely our mother's.

Sonny's and Bret's Messages to Me

Back in the mid-1980s, my former fiancé, Wayne, and I had split, but we maintained a unique connection long after. For years, if I would dream of Wayne, I knew I should call him because something big was happening in his life. One time in particular stood out because I had had a dream that his wonderful Brittany spaniel Sonny and my long-deceased poodle Pinky were together on the other side of the chain link fence that bordered the backyard at the house in which I'd grown up. They were sniffing and greeting through the

Sonny

fence my mother's living dogs that were in the yard. Then they trotted off through the yards adjoining ours until they were out of sight. I awoke fully aware that Sonny had passed away. A call to Wayne confirmed this.

I believe this was either a purposeful visitation from these dogs (or a signal sent by Wayne?) or, at very least my subconscious mind's way of giving me a recognizable symbol for this kind of event. Since then, I've had uncannily similar dreams. Whenever I dream of that fenced-in backyard scenario, if an animal I have known well is on the other side of that fence, I know he or she is or soon will be actually on the "Other Side."

Three years later, I dreamed Sonny's son Bret was trapped in mud and sinking. When I awoke, I knew this was a portent of danger for this dear dog. Sure enough, when I contacted Wayne, I found out Bret had contracted Lyme's disease but was being rigorously treated and was expected to recover. Despite several relapses, he did survive another six years.

Bret

"A Soul can create as many forms as it desires, physical as well as etheric, and is living in many of these forms and alternate realities simultaneously. ... A bit of one's Soul can mix with another's."

–Jacquelin Smith,
Animal Communication: Our Sacred Connection

On the Subject of Reincarnation

Now, I can't run any of my quasi-scientific experiments to rule out a commonplace explanation for this next thing I'm about to tell you. You'll simply have to believe or disbelieve me as you like. But I strongly suspect the author just quoted is right about her theory because when my Siamese cat, Dudley, passed away at age fifteen, I was inconsolable in a way that was substantively different from my usual response to loss. I remember telling my mother, through gut-wrenching sobs, "I don't know why, but I feel like I just lost Dad all over again!" You may remember what I've said about my sometimes saying things that I feel were placed in my brain/mouth to say but weren't of my own conscious devising. This was definitely one of those statements that popped out for me to actually "hear it said."

My father had died of stomach cancer in 1975 at age fifty-seven. Dudley may have had the same disease; I never bothered to have it formally diagnosed because it would have involved a highly invasive procedure and ultimately made no difference in his prognosis, but he vomited continually and lost weight until he looked skeletal, just as my dad had when nearing his end. I felt as though Dudley had only lived three-quarters of his life expectancy, too, just like my dad. Of lesser importance, but just sort of interesting, they both had blue eyes and I often called my cat "Dud," which is quite close to "Dad."

Anyway, when reading the above quote in *Animal Communication*, I felt I'd found the explanation for how I was feeling that day. I don't think Dudley was my father reincarnated, per se. But my dad could

Dudley & his sister Genevieve

easily have sent some of his soul to co-create my wonderful, beautiful cat years after he died, while the rest of him went about doing, or being, whatever he was meant to on the Other Side. He might have left just a smidgen of himself behind in this world to take care of his little girl. (I'd been thirteen when he died.) If this is true, and I honestly feel it is despite how nutty I may sound to some, I was truly mourning a double passing when this kitty died and took my last tangible evidence of my father's love for me with him.

〰️ 〰️ 〰️

SUBMITTED OPINION

An Animal Communicator's Viewpoint
by Diane O'Callahan, Animal Answers

From my experience, if we ask it of them, pets will send us a message that is personal and comforting to us. I received a message from my cat Mistofelles when he passed by first asking him for one, then watching two rabbits hopping over each other outside my window. This to me was Mistofelles and Secret — a cat who had passed before Mistofelles — playing.

Asking, believing, and watching are ways to connect with the spirit world. We took a walk on the beach when the cats passed and have a memorial site in our yard with a cat statue to mark the gravesite. I talk with the other cats about Mistofelles and Secret and have had dreams about Mistofelles, which I love to receive.

I have thought about taking a day off from work to honor my

pets' passing and have encouraged other people to talk about this experience and to honor their time together. People are getting more sensitive to others who are deeply connected to their pets, but still there are people who minimize this bond and say things like, "It's just a pet" ... or "Get another one."

Other ways that the animals communicate are through the animals that have lived with them in their homes. When I intuitively contact the animals who have passed, they will tell me they are around in certain places ... such as in a closet or on the stairs, which is then confirmed by their people who, once alerted, watch their living pet and then feel the presence for themselves of the one who has passed. This brings great comfort and reassurance that the pet is okay on the Other Side.

The animals who have passed give messages through songs and words to their people to help them in their grief. Sometimes the pets give a brief yes or no to questions asked; other times the messages are philosophical, like: "Love Is All There Is," "It's All About Love," or references to a Joni Mitchell song, "Both Sides Now," to help the people adjust to life without them.

~~~ ~~~ ~~~

SUBMITTED OPINION

Counterpoint: About the Afterlife of Animals and Humans

by Bonnie Illies, Animal Intuitive and Healer, of St. Paul, Minnesota; www.bonnieillies.com

I know how painful it is when an animal companion dies. I understand the need to communicate with that animal and the desire to have them come back to you. I believe we are all recycled, so to speak (reincarnation); therefore, it is possible that our deceased animal could come back to us.

People are often told by communicators that their deceased animal is still with them or visits them. And the person is thrilled to hear this, which I can understand, but how often is it true? And if it's true, is it a good thing? Think about it — if we were told that a deceased human was still with us, we would recognize that this may be something to be concerned about versus happy about (i.e., they may be trapped between worlds). Yet with animals, people are often told these things.

John Edward,* a communicator who speaks to the dead (humans), has said that humans do not come back to Earth as soon as people think. I suspect it's not that much different regarding animals. Also, when I talk to psychics/communicators who work solely with humans, most of them agree that animals do not come back to us as often and/or as soon as people are told or believe. Again, I'm not saying deceased animals do not come back or never come back to us, but I do not believe it happens as often as or as quickly as people are told by many animal communicators.

I could have more clients if I were willing to do this type of communication, but I usually only do it for longtime clients who know and trust my work. If it's someone who has never worked with me before and they are calling solely to have me do a communication with their deceased animal, I will not take the case because I fear they will want to hear what they want to hear; i.e., their animal is still with them or is coming back, and that their animal is romping in green grasses, etc. I will not tell them something that I am not "seeing," even though I know that is what they want to hear.

Also, our world is usually projected into the afterlife. People are told that their deceased animal is running through the grass and there are trees, etc. Maybe the afterlife does look similar to Earth, but again it is something I fear is only a projection of what our minds know. For example, if a communicator with deceased animals had never visually seen what Earth looks like, would they be seeing those kinds of scenes while communicating with a deceased animal? How much is only a projection of what the mind knows and what the heart wants to hear?

I don't know if there are grass and trees in the afterlife. I don't know if my deceased animals will come back to me. I believe what continues is the love.

*Editor's note: For the sake of full disclosure, I was a self-professed fan of John Edward's show, "Crossing Over." Over the years of watching the program, I noticed the medium frequently perceived the very specific spiritual presence of pets, sometimes long passed, when doing readings for audience members. Assuming he has a legitimate gift, of course, this would make a nice argument for the afterlife of companion animals and our ability to be reunited with them somehow. (I think the fact that they're given familiar physical or behavioral attributes in these readings may just be so we can recognize them and receive their message of love and comfort; it may or may not be how they actually exist on the Other Side.)

Edward also once picked up on the group presence of four husbands whose wives had remained friends after their being widowed. What interested me was that these men were of widely different religious backgrounds (i.e., Catholic, Protestant, and Jewish, etc.) yet they were all sharing the same afterlife experience together. Makes you wonder about the validity of any one religion's claim to have the ONLY key to the soul's continuance. Perhaps if we could accept the notion that we all end up as loving energy and are inherently interconnected as spiritual beings, wars fought over religious beliefs could be avoided. It's just a radical thought I've often had.

Submitted Stories

The following section of the book is dedicated to the retelling of the stories of people and pets around the globe that have shared this loving connection beyond the veil that is death. There is no inherent difference between the people in these stories and any of you readers, with one possible exception. All of us who share our stories here have demonstrated an openness to receive and recognize the communications that are actually there for all of us all the time. What a skeptic might pass off as coincidence, we might well take as evidence of a miracle. It's all a matter of perspective. I know my belief that these experiences stem from that loving energy that is greater than one's Self and yet a part of one's Self at the same time has saved me from despondency innumerable times. I am forever grateful that I can know with certainty that love cannot be destroyed simply because someone's spirit is transformed to another state.

SUBMITTED STORY

Katie (Beardo)

by Rachel Taubert of Anoka, Minnesota

Katie (Beardo)

My dog's name was Katie (a.k.a. Beardo). Katie was a rescue mutt that was given to me by a friend that could no longer care for her, so I'm not sure of her breed. She looked sort of like a wirehaired mini dachshund, but she definitely was a Heinz 57.

She had passed a few months earlier and had been buried in the yard when, on this particular occasion, I had been having a rough day and was crying. I told her that I wished she was still around for hugs. The next morning, I saw a sunflower, about a foot tall and with a giant six–seven-inch head on it, had appeared exactly on her grave — overnight! I know it wasn't there the day before. I really felt as though Katie heard me and showed me she was still around in this astounding way.

SUBMITTED STORY

A Visit from Hunter

by Sandra Slayton of Ingleside, Texas

We got our golden retriever puppies, Hunter and KayCee at age seven weeks. KayCee became a foot and leg licker, her tongue fairly dry, her licks slow and deliberate. Hunter preferred arms, face, and neck, and his tongue was like a wet lasagna noodle, all over the place, leaving enough "slurp" that you would have to dry off.

He and his sister were always close. When she had knee surgeries fourteen months apart, he'd spend hours lying with her, licking her face. I saw more compassion in that dog than I see in most humans.

Hunter & KayCee

I loved him no more than I loved our other goldens, but there was a bond between us that everyone commented on. At night, he always had to sleep where he could see my face. If I turned to my other side, he would cross over me to be where my face was. I would sometimes wake with the feeling of being watched and would find I was on the edge of the bed and he would be sitting on the floor watching me. I would move over and he would get in bed. He would wake me in the mornings by licking my neck and ear and getting my hair all soppy wet. That was every morning.

A new heartworm prevention medicine came out, a six-month injectable, and I decided to switch our dogs one at a time from the monthly pill to the injection. Just after he turned four, Hunter was dead of an adverse reaction to that injection. I was totally guilt-ridden. Why had I not researched that injection before allowing Hunter to have it? Had I done so, he would never had gotten it; he would be alive. I had killed him. I was so guilt-ridden that I had trouble eating and sleeping and I lost forty pounds over the next eight months.

Then one night, I was awakened by Hunter drenching my hair, ear, and neck. I was half-asleep, but then as I fully woke I realized Hunter had been gone for eight months. It was his sister, KayCee, doing the slobbery licks, something she had never done before. And suddenly I knew without a doubt it was Hunter using KayCee's body, and he was telling me that he loved me as much as ever, he didn't blame me for his death, he knew I loved him as much as ever, and he didn't want me sad.

Hunter & KayCee

Now here I have to say I had never believed in ghosts or visits from beyond and used to laugh at the ghost stories on unsolved mysteries. But that night I knew without a doubt Hunter was visiting me to remove my guilt.

When I told family, they thought I had finally gone off the deep end. But they soon noticed that I could talk of Hunter without crying, I smiled again, I was happy.

They no longer doubted. I have hoped and wished for another visit from him, but it has never happened again. But that one time removed my guilt.

≈≈≈   ≈≈≈   ≈≈≈

Samples of Visitations
from *Animal Communication: Our Sacred Connection*
by Jacquelin Smith

- When the vet euthanized her, one cat's spirit shot out of her body —through a dolphin light catcher, which fell and shattered. The vet and her technicians witnessed this and were stunned.

- Later, at the aforementioned cat's owner's home, a yellow-and-black butterfly flapping behind a window shade above where the cat had slept was a visitation. The owner reported that her bed sheets had moved on their own, and she heard pawing at the cat litter when no cat was visible.

- A stray dog came to a woman's door after her dog passed. It came in her house, sat where her dog used to sit, and went into another room and got the deceased dog's only remaining toy. All others had been tossed out.

She and the dog played awhile, then he pawed at the door to leave. Her dog had "borrowed" the stray's body to play once more with his person before moving into the light.

≈≈≈   ≈≈≈   ≈≈≈

SUBMITTED STORY

Hannah

by Gretchen Anderson of Minneapolis, Minnesota

We get to know people in certain situations and do not look beyond into other lights. I have a colleague, a friend, whom I have known for years. About a year ago, I emailed him for some advice. He sent back that he could not help, that he had just had to put his old girl down after a long illness. He had three Labs, a young chocolate, a middle-aged black, and the old yellow girl. He said he would talk to me later. I sent back my condolences, said I understood, and told him he should take the time to heal. Later he told me her story. She was the dog that took care of the rest, the alpha, the one that took care of everyone. She was the one who straightened out the conflict when the youngest was brought into the house. Considerate, in control. He told me that coming home, after taking her to the vet that last time, they saw a bright shooting star sail over their house — and they knew it was Hannah letting them know it was okay, that all was well.

SUBMITTED STORY

Chicklet, Roxanne, and God

by Roxanne Saunders, R.N., of St. Petersburg, Florida

Chicklet was my baby girl for exactly three years to the month. She didn't look like a normal kitten; she had big round eyes and huge ears! Everyone called her Yoda. My house was pretty busy at the time, with one nine-month-old and one eight-week-old feral rescues I caught in the hurricane that was blowing through my area. The feral

Chicklet

boy, Mac, took to her like glue. Chicklet was the love of his life. My other fur kids each loved her, groomed her, and took care of her. I think they knew all along, Chicklet was destined for something important.

She grew up looking and acting different than my other cats. She had very thin fur, and you could see the pink of her skin through her fur. She didn't meow like a regular cat; she whined and spoke so you knew what she wanted.

Over the last year with Chicklet, my faith in God was fading. I was born and raised Catholic and had never before wavered in my faith. But things kept happening: the loss of my twenty-year-old cat, Misty; dislocating my knee; and having to miss four months of work, with bill collectors calling all the time. I also had/have been suffering from Gulf War Syndrome for many years and getting physically worse.

Chicklet was always there with a meow of love, her silly antics, crawling under the sheets to sleep against my back. Of course, this was only when she didn't have the sun shining on her in her screened-in porch.

She had her vaccines in July and was given a clean bill of health. On September 27, she was fine; on September 28, I couldn't find her for breakfast. I finally found her lying down, having crawled out of the laundry room. She was breathing so hard, I grabbed clothes and scooped her up, knowing she was very ill. I ran her to the ER vets. I figured she had a bad bug that came on suddenly. The vet came out and showed me her X-ray; her lungs were seventy-five-percent collapsed on both sides, and her chest was filled with fluid and probable tumors he told me. How could she be fine one day and dying the next?

I was so mad at God, it was the breaking point. The vet said she was suffering and didn't think he could keep her alive another four hours. He gave me the option of trying to drain her chest to see if it was cancer but didn't think she would survive the procedure. She would always like for me to cradle her like an infant in my arms, close to my chest, but I couldn't even do that as she was trying so hard to breathe. I tortured myself with questions: Did I miss the signs? Could I have gotten to her earlier?

The vet said she was suffering and the best thing for her was to put her to sleep peacefully. I held in her in my arms, begging her to forgive me, but I didn't want to put her through something she might not survive and then not be with her mommy when she passed. I held her, sobbing on her sweet fur, and told her how much I loved her. My heart was breaking and I screamed at God, "Why not me? Why don't you give this cancer to me instead of my innocent little girl?"

I did this alone as I don't have any family within 3,000 miles and no one to call to be with us. I was so angry, and I felt and still feel as though a part of my heart died with her. I took her home wrapped in a towel, carried like a baby in my arms for the ride home. I was lost, devastated, as my fur kids are all I have and my baby was no longer with me. I had to have a neighbor take me to have Chicklet's beautiful body cremated, as I couldn't drive.

A few days later, I was still not emotionally well but could not cancel my mammogram appointment. I got a call that the mammogram was abnormal, and I had to go back in another few days for additional tests and pictures. The doctor came in and told me the mammogram showed a highly suspicious growth and, most likely, I had cancer in my left breast. I was a bit in shock, but I said to myself, "Well God, You did give me the cancer Chicklet had and now she is gone, so I don't understand. Who is going to take care of my other fur kids? How am I going to do this with no one to help me?" I was more scared of having the surgery than of the diagnosis itself. I was worried about my fur kids and how they would all have to be separated. I had nightmares every night, was sick to my stomach, etc.

Then my sweet baby came to me the week before surgery while I was in bed sleeping. I knew Chicklet was there, lying next to me, letting me bury my face into her sweet unique fur, hearing her singular meow/talk, so I knew it was her without a doubt. I missed her so much I cried, cried like I did and still do each and every day.

A few days before surgery, she came again at night, but this time I was able to understand the message she was telling me. I was no longer scared of cancer because I knew what I had was not cancer. Chicklet took the cancer out of my chest when she knew I had it. Everyone was so worried about this cancer, but I was not. I stopped telling people because they did not understand, and I know they thought I was losing it. Chicklet was fine one moment and then full of cancer in the chest. But I knew what she had done for me. On November 2, they operated and took almost half of my breast. I had some complications from anesthesia and a post-op infection as I waited for the results. I was not worried. Thirteen days later, the pathology came back clean.

I know somehow Chicklet knew, as she was always on my chest when I held her or when I would read in bed. She had her own talk with God and sacrificed herself for me by taking the cancer out. Both doctors were simply amazed that the mass was benign. But then they didn't know Chicklet. My faith over this time was restored in God. Chicklet did that. She showed me God is loving and kind and He gave me three beautiful years with my baby. She showed me that God does listen; I asked for the cancer from Chicklet when in fact she had taken it from me. I know, too, we will be together again for eternity when my job on this Earth is done.

In memory of Chicklet Veronica, my beloved fur baby. May you bask in the love and sunshine of the Rainbow Bridge until I come to meet you someday.

〰 〰 〰

Samples of Visitations

from *Animal Immortality: Pets and Their Afterlife*
by Bill D. Schul

- A veteran returning from war was met by his dog, wagging its tail and barking excitedly. He was told the next day his dog had died nine months earlier and was buried in the garden.

- Collie breeder and novelist Albert Payson Terhune wrote in *The Book of Sunnybank* about his collie, Rex, that a year after Rex died, a friend came to visit for the first time in several years and commented that he thought he knew all of Terhune's dogs but hadn't recognized the big dog with the scar across his nose playing with the other dogs on the lawn. It was a perfect description of Rex, though the two had never met. Other guests at Terhune's house also saw Rex several times after his death.

SUBMITTED STORY

Raja's Road Trip
by Camille Olivia Strate of Valley Center, California

How in the world do you let such a creature go? Twelve years is a mighty long time (about a quarter of my life!) and this puppy was really a treasure. NO. Wait. This puppy IS a treasure. And the lessons she taught continue even now, from wherever she is.

Raja's Messenger

I met Raja when she was six hours old. She wouldn't take the bottle and the darling galoot of a man who had her mama had no idea what to do about it. Her mama died trying to have those puppies (there were thirteen of them!) so he was pretty devastated. He called ME. And he was crying like a baby, which was quite a shock. So I dashed over to his house and got her to eat off my fingers. I took her home three days later and she was with me the rest of her life.

The day came when I had to let her go, and I insisted on holding her while the doc did his job. When I left his office, not half a mile from my house, this huge red-tailed hawk flew out of nowhere and hovered in front of my windshield a mere fifteen feet in front of me. With its wings spread wide and tail feathers tilted forward, it looked right at me (I swear! I even have a witness!) for those few seconds, and then flew straight up into the big blue sky. Only God knows how

I didn't crash my truck. But there it was ... clear as day ... and I knew it was Raja. I knew she'd come in the form of a red-tail because that's my "totem" critter, and she always knew how much it meant to me. In fact, the canyons we used to hike were filled with them, soaring way high on the air currents, looking down for their next meal. We used to sit on the mesa at the top of the canyon and watch them for hours. Just me and my puppy, taking it all in.

Right after that hawk flew away, I looked at my friend and hollered, "DID YOU SEE THAT? OH MY GOD.... DID YOU SEE THAT?" I was afraid I'd imagined it, maybe hallucinating in my grief. But she'd seen it, too, and we both started crying all over again. Only this time, I was laughing at the same time. BOYHOWDY! That RajaPup sure was clever. She always knew exactly how to get my attention. Such a smart puppy.

So, here we are, her kitty and me, trying to adjust to life without her. It's not easy. She was such a huge part of my life. How do you get over something like that? How do you keep breathing? How do you laugh again? Not sure, really. But I do know this—she gave me more love than any two-legged being ever did, and I will always remember her. Even when the next puppy comes along, and there will be another puppy one day, none will ever replace my Raja. I miss her now, and it's likely I always will. But any time it gets too hard, all I have to do is step outside and look up. There will always be a hawk for me to watch ... and I'll remember that moment when she came to give me one last glance before she took the road trip back home.

Corky was a dog saved after having been shot. Two years after Corky's passing, his human was awakened by his bark only to find the apartment was filled with smoke. It was theorized that "maybe Corky was just repaying you for saving his life."

– Paul C. Dahm, *Rainbow Bridge*

SUBMITTED STORY

Chelsey

by Wanda Andrews of Bellefonte, Pennsylvania

Chelsey

It took a few weeks, but after my grief settled down a bit from losing my precious eighteen-year-old rat terrier, Chelsey, I began to have dreams of her. In a few of them, she was once again young and vital and running around as if she were a pup. In a few of the dreams, she was with my mother, who had passed away a number of years ago. I like to think Chelsey has taken up residence with her on the Other Side and will be there, waiting for me, along with other loved ones.

Also, one morning about a month after she passed, I distinctly heard her barking. It was loud and sounded like she was barking right into my ears. I remember thinking, "Chelsey's back." Then I remembered she was gone. I feel she had contacted me in that "Twilight Zone" — not fast asleep yet not quite fully awake. That was truly a gift.

I also remember two distinct occasions in which I could "smell" Chelsey. She had a certain odor (even with her baths), and I would smell that on occasion. I thought perhaps it was just something lingering in the carpet or chair, but when I would try and smell it at chosen times (in the same place), I could not.

John Gambill of Paris, Texas, nursed a wounded goose back to health. The next year, she returned with a gander and goslings. This went on for many years, until eventually more than 3,000 geese and ducks wintered in Paris. When Gambill died in a Paris hospital, hundreds of geese circled round and round the hospital.

–Paul C. Dahm, *Rainbow Bridge*

A stray cat we call Red eventually became our indoor cat. One night around 11:00, I was sitting on the floor with him when I noticed he seemed to be looking at "nothing" very intently. His eyes were following "something" across the kitchen floor and right over to my lap area. I kept whispering, "Chelsey, is that you, here for a visit?" Red also kept looking up at a certain spot, as if he were looking at another human. This went on for quite a while. I couldn't help but wonder if perhaps my mom came for a short visit, along with Chelsey, and Red just happened to "tune in" to them. I hope someday to verify that.

SUBMITTED STORY

Buddha in a Cat Suit: Bodhi

by Polly Klein, Tonglen Healing Arts for Animals, Issaquah, Washington

Bodhi

I've always loved being with children. I've worked in camps, run support groups for children, and the sound of squealing giggles is simply joyous to me. There was never a doubt in my mind that I wanted children of my own one day. However, there were many personal obstacles that stood in my way when I was in my twenties. When I turned thirty-four, I was ready to try for a child of my own.

After a year passed and no pregnancy had occurred, I started having questions about my fertility. This is when I began the trip down Fertility Specialist Lane, a road you don't want to travel if you don't have to. There was testing for myself and my husband, medications, and many intrusive medical procedures. Two years and two miscarriages later, I sat on the other side of a desk from a fertility doctor who told my husband and me that I had almost no chance of conceiving and carrying a pregnancy to term.

As I listened to the doctor, the feeling of devastation ripped through me. It was as if someone had told me that my future, the one I had worked so hard for and the one I had overcome so many obstacles to be ready for, was gone. The story could have ended there but it didn't.

A cat came to live with me during this period in my life. Bodhi was a silver Maine Coon kitten. He and his littermates had been rescued from deplorable conditions when they were several months old. They were so malnourished at the time, they looked more like they were weeks old rather than months old. When I met Bodhi, he was a scrawny seven-month-old ragamuffin.

There was something different about Bodhi from the first moment I saw him. Though his skin was the size of a Maine Coon, it looked like someone had forgotten to add the stuffing. I called him my walking bag of bones, but that wasn't what made Bodhi unique. When I was in bed, Bodhi would curl up and sleep on the top of my head like a kitty turban. His purr speaker was always set on high and the vibrations would run through my body, soothing my soul.

Gazing into Bodhi's eyes was like looking at pure wisdom. He was also unflappable when my three large dogs leaped and galloped around him. He was calm in the middle of this dog storm, and he also became my calm.

By profession I'm an animal communicator and have a healing practice for animals. Whenever I would ask Bodhi how he was, he would simply say he was fine. He would tell me he was not his body and so he was okay no matter what was going on with him physically. The sincerity and peacefulness Bodhi conveyed when he told me this always made me feel like I was talking with a Buddhist monk. He was an amazing teacher for me in this regard because Bodhi had numerous health issues over the first year he lived with me. He had several major surgeries to remove polyps in his ears that pressed on his brain. Bodhi spent much of that first year wearing a yellow-and-blue-plaid Winnie the Pooh button-up shirt made for premature babies and a cone collar around his neck to allow his surgery sites respite from his pin-sized claws. Even festooned in this costume, there was a delightful sense of dignity that always shone through. He was completely content despite the state of his body.

Sadly, about a year after Bodhi's arrival I discovered that he had been carrying FIP (feline infectious peritonitis) and the disease had progressed to an active infection. As it turned out, all of his litter-mates had it, and with the exception of one other kitten, all died from the disease within the first two years of their lives. Bodhi was no exception. In September of 2004, Bodhi's little body simply wore out and I helped him to let go of it.

Two days after Bodhi died, I was teaching a Reiki class. While my students were practicing an exercise, I felt the sinking despair and pain of missing Bodhi wash over me, so I decided to sit quietly and compose myself by practicing some self-Reiki. I put my hands out in front of me as I contemplated where I wanted to place them on my body. Suddenly, I felt that unmistakable purring vibration between my hands. It was Bodhi! He had come back to me in spirit form.

As I sat there taking in his presence he told me, "It's okay now." Bodhi was such a wise old soul that I knew he was okay, so I took his message to mean that I would get through the grieving of his death and that I would be okay. I then felt an immense sense of peace flood over my body. Never before had I experienced a sensation like that.

Two weeks later, I stood in my bathroom transfixed by a home pregnancy test. I was pregnant. I realized I had gotten pregnant the old-fashioned-way the same evening as Bodhi's spiritual visit. I went back to the fertility specialist and she confirmed my pregnancy with an ultrasound. I told her the story of Bodhi. She wrote in my chart, "Spontaneous pregnancy with cat intervention."

Nine months later, on July 10, 2005, my beautiful healthy daughter Melissa Sage was born. Her middle name was chosen to honor the wise sage Bodhi, who, after his passing, had given me a final gift in the form of Melissa.

Back when Bodhi died, I had tried to make sense of why he had graced my life with his presence for a mere year and a half. I thought it might have been so I could help him. I thought perhaps he came to me so I could care for his physical, energetic, and emotional well-being. As it turned out, it was never really Bodhi who needed help. Bodhi was already a Buddha, an enlightened being. It was I who needed help from him.

Blessings to you, my sweet cat man. Thank you for bringing me my baby.

SUBMITTED STORY

Yellow and Grey

by Beverly Rice of Charlotte, North Carolina

Yellow

It's 10 p.m. Time for my cat Yellow's late-night milk break. She would go to the kitchen and nudge or stand by the fridge. After Yellow passed on, my TV would sometimes cut off mysteriously around the 10 p.m. hour. I'd like to think it was Yellow, reminding me of her late-night snack break. That was in 1997. I still have the same TV. Every blue moon or so, it will cut off during the evening. I like to think it's Yellow stopping by to say hi.

Yellow facts: She was a "Morris the Cat" look-alike born in Houston, Texas. Yellow found me in the late '80s. I was taking out the trash one Sunday when she and I saw each other. From then on, she'd greet me when I came home, follow me to the laundry. I moved from Houston in '89 and decided to take Yellow with me. We were together till cancer took her away in 1997.

I lost my handsome boy, Grey, suddenly last week due to an undetected cancerous mass that ruptured his bowel on September 30, 2007. I made the toughest decision of my life to let him cross over the Rainbow Bridge on October 1, 2007, in the early evening.

Grey

It's never easy to lose your best buddy, but it's doubly hard when it's unexpected. Words can't really express my sorrow and how much I miss him. I was driving home from work this week and looked up at the clouds. I saw one in the shape of a cat's head, with its pointy ears. I hope that was Grey, saying, "Hey Mom, I'm watching over you."

Grey facts: He was adopted from a Charlotte, North Carolina, animal shelter. I went there for a cat I saw on an adopt-a-pet TV segment. (It resembled my cat Yellow who'd passed away.) But someone else had taken that cat, and guess who I spied rubbing up against his cage? A beautiful grey wonder with the cutest big head you've ever seen. I adopted him on the spot and took him home from his neutering procedure the next day.

Ways I've memorialized/honored my pets' lives: My parents have a farm where many of my past pets are buried. Once a year, I clean the graves of my beloved angels and place flowers or a cross by them.

I've also kept the collars from sweet, gentle Ryan, the last dog I had before going off to college, and from my two cats, Yellow and Grey. I found Ryan's food bowl in my dad's shed when she passed. I've kept it by my bed ever since. The collars hang on my bedroom doorknob; I hold them close for a hug or just touch them often.

I'm financially strapped but have a half-dozen animal welfare charities that I send small donations to when I can. It's my way of helping and honoring all the dogs and cats that have enriched my life over the years.

SUBMITTED STORY

Gizmo

by Kathi Sherburne, Animal Communicator, of Henderson, Nevada

My friend Lynn had a small elderly dog named Gizmo. I did a BodyTalk session on Gizmo because he was barking too much and had recently gone through a very traumatic event.

Lynn had left for a few days and had someone checking on Gizmo. Meanwhile, someone else broke into Lynn's home and locked Gizmo in the bathroom. Gizmo was blind in one eye and often bumped into walls and furniture. The poor little guy was running around in circles and running into everything in the bathroom, until the person who was checking on him found him. I knew some of Gizmo's barking was emotionally based because of this event.

Gizmo's body addressed an emotional release and the active memory of the traumatic event and all the emotions that were involved in the event so his body could heal itself. Lynn reported that Gizmo was much calmer after that.

Approximately three months later, Lynn called to tell me she had to put Gizmo to sleep the day before. I told her I would contact Gizmo to make sure he passed quickly and hadn't suffered, and I said I would email her the results of that communication.

I asked Gizmo if he'd been ready to cross, if his passing was quick and pain-free. Gizmo confirmed all three. He wanted to thank Lynn for letting him go and added that he would watch over her. I asked him if he would send another animal to Lynn and he said, "No." Instead, Gizmo told me he would move things out of place as a sign that he was around. I emailed Lynn to "pay attention" for such signs from Gizmo.

Gizmo

The next day, Lynn emailed me back saying that she'd noticed a stereo speaker was moved and a picture on the TV stand was out of place. She was so happy about Gizmo's signs and it comforted her.

I expected it to take a few months before Gizmo would move things around! I'm always amazed at what animals are capable of doing in spirit form if only we pay attention.

Part Four:
Memorializing Methods

Coping in Public, Crying in Private

"I must just be weird, but I prefer to do my grieving in private," my sister Diane said to me when we were discussing holding funerals for companion animals we've lost.

She most certainly isn't "weird" in this sentiment. There is no right or wrong way to meaningfully memorialize a dear companion's passing. Your method may be as quiet as meditating on what he or she meant to you (with a box of tissues nearby), writing him or her a loving letter of goodbye, or planting a tree or flower garden in your pet's honor. Conversely, your method may require the participation of another person or pet, who may be in mourning, too; a select gathering of like-minded, animal-loving people or members of a support group; or it even could include reaching out to the whole world via the Internet. The method you choose may simply have to do with whether you yourself are an introverted or extroverted person, which means, beyond saying one is simply shy or outgoing, that you are someone who processes thoughts and feelings inwardly and alone or out loud and with others present, respectively.

We all fall somewhere on that continuum. For instance, Diane and I shared a quiet time walking our four remaining dogs in a lovely park and sharing memories of her dear pug, Mr. Moto, on the afternoon of his passing. That's what I'd call semiprivate grieving. Not exactly open to the public, but not holed up alone either. It's what was perfect for that person and that pet.

Other people, myself included, seek a bit more support, at least at times. (I don't save all my tears for an audience, of course. I do allow time for plenty of solitary sobbing.) But still, I think it's important for many of us to know support is out there if we need it and that all we need do is ask for it.

Sophie Louise

I considered it a sacred duty as I rolled out my special lavender short-bread dough because, on this day, I was making schnauzer-shaped cookies for a special family member's memorial service. A couple of days earlier, my husband's Aunt Marie and Uncle Dale lost their most-precious miniature schnauzer Sophie Louise to advanced kidney failure, making the selfless decision to end her suffering on what happened to be her thirteenth birthday.

The day after Sophie's passing, I'd stopped by to see Marie and Dale and was struck, as one always is by the passing of a once-vocal pet, by the deafening silence that followed my ringing of the doorbell. No welcoming/warning barks would be heard from her anymore. Marie bravely shared with me their experience of making the heart-breaking decision to put their baby to sleep, the peacefulness of her actual passing, and the details of how they planned to send her off in style.

They opted out of cremation, so, by way of a coffin, they'd chosen a large Styrofoam cooler into which she'd be placed on her favorite blanket, positioned lying down on her tummy with her head on her front paws, and wherein she'd remain perfectly preserved.

With her were going to be placed two rosaries, one black and one white, "because those were her colors," Marie said. A prayer card featuring the poem "Footprints" and some laminated photos of her human mommy and daddy would also accompany her.

My sister Diane, a fellow schnauzer parent, came by to offer her condolences and some flowers from her garden. She also gave them a lovely handkerchief, which they told me they'd draped over the cooler as it was lowered into the ground at the burial site.

(NOTE: Take the gas company's advice and call before you dig. Also, be sure to check first with your city officials as to whether it is legal to bury animals on your property or elsewhere within city limits.)

Sid's Lavender Shortbread Cookies

(May start preparing these the day ahead, or at least allow 2 hours flavor-blending time for the lavender/powdered sugar coating.)

1 cup powdered sugar
2 tablespoons plus 2 teaspoons dried lavender flowers, cut finely or
    ground with a mortar and pestle
1 cup and 2 tablespoons butter (not margarine), softened
⅔ cup sugar
2 cups all-purpose flour
½ cup cornstarch
⅛ teaspoon salt

In a small bowl, mix together the powdered sugar and the 2 teaspoons of lavender; cover and set aside at room temperature to blend flavors, at least 2 hours and up to 24 hours.

In a large bowl, cream together butter, sugar, and remaining 2 tablespoons of lavender. Combine flour, cornstarch, and salt and gradually add to the creamed butter mixture. Stir only until blended thoroughly. Too much mixing can make the dough tough.

Divide the dough in half, and wrap each portion in plastic wrap and refrigerate for an hour or until easy to handle. Preheat oven to 325° F. On a lightly floured surface, roll out half the dough to ¼-inch thickness. Cut into desired animal (or other) shapes with cookie cutters. Place cut cookies on an ungreased cookie sheet. Gather scraps and re-roll to cut more cookies until most of the dough has been used and there isn't enough to use the cutter again. You may either just press that remnant into a flat, round cookie to bake or discard scraps.

Bake for 18–22 minutes. Watch carefully at the end so that the cookies just barely turn golden on the edges. Do not overbake. Remove from oven and cool 1–2 minutes and place on a wire rack to cool completely. Sift the powdered sugar and discard its lavender. Dust cookies with the powdered sugar. Hint: For easier cleanup, place an opened newspaper or towel beneath the rack to catch the scattered powdered sugar.

Store in airtight containers. Makes 4–5 dozen depending on the size of the cookie cutter used.

The very act of planning a funeral service or memorial gathering can, oddly enough, be a welcome diversion from the pain and emptiness in which we otherwise might wallow. There's also a heart-lifting sense of purpose in knowing our efforts are to honor someone else, in this case our beloved pet. I know firsthand how enormously healing this can be, as I've had to plan and execute numerous funerals in recent years, for humans as well as for companion animals. The superfluous things of life recede into the background, and all we focus on is what is most meaningful to us and to those we've lost. What we want our pets (or any other loved ones) to take with them into eternity and how we plan to commemorate them is very revealing of not only our bond with them, but our own values and sense of spirituality as well.

Usually, unless the relationship is strained for some reason—and sadly, this is usually only possible in human relationships because we infrequently find reasons to resent the animals in our lives—what motivates those choices comes from a place within us, far deeper than just the conscious mind. It's a prime opportunity for us to put that other being's/person's desires before our own, to bring a profound sense of purpose to the ceremony. (More on this concept can be found in the section on Animals and the Afterlife.)

The funeral itself was a private affair, but days later, a memorial to celebrate Sophie and all her wonderful years with Dale and Marie was held with only human family and friends specifically chosen for their shared animal-loving traits in attendance. I had advised Marie to try and feel no animosity toward, but to simply not invite, those she knew would not understand Dale's and her immeasurable sense of loss, so as to avoid creating any undue hurt feelings or resentments from either party. (See Part One: The All-Important Grieving Process.)

At this gathering, my brother-in-law, John, who is especially close to his aunt and uncle, shared stories of how Sophie had been there to help both him and Dale recuperate after their recent respective surgeries, (John's shoulder/rotator cuff repair and Dale's sequential hip and knee replacements).

Sophie intuitively knew when Dale was in pain, John explained, and she'd approach him on the bed unusually slowly and carefully, positioning herself to lie beside him with a paw outstretched and just resting against her daddy's arm to comfort him. These poignant shared memories of the human/animal bond are the most healing things a person can bring to a service like this. It feels wonderful to know that what we valued as unique about our beloved companion animal was noticed and appreciated by others, too.

What's more, it doesn't take a grandiose gesture to truly touch someone whose heart is hurting. For instance, Marie and Dale repeatedly expressed their thanks to my sister for what they called her too-kind gesture of delivering the flowers and handkerchief. Diane shrugged it off, saying, "There's no need to thank me. It was just human decency." Maybe so, but would that more people understood that and acted accordingly, right?

Carefully chosen or heartfelt words can really resonate with the bereaved as well. For instance, I'll always remember the day in 1979 when I lost Pinky, the totally devoted-to-me miniature apricot poodle with whom I'd grown up — and who my mother had obviously let me name when I was about three

Pinky

years old — to the autoimmune disease pemphigus. My high school boyfriend, Troy, though not a pet owner himself, did and said the perfect things to help me through my loss: He held me as I bawled and bawled and simply whispered, "He was a good dog." Those unadorned words validated my feelings perfectly, as they were spoken in a tone that held sympathy and not a trace of sarcasm. Thanks, Troy. Pretty wise behavior for a teenaged boy. No wonder he went on to become a successful counselor.

So, I included with my platter of Sophie-shaped cookies a small sheet of gold paper with an illustration of a schnauzer on top and the words:

*Celebrating the life of
Sophie Louise
June 12, 1995 – June 12, 2008
A dear schnauzer-child
who made our lives sweeter.*

Sophie Louise

It took me five minutes to make this on the computer, and yet Marie and Dale told me it meant so much to them, they framed it. When they look at it, I hope they'll know their feelings were understood and shared. They'll know their Sophie was important to and will live on in the memories of others, too.

As at many American funeral services, there was a touching array of photos of Sophie and her human parents on display, as well as a terrific spread of foods to share. I think a morphed version of "the way to someone's heart is through his/her stomach" comes into play here. Sharing food at a memorial can be both a soothing act for our own saddened hearts — filling the void, as it were, created by our companion's passing, on this special occasion,* with shrimp and cocktail sauce, cheese and crackers, dog-shaped lavender shortbread cookies, what have you — as well as a pledge to those we've lost that we understand our lives here on Earth must continue, just as they would have wanted for us. It's as if, in choosing to fuel our bodies, we're making the tacit commitment to go on living despite how much we'll miss the one who is no longer with us in physical form.

At the memorial, Dale expressed the belief that he can never have another dog because the pain of loving and losing one is too acute. This is a very common reaction among those who are deeply attached to their companion animals. I assured him he is not alone in that feeling but that it just might prove a temporary thing, necessary to keep him from jumping too soon into another human-animal relationship before he had grieved sufficiently. I told him that someday, if and when the time was right and his heart was duly healed, his personal doggy angel Sophie just might surprise him and send him someone new to love. (Opinionated person that I am, I encouraged him and Marie, as I do everyone who will listen, to consider adopting a rescue animal at that time rather than bring profits to a puppy mill.)

* Please note, however, we're all especially vulnerable when we're hurting, so this take on the concept of "comfort eating" in no way advocates abusing yourself through your relationship with food (or drink, drugs, anything done to excess to provide pseudo-succor) by either stuffing yourself to tamp down your emotions or starving yourself to prove your devotion to your lost loved one or going on a weeklong bender to forget the pain. I'm talking about sharing a meal and memories with caring friends and family at a memorial service, not a long-term commitment to unhealthy eating habits or an excuse to slide into addictive patterns of behavior. That's something no beloved animal companion wishes for his or her human.

In the meanwhile, however, he committed to a wonderful, healthy, wise plan to show his gratitude to the University of Minnesota Veterinary Hospital for its excellent care of Sophie through her last years by volunteering as a dog walker — giving exercise, attention, and affection to other dogs in need who are patients there; thereby helping his own grief abate just a bit and honoring Sophie in a beautiful way.

*ADDENDUM — Despite their best efforts to forestall another dog's entrance into their lives, Marie and Dale looked into Second Chance Animal Rescue and volunteered their services as providers of a temporary foster home for needful dogs. They were instantaneous "foster failures," we're all happy to say. They were told of a young schnauzer-Yorkshire terrier mix who would have to be euthanized the following day if they couldn't take him in. Naturally, they stepped up to save the little guy; but their foster failure occurred as soon as they saw him and said, "Hand over those adoption papers.

We're keeping him." The dog's name was Jack Murphy, another sign from the heavens above that this was meant to be their new baby because, all her life, Marie's nickname has been Murph. Welcome to the family, Murph!

Murph

More Ways to Share

When Ludwig, my Westie, passed away in November 2005, my husband Anthony and I decided to have a memorial service the first weekend in December. But what started out as just a celebration of our sweet boy turned into something even more profound. We decided to make it an All-Pet Memorial event.

Ludwig and Tuppence, my first Westie who'd preceded Ludwig in death by just over two years, both were prominently featured in a shared shrine of photos and mementos. To open up the ceremony, everyone who attended was asked to bring pictures of their own beloved animal companions who'd passed away to be featured on a big foam board display on an easel.

Included were pictures spanning six decades, such as our sweet friend Char's St. Bernard from her childhood in the 1940s. Sadly for us who miss her terribly, but no doubt happily for Char, she has since been reunited with her long lost pet on the Other Side.

Particularly poignant was the portrait of Mollie, our dear friends Lisa and Adam's beautiful greyhound, who tragically fell ill and had to be put to sleep just days before this memorial. Because of the freshness of their loss, Lisa said she couldn't bring herself to come to the memorial itself, but having Mollie's photo there and us to share

Mollie

stories of her for Lisa and Adam helped her feel spiritually included in the healing process.

There was also one of Dexter, my boss Janis' black cocker spaniel, a.k.a. the *Southwest Journal's* company mascot, who would visit me in my office at work almost daily. He'd push open the door with his nose whenever he saw me through the glass wall facing the hallway, ever-ready for a love fest. For around a week that late summer, though, I hadn't seen him around. This wasn't unusual; it periodically happened for stretches of time when my boss was on vacation or otherwise out of town and Dexter was being cared for elsewhere, so I didn't think much of it.

However, what was highly unusual was that I kept hearing his collar's familiar jingling coming down the hallway toward my office that whole week anyway. I'd repeatedly look up from my work, sometimes saying something like, "Hey there, Dexter. How ya doing, sweet fella?" expecting to see him opening the door.

Dexter

Nothing. It wasn't until I mentioned this to the receptionist, Linda, that I was told Dexter had died a week before. I hadn't even been aware that he'd been sick. (See the section called Animals and the Afterlife for more such stories.)

Also featured were photos of Flint Fredstone (gotta love that name!), Ludwig and Tuppence's vet tech/our good friend Tai's cat from her youth; an invitation for her hamster's funeral drawn by our friend Beth when she was a child of nine (See page 149); and more. All our thirty or so guests readily shared memories of both their own pets and Ludwig. It's astounding how healing it is to have caring people tell you they'll miss your dog, too. After a moment of silence, there came lots of tears, laughter, and, of course, food—including frosted ginger-molasses cookies (recipe follows) I'd cut out in the shape of (what else?) Westies.

In the foyer, I had set out a large Christmas card holder with little wire spirals at the ends of its many prongs, into which guests inserted little slips of paper I'd prepared for them—each one preprinted with, "In loving memory of…"—upon which they'd written the names of their beloved furry (feathered, finned, etc.) friends who'd gone before. Each person was provided a tea light candle to light in the name(s) his or her pet(s). We wound up with close to 100 companion animals named and honored!

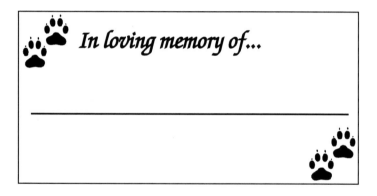

We kept up the All-Pet Memorial display throughout the holidays, until Jan. 1, 2006, when Anthony and I built a fire in our wood stove and sent out individual prayers of thanks to each and every animal listed on those slips of paper. It took us more than an hour and was both tearful and cleansing. This action had magical effects; see the Animals and the Afterlife chapter's story of Mortimer.

In 1988, nine-year-old Beth Jones invited friends to her pet hamster Teddy Fuzzy Hamsterham Jones's funeral.

In 2005, now Beth Engelking, she brought this along to share with those in attendance at Ludwig's All-Pet Memorial Service.

Cover art above, interior below.

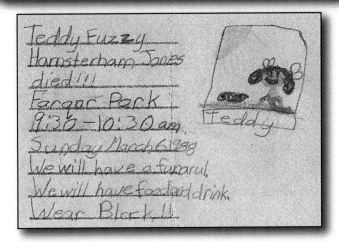

Sid's Ginger-Molasses Animal Cookies

¾ cup shortening, melted
1 cup sugar
¼ cup molasses
1 egg, lightly beaten
2½ cups all-purpose flour
2 teaspoons baking soda
¼ teaspoon ground cloves
¼ teaspoon grated nutmeg
½ teaspoon ground ginger
1 teaspoon ground cinnamon
½ teaspoon salt
raw sugar or powdered sugar icing, optional

Melt the shortening in large covered microwavable bowl in the microwave at 30-second intervals, mixing between each interval. Add sugar and molasses and mix well. Lightly beat the egg and add to the mixture. Stir well.

In a small bowl, combine all dry ingredients, flour through salt. Add to molasses mixture, mixing well. Chill for at least one hour, until easily handled.

Preheat the oven to 350° F. Roll out the dough on a lightly floured surface to about ¼-inch thickness. Spray cookie sheets with nonstick cooking spray. Cut cookies with flour-dipped, animal-shaped cookie cutter. If using the raw sugar crystals, sprinkle them on now. Omit this if you plan to frost the baked cookies.

Bake 8–10 minutes, until set. Cool 1–2 minutes before removing them to wire racks to cool completely. Makes approximately 3 dozen cookies, but this number will vary with the size of cookie cutter being used.

If frosting, wait until cookies are completely cooled. Use your favorite icing recipe or the one below. Food coloring may be added to portions of the icing and "painted" on to resemble the pet being honored. Add a miniature chocolate chip for the eye or nose if desired.

1½ tablespoons meringue powder
2 cups powdered sugar (about ½-pound)
3 tablespoons warm water*

* For stiffer icing, use ½-tablespoon less water. For thinner icing, add ¼-teaspoon water at a time until you reach the proper consistency.

Beat all ingredients until icing forms peaks (6–9 minutes at low speed with a heavy-duty mixer, 8–10 minutes at high speed with a hand-held mixer). Recipe makes 1½ cups.

Wrapping Her Arms Around the World

It's no secret that reaching out to make others feel better often facilitates our own healing. Gail Heller found this to be true when, after suffering her own devastating grief upon the death of her dog, she decided help others who have lost pets process their pain and help each other heal when she started the website "Chance's Spot." But she didn't stop there …

SUBMITTED STORY

Chance's Spot

by Gail Heller of Clarksville, Indiana
Founder of www.chancesspot.org

"I sure am taking a chance," I said out loud as I looked down at the English setter puppy I'd instantly fallen in love with back in 1984. Chance it was.

Fourteen wonderful years together later, my beloved Chance succumbed to lymphosarcoma.

I don't think I've ever been as devastated as when Chance died. I couldn't sleep, much less stop crying. So, I did what I usually do when I'm upset. I began to create. I'm a graphic designer, and art has always been a way for me to

Chance

express myself and to cope. In the fall of 1998, I decided to make a one-page Internet tribute to Chance. I called it Chance's Spot.

Initially, the page was intended only as a way for me to work through my grief. But, as I expanded the contents of the site and eventually went back to school to learn website design, I began to notice that others were visiting and finding comfort there. I had begun to heal and, although I still thought of Chance daily, I had created a place where people could share their grief. So, in 2005,

Chance's Spot became a nonprofit organization that focuses on helping those who are trying to cope with the loss of a pet.

Today, I share my life with two other special dogs, Moses and Mazie. I give presentations on pet loss throughout the community, as well as provide support to area groups and professionals that rescue and care for animals. [In the summer of 2007], Chance's Spot held the first-ever Honoring the Animals Candlelight Vigil. It almost took place in the rain, until, as we say around here, 'Chance wagged his tail.' Because just before it was time to set up and begin the vigil, the clouds disappeared and the sun set perfectly.

How Do I Love Thee?
Numerous Ways to Honor Your Beloved Animal Companion's Life

Memorializing our beloved animal companions can be a small, private affair or the impetus for a permanent change in the course of one's life. From a wide variety of sources, I've compiled a list of suggested ideas to help you memorialize and honor your past pets.

Tweak any of the following suggestions to suit your needs and/or tastes. (Note: Any website listed for items noted here is meant to get you started in your search and does not imply an endorsement of any company, service, or product.)

1) If there was a spot in your yard that was your pet's favorite, plant a tree, bush, or perennial flower there with which to remember him or her. (See *Catnip and Dogwood* in the bibliography for great ideas.)

2) Scatter your pet's ashes in a favorite park, woods, or spot in the garden.

3) Donate to an animal-rescue organization in your pet's name.

4) Write a thank-you note to your pet and bury it with him or her.

5) Create a memorial shrine with photos, beloved toys, name tags, etc. May be temporary or on permanent display.

6) Light a candle and let it burn (somewhere safe) continuously for several days, lighting new ones from this one as it burns down, and meditate on the thought of this light guiding your pet's path to the Other Side.

Memorial shrine for Ludwig & Tuppence

7) Volunteer at or donate to shelters that take in "unadoptable" animals (i.e. older, terminally ill, crippled animals, and animals whose owners have passed away) and give them a place to live out the rest of their days, such as is the case at Home for Life Animal Shelter near Star Prairie, Wisconsin, and their Angel Care program.

8) Draw or paint a picture of your pet or have a professional paint a portrait from a favorite photograph.

9) Embroider, needlepoint, or cross-stitch a pillow with a likeness of your pet.

10) Decorate your pet's urn or casket/burial box with meaningful items.

Drawing created from a photo

11) Create a photo collage and include words cut out from various magazines that make you think of your pet's personality.

> "Each of us has a unique, loving bond with our pets. It is a beautiful act of love to memorialize your pet, no matter what means you choose."
> —by Eleanor L. Harris, *Pet Loss: A Spiritual Guide*

12) Take a pottery class and make your own urn for your pet's ashes.

13) Make art of reused / recycled items and display it in a meditation garden dedicated to the memory of your pet. (For instance, paint a picture on the glass panes of an old discarded window and mount it on a fence or wall outside or indoors if appropriate.)

I painted Tuppence beneath bleeding hearts, my mother's favorite flower.

Memorializing Pets Isn't a New Concept

- Egyptian noblemen have kept pets for thousands of years, as depicted in a painting from the side of a 3,000-year-old coffin showing a man with a dog on a leash. And cats were considered so sacred in ancient Egypt, they were mummified at the time of their owner's death so as to accompany their human into the next world.

- "Thrice has this dog saved his little master from death — once from fire, once from flood, once from thieves." — Inscription on the collar of a fossilized dog found in the remains of Pompeii's volcanic eruption of 79 A.D.

- A fourteenth-century painting of the Last Supper by Pietro Lorenzetti includes pets shown cleaning the plates of their guardians.

- Illustrations of noble ladies in a book on medieval times shows them with lap dogs kept for their company.

Dr. Milani, a veterinarian, wrote of one family that had simply dropped off their dog, Buddy, to be euthanized at her office and left to go to dinner. Somewhat taken aback by what seemed such callous behavior toward a dog they'd obviously loved dearly for years (they were longtime clients), the vet and techs became increasingly upset. They later noticed that the family had provided a box for Buddy's body. They opened it and discovered it was filled with his collar, leash, toys, blanket, and lined with photos from his whole fifteen years. There were also "four sealed envelopes bearing Buddy's name, surely filled with the very best good wishes with which each family member wants to surround their dog on his final journey." The entire clinic staff wept with relief that Buddy had been assured of his family's love in this way.

The vet later learned that the family had bidden Buddy their tearful goodbyes before dropping him off, didn't want their sorrow and anxiety to cause him stress at the very end, and instead wanted to go to a restaurant and talk about and celebrate his life together, remembering him as he would always be, alive in their hearts.

–Adapted from *Preparing for the Loss of Your Pet*
by Myrna Milani, D.V.M.

14) Volunteer as a foster family for a no-kill pet-rescue organization. (See the Resources section for a list of these.) You can have the benefit of a worthy animal's loving energy in your home without the long-term commitment of owning it if it feels too soon.

15) Join a pet loss support group. (See list Resources section.)

16) Organize a garage or rummage sale to raise money for an animal-rescue organization of your choice.

17) Start an online blog about your pet, and upload photos of him or her. This can certainly start while he or she is still alive, of course.

18) Volunteer at a wildlife rehabilitation clinic, where you can help animals that aren't meant to be personal pets while you heal from your own loss.

19) Pay upwards of $950 to the company that will launch your pet's ashes into orbit, where it will be 60 million years before they decay. Seriously. www.celestis.com.

20) Develop your own private ceremony or ritual.

21) Create ceramic tiles with a likeness of your pet or his or her name inscribed, and include it in a remodeling project (such as in the backsplash of your sink).

22) Create a shadow box with such items as a lock of your pet's fur, photos, toys, treats, etc.

23) Make a screensaver slide show on your computer starring your pet.

Harley Davis

Harley, of Southern Pines, NC, lost his battle with cancer on Tuesday, September 2, 2008. Harley was the beloved pet of Debbie and Eddie Davis, Jay Guinn and Holly Tripman. He loved life, mealtime and visiting his extended family of human and furry friends in the Weymouth Heights neighborhood. He was known for his loving personality, excellent behavior, and 'warming the hearts of everyone who knew him. He was preceded in death by his brothers and sisters, Anya, Benjamin, T, Betty and Jigger. In lieu of flowers or donations the family request you give your pet, if you are fortunate enough to have one, all the love and hugs you can possibly give.

24) Place a death announcement in your local paper's obituary section.

25) Ask for a visitation from your pet in your dreams, and keep a dream journal until you get one.

26) Keep a grief journal for a predetermined amount of time, say six weeks, and at the end of that time, review the earliest entries and contrast them to the latest entries. If you see sufficient progress in your healing, thank your pet for all the love and companionship he or she gave you and burn the journal pages to release yourself of any stuck emotions.

27) Write a book about your experience and self-publish it for yourself, friends and family, or the pet-loving community at large.

28) Invite over friends and family to look at your pet's photo albums, have a potluck, and share stories about all the companion animals you've each had and loved.

29) If you have a date scheduled for euthanizing your pet, invite over friends or family members who also loved him or her while he or she is still alive to say goodbye in person.

30) Hold a formal funeral with a burial and someone to speak some words over the ceremony, be it a member of the actual clergy, an animal chaplain, you yourself, or a caring friend.

31) Write a eulogy for your pet and share it aloud with supportive human companions to hear it. Don't worry about your writing or public speaking skills. The main thing is to lovingly express your thanks to your pet and affirm your own spiritual values.

32) Write a poem about your animal companion.

Ode to Meme

I learned much about character
from a tiger I once knew
dignity, forgiveness, appreciation,
patience and especially
joy in small things

slow down and see
feel me in your heart
where I will always be

— Christine, supporter of
The Wildcat Sanctuary,
in honor of Meme, a Bengal tiger
who passed away in 2006.

33) Say a prayer for your pet. Have him or her blessed by a clergy member or animal chaplain of your choice.

Basilica of Saint Mary's Blessing of the Animals
October 2007

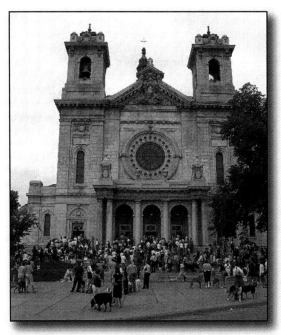

**Hundreds of Humans and Their Pets
Gather for a Mass Devoted to Animals**

**The Priest Blesses
Mortimer & Blanche**

Basilica of Saint Mary's Blessing of the Animals
October 2007

Nigel the Ferret

Bunny Named Carrot

A Pair of Parakeets

Black Swallowtail Chrysalis

"The World Is Filled With Creatures"
by Thomas Hassing &
Mona Lyn Reese

Marybeth, a Box Turtle

West Highland White Terriers

A Hermit Crab Named Leah

34) Write a song about your pet. Record it if possible or perform it for friends and family. It could be the next "Fifty Ways to Leave Your Rover"! *(Sorry.)*

Think this is unusual? Well, think again. Here are just a few examples of songs inspired somehow by our animal companions and the folks who made them famous. Get your iPod ready for a hefty download! • "Old Shep" by Elvis • "Old King" by Neil Young • "Martha My Dear," by the Beatles • "Ben" by Michael Jackson • "I'm Gonna Buy Me a Dog" by the Monkees • "Quiche Lorraine" by the B-52s • "Me and You and a Dog Named Boo" by Lobo • "Shelly's Dog" by Peter Himmelman of Sussman Lawrence • "How Much Is that Doggy in the Window" by Patti Page • "Mona" by James Taylor • "Old Tige" by Jim Reeves • "Fido, Your Leash Is Too Long" by The Magnetic Fields • "Bron-y-aur Stomp" by Led Zeppelin • "Jet" by Paul McCartney and Wings • "I Love My Dog" by Cat Stevens • "Out There in the Night" by The Only Ones • "Lester" by Crowded House • "Delilah" by Queen • "Mr. Bojangles" by the Nitty Gritty Dirt Band • "Lily's Garden" by the Wildhearts • "Sometimes I Don't Mind" by the Suicide Machines • "Ol' Red" by Blake Shelton • "Dogs Are the Best People" by The Fauvres • "Old Blue" by the Byrds • "Dirty Old Egg-Suckin' Dog" by Johnny Cash • "Wildfire" by Michael Murphy • "The Dog Song" by Nellie McKay • "Lucifer Sam" by Pink Floyd • "My Sweet Dog" by Hi-Standard.

Sample Lyrics

"I love my dog as much as I do you, but you may fade, my dog will always come through."

–"I Love My Dog" by Cat Stevens

"He danced for those at minstrel shows and county fairs throughout the South. He spoke through tears of fifteen years how his dog and him traveled about. The dog up and died, he up and died. And after twenty years, he still grieves."

–"Mr. Bojangles" by the Nitty Gritty Dirt Band

"A four-legged animal so cute he'll take your breath away. When that dog's ears stand erect, you better stand back, stand back, stand back, stand back. They go wild. They go crazy.... All the sharp young kids go wild for Shelly's Dog."

–"Shelly's Dog" by Peter Himmelman of Sussman Lawrence

SUBMITTED SONG

"Holly's Favorite Things"

by Erika Thorne of Minneapolis, Minnesota

written for her mare;
sung to the tune of "My Favorite Things"
from *The Sound of Music*

Green grass, alfalfa, and hay made of clover
Apples and carrots and grain poured right over
Hours of grazing while Erika sings
These are a few of my favorite things.

Trotting on trails and jumping the creek rills
Winning the Fun Show and racing up Cross Hills
Reigning at Tara as queen of the herd
This is the best life a horse could incur!

When my joints hurt, when my leg's stiff,
When I'm feeling down
I simply remember my favorite things
And that turns me right around.

Having two moms and Grandpap and Grandmim
How they kept caring when fetlocks went crampin'
While-away summers with Nifty and Liz
These last years are best years that there ever is!

Now I'm older, aching shoulder
When it's time to pass
I'll simply remember my favorite things
While munching on Heaven's grass!

35) Get a plaque engraved with your pet's likeness and name.

36) Watch any home movies you may have that feature your pet.

37) Have a T-shirt made with your pet's photograph appliquéd to it.

38) Place some of his or her ashes or a photo in an engraved locket.

39) Write a tribute article for your pet and have your community newspaper publish it.

40) Go to Kinko's/Fed Ex or Proex or some other such company and have personalized mugs, Christmas ornaments, calendars, even a throw blanket created from your favorite photo(s) of your pet.

41) Bake cookies or dog biscuits in the shape of your pet. Inexpensive dog-breed and other animal-shaped cookie cutters are available online. Just Google "(breed name) cookie cutter."

42) Write and illustrate a children's story with your pet as the hero or protagonist.

> Immortalize your pet in a series of popular mysteries as Lillian Jackson Braun did for her Siamese cat Koko, who'd been murdered by someone who threw him from a ten-story apartment balcony. To process her immeasurable grief, she created *The Cat Who...* mystery series, wherein a prescient Siamese named Koko helps his human, James Qwilleran, solve murders.

43) Use your pet's ashes in a potted houseplant's soil and tend it lovingly.

44) Ask others to contribute memories or stories of your pet for a personal scrapbook.

45) Honor your pet after his or her passing by sincerely asking his or her help in finding you your next pet. This eliminates any feelings of guilt for moving on because you are not "replacing" your pet, you're accepting his or her latest gift to you.

46) Send away for a personalized headstone or plaque. Some sites to start with might be:

> www.4everinmyheart.com
>
> www.4pawsforever.org
>
> www.oldworldstones.com.

Or, create your own by finding a particlarly lovely stone and painting your message on it.

47) Share your thoughts with others on a pet loss support site. (See Resources at the end of this book for one in your area.)

48) Volunteer to staff a pet loss support hotline. (See list of resources.)

49) Contact a pet chaplain or become one yourself. Go to www.interfaithofficiants.com/CompanionAnimalClergy.html or www.petchaplaindottie.com/.

The Universal Life Church recommends animal chaplains answer these questions for themselves before embarking on this new business or ministry:

- Do you love animals?

- Are you a spiritual person? (It is not necessary to be religious in the traditional sense.)

- Do you enjoy serving others?

- Are you willing to put the time and effort into marketing your services in your community?

- Are you open-minded, nonjudgmental, and willing to learn about the practices of numerous faith traditions?

- Are you a good listener?

- Are you reliable, mature, emotionally stable, and willing to accept the responsibilities inherent in beginning a new career, hobby, or volunteer position?

- Would adding animal ministry to your life offer fulfillment or augment the other things you are already doing?

- Would you like to network with people who share your interests, values, and concerns regarding animals and spirituality?

If you answered yes to these questions, animal chaplaincy may be right for you!

www.animalchaplains.com/BecomeanAnimalChaplain.html

---

50) Make a donation to your local park board or see about having your pet's name engraved on a bench or on a brick used in a building associated with animals, such as at an animal humane shelter that is expanding.

51) Create a website. (Contact Gail Heller at Chancesspot.org for tips.)

52) Volunteer for a breed-specific rescue organization.

53) Solicit sponsors and participate annually in a local Walk for Animals for a humane society or other animal-based charity.

54) Paint a mural on the side of a building that could use sprucing up or graffiti-tagging prevention. You could invite others to include their own artistic skills and make it a community event.

55) Donate your stories to someone such as myself who is compiling them for a book. Or hire a writer to create your own pet's story at www.mybestfriend-petstories.com (1-877-LIFE577).

56) Have a custom 3-D felt figure made of your pet via www.feltpets.com.

57) Take an art class and experiment with various ways of expressing your feelings toward your companion animal(s), either realistically or symbolically.

58) Make a sculpture of snow or sand or clay in your pet's likeness.

Snow sculpture commemorating Tuppence

59) Design condolence cards for others who have lost their beloved pets, using words and images you found comforting when you were experiencing a similar loss. You may personalize these with photos of their pets or yours, using your computer's design program.

60) Make personalized pet stepping stones for your garden. Search the Internet using as keywords Personalized Stepping Stones or Pet Memorial Stepping Stones, or go to these sample sites:

pawsandremember.com/store

dog.com

http://epicmerchandise.com/petmemorials.html

oldworldstones.com.

61) Use clay to make a paw print impression of your pet and inscribe his or her name. Search the Internet using Clay Paw Prints as key words. Or check these sample sites:

www.castinggifts.com/pawprintkit

www.smalldogsparadise.com/crafting-dog-supplies/how-to-make-your-own-paw-print-stepping-stone/

www.CastingKeepsakes.com/ClayPrints

www.clayfactory.com/pawprint-kits.html

62) Include your pet(s) in your daily prayers.

One Family's Prayer

"We take a moment during Sabbath and all holiday meals to bless a sometimes overlooked but very important member of our family, Lily the dog. 'Blessed are you, Adonai our God that created this dog to be a friend and companion to this family. May you always have plenty of what you love to eat. May you come and go in peace and stay out of harm's way. And may you always find your way back home. Amen.'"

–Joan Blinkoff, printed in the *Minneapolis Star Tribune*

Submitted Stories

When I put out word that I was looking for people's stories about the strong and unending bond between humans and their companion animals, I was astounded by the flood of heart-wrenching, soul-enriching stories that poured in, literally from around the globe! Here is a sampling of such tales. I wasn't able to print each and every one, but I thank with my whole heart everyone who took the time to share so important a part of their lives with me and with the world.

From these stories, you'll learn of ways these individuals came to make that final selfless decision to euthanize a dear friend, how they've coped with the pain of loss, how they've chosen to memorialize their pets, evidence of their pets' presence near them from the Other Side, and so forth. Most importantly, you'll learn you are not alone in your feelings toward your dear companion animal(s). That bond of love is unique to each individual, yet it is absolutely universal, spanning geography and even time. The mere act of writing each story, regardless of its content or who eventually reads it, was an act of memorializing these wonderful creatures.

The stories you will read here have been only minimally edited. I tried to preserve the unique voice of each author and let his or her poignant expressions speak to you directly.

Thumper's Tale

by Marisol Diestro of Orlando, Florida

Thumper

Thumper was a little grey dwarf rabbit, an Easter gift I received as a little girl. My mother had a friend that bred rabbits and I went to see them. When I saw Thumper, I knew he was the one. I held him the entire time I was there, and he never once tried to get out of my arms. I didn't know anything about rabbits except that they were cute and looked cuddly. I never would have guessed at how much love they could show. Thumper was the first to teach me about unconditional, unselfish love and the

167

strong bond an animal can develop with their guardian.

Thumper never left my side when I had him out of his cage. He followed me everywhere. If I left a room we were in and tried to hide, he would immediately come and look for me. He would run circles around my feet until I was so dizzy from watching him I would plop down on the floor and lie there. And he would lie down next to me, stretching out his entire body in pure happiness. If I didn't pet him, after a little while he would start running circles again around my entire body until I got up and played with him. He would give me kisses with his little pink tongue and licked my tears away when I would cry. He had so much spirit in him and even as he got older he would continue to run circles around me and jump in the air while doing little twists with his body. I now know this is a rabbit behavior known as "binky," which means they are in a state of pure bliss.

One day into my first year of college, I came home one day and found him asleep forever; my heart broke and I held his little limp body as I cried for hours. My boyfriend at the time buried him outside under my bedroom window, and I said goodbye to Thumper forever.

Almost ten years later, I still miss him and my heart aches when I think about him. From time to time I dream about him still. It took me about eight years to get another rabbit. I finally adopted one from a local rabbit rescue group. But I will never forget my grey little bunny that had so much spirit, and I can't wait until we are reunited again forever.

Thomas' Story
by Betty Johnson of DeBary, Florida

Thomas

My story is about our beloved Thomas. Thomas came to us, or I believe was sent to us, after the loss of our first cat, Sam, the Siamese. We had Sam for almost twenty years before we lost him to kidney failure and old age. The year 2000 was quite an eventful year for us as my husband had to have a quadruple bypass on his fifty-fourth birthday in January, my father had been very ill, and then on April 1st, our beloved Sam had a seizure and we had to have him put down. Of course, this broke our hearts, and we didn't know if we could have another kitty to love because the loss was so devastating. But, as luck would have it, I was looking through the newspaper one Saturday afternoon and there was an ad for a part-Siamese/part-Himalayan kitty to go to a good home. I woke up my husband (he works nights) and told him I felt like we should go and see this kitty. I called the people and she said she had another older woman looking at him, but I explained that our last cat had lived for twenty years, and she was impressed with that and told us to come over.

Thomas was lounging at the front door enjoying the sunshine when we came in. He didn't want us, or anybody for that matter, to hold him for very long, but he kept walking by so that we were sure to get a good look at him. He was precious, with beautiful blue eyes and a big fluffy tail. His presence was almost angelic. He loved for us to walk him to his food, even though it was always in the same place, and he could talk just about anyone else who came to visit into doing the same thing. Even friends of ours who were never cat lovers loved Thomas.

Thomas was seven years old when we got him and had already had two homes, so we wanted him to know that this would be his forever home. He was our child since our daughter was grown and lived away from home. Over the next few years, we began to notice that he was slowing down a little and didn't do some of the things we had been used to having him do, but he was still healthy, according to the vet. During the last year we had him, he began to lose weight and when we took him to the vet, we found that he had liver failure. By that time he was nearly thirteen years old, so the vet suggested we treat him symptomatically rather than doing any invasive surgery because of his age. Despite a diet change and IV fluids, eventually, he stopped eating again.

My husband, Johnny, and I both knew he had been sent home from the veterinary hospital to enjoy his last couple of days, though we couldn't talk about it. Our agreement had always been that we would keep him as long as he had quality of life and we felt he could be helped. On Monday morning, we realized that quality was gone. He couldn't get up to use his box, and we weren't going to have him lose his dignity, too. At this point, we knew it was time to help him be in a better place. We took him back to the clinic and Dr. Blake, our veterinarian, was visibly upset that he could not help Thomas. We stayed with Thomas until the last and watched him go to sleep. His beautiful blue eyes had turned a glorious green from the jaundice. Dr. Blake shaved a tuft of fur for us to keep. Thomas passed on August 29, 2006.

We had him cremated and bought him a beautiful little tapestry box for his ashes. He sits alongside Sam, whom we'd had cremated also, in our office at home. We have lots of pictures of him, and I talk to him daily. I did a memorial candle for him on the Rainbow Bridge website and still can't talk about him without bubbling up.

After he was gone, the house almost seemed haunted, as everywhere you turned you would see him there. When our daughter came home, she said the same thing. It was like his little shadow of a person was still among us. Life was so empty; it is hard to explain. Johnny and I both agreed that we grieved over Thomas more than when we lost both of our parents, which seems weird, but he was just such a total part of our lives and such a loss that it was hard to fathom. Yes, people thought we were pretty crazy to be so upset over him, but we didn't care and still don't. Losing Thomas was like losing a child to us, and I don't think I will ever completely get over that, and I don't apologize for those feelings either. So Thomas will always be memorialized in our hearts. If you haven't had a Thomas in your life, you are really missing an experience of a lifetime.

Zelda's Story

by Isabelle and Austin Foster of Spokane, Washington

Up until Saturday, November 3rd, our life was full of fun, games, and laughter. Our little family consisted of my husband and myself; our sixteen-year-old son; a ten-pound, furry, white, nine-year-old

Zelda & Isabelle

mixed-breed girl called Sweetie; and a twenty-pound, furry, brown, nine-month-old girl called Zelda.

Zelda was full of energy and fun. She brought out the fun in Sweetie, who was getting older. Zelda had a huge head and paws for such a little dog. Her front paws were turned in slightly, which made her look like a seal when she was sitting. She was also more vocal than any other dog that we have ever had.

On the other hand, Zelda also had a naughty side to her. She had chewed a dozen pairs of my shoes, a checkbook, my purse, an electrical cord to a heating blanket, pens, pencils, car upholstery, notepads, and books. I would swat her with a rolled paper each time and tell her no, but it was immediately followed with hugs and kisses. I truly loved her no matter what she did. In my eyes, she was perfect and beautiful.

Then on the morning of Sunday, November 4th, 2007, our life changed. My husband let Sweetie in from being outside, when Zelda, who was in the house, wanted to go outside. That was the last time we saw her. We live on ten acres in the mountains north of Spokane, Washington. We have a lot of wildlife around our home, and I assume that she chased some deer or turkeys and never came back. We looked for her all day. We looked for her again the next day and even went to four different neighbors to let them know she was missing. We posted ten signs all around the area, and posted an ad on craigslist in the lost-and-found section. Today, as I write this, is Wednesday and we still don't know what happened to her.

Did she get attacked by coyotes? Did someone decide to keep her? Is she too weak to make it back home? Is she hurt? What could have happened to our beautiful little girl???????

As you can tell, I am truly heartbroken. I am a forty-six-year-old woman, and I can't stop crying like a baby. My husband and son were saddened about the loss initially, but they have gotten over it. I depend a lot on my best friend, Nancy, who lives in Colorado. We talk about how I feel on the phone and chat about it on the Internet. It helps to know that she understands. I know that this will take time to get over it, but for now, it hurts like hell.

Micah

by Shari Boyd of Nashville, Tennessee

Shari & Micah

My story is not so exceptional but my fur-baby's story is. She overcame being a trapped in a puppy mill, lived a good (though far too short life), and in my humble opinion, is about the most amazing creature I've ever known. She was an eight-pound Maltese named Micah. I was a volunteer helping out after a puppy mill seizure. I was there to help, not to bring one home, but she stole my heart. In August 2007, I lost her to a brain infection, and the heart she stole is now broken and I'm in search of a bandage big enough to fix it.

From my blog, Sleepless Ramblings (enter at your own risk):

I just have this heavy heart and I can fake it, but I just can't shake it.

The last time I posted something was the morning Micah left me. It wasn't much, but it was like I had to write it out to believe it. She just broke my heart into a million little pieces. Here I was trying to be better about my health so I'd always be here for her and she up and leaves me!! Needless to say, the [quitting] smoking thing went to hell fast...

Yesterday, I met with someone about her urn and took the pictures they'll use to etch her beautiful little face into the bronze. This last month just seems surreal to me, especially the last two weeks without her here. A month ago we were playing, chasing each other around the house, and working on "our" weight (damn, even my smoking was down to two packs a month!!!) then BAM!! She couldn't walk, then she wouldn't eat.... But her spirit was high. If I left the room I had her in for more than a minute, she used what little energy she had to "bitch" (bark) at me till I came back. And when I walked back in and asked what on earth she was bitching at me about, she'd lift her head, look my way, and wag that tail ... like I'd been gone for days.

I started working outside the house, which helps. But then I come home and there's nothing, no sound, no wispy Katharine Hepburn bark, no little nails clipping around on the kitchen floor, waiting for the gate to come down, no toy squeaks in anticipation of playtime — it's just dead silent. The nights are the worst — after years of bitching about her snoring like a damn freight train — I'd give anything for THAT to be what's keeping me up nights. Not all the guilt and "what ifs" that run circles through my head no matter how hard I try to block them out. Since I can't turn them off, I'm still not sleeping right. Sometimes it feels like I haven't really slept since July.

Some of you are probably thinking, "My God, woman, you are talking about a dog." But the fact is, she was so much more to me than my pup. She was my "kid," my fur baby, my buddy, my travel partner, the most loving little creature I've even known. She was my reminder everyday of just how beautiful life is. How the simplest of things can bring excitement and a smile (wag wag). Watching her evolve from a timid, scared, caged tragedy to a playful, curious dog that loved playing with her toys, chasing fireflies, greeting our neighbors, and actually smelling flowers ... was just a wonder to behold. I told her all the time she was my amazing baby girl, and the house just isn't the same without her around.

Here's what happened:

When I took Micah to the ER, I explained her separation issues when they said they were going to have to keep her. I had one of her toys with me so I asked them to keep it with her at all times. I was informed I wouldn't hear anything from them till probably the next morning.

At 1:58 a.m. my phone rang (scared the crap out of me) and it was the vet, the one I didn't expect to hear from, calling me to touch base and provide me an update (something he said they typically don't do). He said he had put Micah in an oxygen area to help her breathing and told me the things they were doing. Then the conversation drifted to the Jennifer Siliski Puppy Mill case (this is the one I worked on, where I found Micah) and it turned out his wife and he had adopted their Maltese from our rescue.

As we chatted about that (now realize, if not for that extended conversation we would have hung up after discussing Micah) a tech came in and got the doc. He said, "Hold on," and literally dropped the phone. I could hear his footsteps as they ran out of the room. I started crying, praying it wasn't anything to do with Micah. Those ten minutes were the longest of my life. But I sat there, crying, praying, hoping they were doing everything they could to bring my baby back. When he came back to the phone and told me she had died, I fell apart. I felt like my heart had been ripped from my chest.

After giving it a lot of thought, I'm convinced of two things:

1) The vet didn't make the call that night on his own; Micah made him do it, as it was as close as she could get to me to say goodbye; and

2) She was never "getting better" but found a way to take a decision I would have found impossible to make out of my hands.

They say God works in mysterious ways, and I believe this is true. I also believe that, due to our society as a whole, people that lose beloved pets cannot mourn properly — especially people in my position (single, living away from family) where the companion animal was more a part of the person's everyday life than any human. When a human dies, we encourage others to cry, to mourn, to take time. We tell them holding it in is bad for them. When someone loses a pet, it's not socially acceptable to mourn. We are made to feel as though we are not in our right mind if we actually mourn the loss.

Even some of my closest friends don't understand how I'm feeling, and I don't think they want to. They are not BAD people, they just don't UNDERSTAND that Micah wasn't "just a dog." In fact, three months after the fact, I feel this loss has hit me even harder than losing my father, but now I see why — I was ALLOWED to mourn my father. I had people around all the time offering me love, support, and understanding. With the exception of a few people (mostly those that also worked the rescue), I don't have that support network. This is why your book is important, not just for pet owners but for their friends, family. People need to understand the pain their friend is going through and not wave it off.

I'm sharing with you the following website, as this woman might be a reference to use. I know it made me feel like I AM NORMAL, which is an alien feeling to me these days. She's a grief therapist/counselor who expanded her treatment to include pet loss: http://www.griefhealing.com/healing-courses2.htm

〜〜〜 〜〜〜 〜〜〜

SUBMITTED POEM

This poem was written by Roxanne Saunder's friend, and Dusty's mommy, inspired by Roxanne's own story of how Chicklet's life touched her life during the years they were together. (See this story in the Animals and the Afterlife section.)

A Poem for Chicklet

by Karen Michaels

When you were young, sweet Chicklet, your ears were quite a size,
they matched though, didn't they, sweet babe, your big expressive eyes ...
Your coat was thin and so your mom saw right through all your fur,
she'd cuddle you close, though, just the same, until you'd start to purr ...

Mom baptized you, her faith was strong, she believed so much in you
she felt you had a purpose grand, a special job to do ...
You let your mommy cradle you, like a baby in her arms
perhaps you felt the nudge back then to protect her from all harms ...

Three years you spent with Mommy, strong bonds from the first day
Even the other kitties knew you were special in some way,
But then that bleak September day your mommy found you ill
with cancer throughout your body, your lungs that day turned still.

A few days later your mommy's test was a scary thing indeed
A mammogram suspicious now, your mommy was in need
But you weren't there by mommy's side, and she was down and blue,
how would she ever get through this, without a touch from you?

But you knew your special purpose had already been fulfilled
that purpose long ago just maybe God himself had willed.
You knew your dear sweet mommy would be diagnosed okay
for you took all cancers with you, that day you went away.

So Chicklet, you took a journey, to the rainbow in the sky
where you soar on wings as eagles, on your angel wings so high.
Mom took a journey through this, too, a journey that renewed
her faith in God, and in herself, and in her love of you.

May you always feel the faith in God and in yourself that
Chicklet renewed in you, Roxanne ... God Bless

〰〰 〰〰 〰〰

SUBMITTED STORY

Suki

by Julie McLaughlin of Naples, Florida

I was diagnosed with acute myelogenous leukemia at the age of twenty-six and six months later had a bone marrow transplant. My dog, Suki, helped me through all of my stages with the disease, transplant, and recovery. Included at the bottom of this story is a link to my Light the Night page (a fundraising walk). On it is one of my most precious, meaningful photos. It is of me, a couple of months after my transplant, with no hair, and with my dog Suki lying in bed with me. Her head is on my side, watching over and protecting me. In my face, even with all the horrors that I had just been through, I have one the happiest smiles and the feeling of being loved by such a dear dog and spirit. I miss her terribly. She helped me through so much, was there with me every step I took to regain my strength and teach my muscles to walk again. She was the one I told all of my fears and hopes to. She was always there to comfort me.

In May 2007, she was eleven years old, old for a yellow Lab. She started failing, and we learned that she had cancer. This was such a blow to me, and I was determined not to put her through what I went through. I could not see her go through chemo. When she looked at me, she was asking

Julie & Suki

me now for help and support. She was asking me to let her go peacefully. I helped her with that and was there with her to the end, till the vet gave her the shot. It broke my heart. But, I was truly blessed to have such a wonderful dog, soul, in my life. She was actually my dad's dog, as I surprised him with her eleven years before. But as she grew, she became both his and mine, always splitting her time between us. When I got sick, I had to move back into my parents' house. Suki would spend half the day in my room with me and the other half with my dad in his office. She will always be the best dog.

www.lightthenight.coremedicalgroup.com

www.active.com/donate/ltnbcom/JuliesCore_2007JBM

〰 〰 〰

SUBMITTED STORY

When You Have a Friend Like Skippy

by Willie McNee,
with an introduction by his mother, Casey Quinn,
of Eden Prairie, Minnesota

I received your solicitation for pet stories from our friends at "Little White Terriers." I have attached an essay that my son wrote a little less than a year ago when he was in the ninth grade, age fourteen. It is about the death of his beloved pet RAT (of all things), "Skippy." It is very sweet.

From my perspective, I couldn't even believe how many tears

were shed over her passing. We buried Skippy behind our cabin in Cohasset, Minnesota. We cleared a path and put down stepping stones. I painted a large rock with her name on it and a picture of her peeking out from inside her purse (she loved purses). We purchased a solar lantern so that we could see her from the house.

Every time we go up to the cabin (many times this summer), both of my boys (Willie, fifteen, and Gabe, twelve, in 2007) run out back to say hi to Skippy. It makes me cry just thinking about it!

P.S. Skippy was part of the sixth-grade curriculum. We "won" her in the drawing at the end of the year.

Skippy

We had a little girl, Skippy the Rat.
She lived in a miniature habitat.
A glass-bottom condo, three stories tall,
Enough room to scurry, walk, run, or crawl.

She fancied her purses, a real fashion gal,
And we fancied her, our favorite pocket pal.
Skippy was raised by the sixth-grade class
No lack of attention for this wee lass.

by Willie McNee

I was about to win first place! I ran towards the finish line. Only ten meters from it, a familiar beeping noise filled my ears. It was my age-old alarm clock ripping me from my dreams. As I turned it off, I looked at the time. It was six o'clock. Of course, I thought to myself,

I have chamber orchestra this morning. I had overslept, but not by much. I took a shower and got ready for the day. My mom was still sleeping. My dad said he'd give me a ride. I ran out the door without having time to say goodbye to my dogs or my rat, Skippy.

Then came the call. My dad answered the phone. As a heaviness crept into his voice, I heard him say to the caller, "Should I tell him now?" The way my dad looked at me at that moment, I knew something was wrong. He said that Skippy had died in the night. I just looked out the window. I didn't know what to do. Nothing close to me had ever died before other than our family dog when I was two years old. Normally my family talks a lot, but now the car was silent. I just sat there looking out my window thinking of the past three years that I had cared for her. We had gotten her from the sixth-grade science project at Oak Point.

I arrived at school and had what would have been a normal, if not good, day. It all meant nothing to me; not the score on my geometry test or how well I did in Pin Guard during gym. I just wanted to get home.

The feeling in my gut when I walked in the front door of my house was a new one, a feeling of the darkest foreboding. As I walked in the house, my mom said, "In the big freezer." I opened the freezer to discover a small, white box. It had a sheet of scented paper in it. I unrolled the paper to find my rat. She was cold and her eyes were faded, unlike the bright red ones I looked into only yesterday. I started to cry. It was the first time I had cried in years.

My family was going up to our cabin the next day. This would be our first trip up there without Skippy. We had decided to bury her up there. We piled into the car and started another silent car ride. It is a four-hour drive up to our cabin. The whole time no one said anything.

When we arrived, we took some tools out and cleared an area behind the cabin. I dug a hole just large enough for our precious pet. We opened the small, white box to say our goodbyes to the little rat who had made our family complete. We rolled the paper back up, closed the lid, and placed the box down in the hole. We had a moment of silence as I covered the box with dirt. We placed a few stones around the grave and one big one in the middle. We made her a little shrine with a light in it.

I will never forget those two silent car rides or the way my dad looked at me when he got that phone call. I still think of Skippy often. I miss her.

In Memory of Shana, Companion and Friend
by Michelle J. Bloom Hockersmith of Mabel, Minnesota

20 January 2003

Woke up to a grey though beautiful day nonetheless. It is a very sad day, as have been the past few days, as we have to put Shana down. We have always known that there was a chance we would have to do this long before her time; it would have been irresponsible of us to not have prepared and talked about this possibility. As hard as it is, this is the only way to be responsible.

This weekend, we were in the Cities and brought Shana to be with us at my sister-in-law's brother's house so that she could meet, stay, and play with Mazel (their 100-pound German shepherd mix). Needless to say, it didn't go very well. Mazel left the scene with a gash in her neck the size of a quarter and had to be taken to the emergency vet to get it stitched up. The thing is this: What my husband, Alan, saw in Shana during that whole incident was far beyond any acceptable limits. There is no question about what he saw. Mazel was being submissive and Shana would not let go. Period. The decision is made. When Alan and I saw the gash ... at exactly the same moment ... we both knew, without saying a word, that this was it; that it has come to us putting her down.

She is a family member; and we have to take our hearts out of ourselves and do what is right ... the pain is excruciating, absolutely excruciating. She has such a wonderful and loving

Shana

personality: funny, cuddly, honest, and intimate. The humans who had her before us have absolutely no idea just how much injustice they have done to her ... this is in large part their fault. Never having socialized her to other dogs and abusing her has fed the fuel of what is in her because of her rottweiler and Doberman breeds. I firmly believe that you can train and work for steering a dog with breeds such as Shana's away from some of their "natural" tendencies if you start from the very beginning.

There is no question that things will be much easier, but this is not what we're looking for ... had it been what we were looking for, we would have given up a long time ago. Easy is not fulfilling; our relationship with Shana was so many things ... including very fulfilling. To not have her spirit with us will be so difficult and sad.

22 January 2003

I have everything set up for the day. Our cat Pitzl is in her basket on the table, and Shana is sprawled out on the sofa dozing while waiting for the sun to catch up with her for a good sunbath. All is well except that tomorrow at 10:00 a.m. Shana will be put down. We are keeping things as normal as possible except that we are giving Shana everything she wants. Playing. Eating. Being on the sofa. We'll go for a walk in the woods later today, and she will get a bone with a ton of meat on it this evening. It is going to be a difficult night. G-d, the pain; it is excruciating.

I just can't imagine the days no longer being punctuated by Shana's needs, desires, naggings, nudges for attention, and hugs. This is so hard. She isn't even gone yet and I am getting a taste of her absence: Alan has her with him for a ride in the truck.

23 January 2003

7:25 a.m. We had a very beautiful morning; I was up at 4:45, unable to sleep any longer, and Alan was up by 5:15, at which time we invited Shana into bed with us. We all cuddled, Alan and I reminiscing, crying, and laughing while Shana snored and ran in her dreams next to us. We will go for a walk in the woods before we leave — she will like that immensely.

A really neat thing: Baby decided to show even Alan that she/he was really in there! He felt Baby kick! Thank you for that, Baby; especially on this particularly poignant morning. [Michelle was pregnant at this time with her son Asher.]

Shana loved her walk in the woods, as did we. It was beautiful—the bright, winter-sharp sunlight gleaming off the creek and between the trees. Our breath hung in the air around our heads with every exhalation ... including Shana's. She ran in between both of us and up and back from the ridge, intent on the things she heard and/or saw that were nothing we could hear or see. I am so glad and thankful that she had a great last day. I am also thankful that she was able, for the last couple of months of her life, to truly enjoy herself.

Later

It's done. It was horrible. Saying goodbye to her body was so unbelievably hard. Seeing Alan in so much pain was heart-wrenching, beautiful; I loved him more than ever at that moment. There will be a hole in our lives now. As I look out the window, the landscape is missing something. Such a big, strong dog brought down in seconds to a weak, vulnerable frame. She trusted us—Alan, actually—to the very end ... looking into his eyes as she got her shot, trusting him that we would never do anything to hurt her; this was good. It is better this way that she believed this to the very end.

There is a way in which this kind of pain brings everything into focus.

31 January 2003

Woke up to a "hoo, hoo, hoo" just outside the window and a veritable winter wonderland: three inches of snow covering everything from the bird feeders to the branches to the table. Stunning. The creek literally glistened against the brightness of the snow even though the morning is overcast.

Shana's footprints are all gone now from the land due to the snow ... beautiful nonetheless. There will always be something missing from the landscape now. It hurts every time we come home ... something is so obviously missing.

Sebastian

by Bruce Cochran of Minneapolis, Minnesota

National Night Out takes on a whole new meaning for us now. We lost Sebastian at fifteen years old that day. Of course, we still haven't found the courage to conduct any formal service. I had to work through the pain the only way I knew, which was a little bit at a time. I don't cry several times a day anymore. This hit me more than when I lost my father. That doesn't bother me though. I was quick to realize how important that connection was to our little Yorkie.

Sebastian Joe Foss-Cochran

Big Love

15 years, 1 month and a day...a day that Sebastian passed away–August, 7th, 2007.

We had a contract. We treated him with the love of a family member and he gave us unconditional love.

As we watched him bite squirrels and run 8 minute miles he taught us that size is all in your head. As we strolled around Lake Calhoun we witnessed even the most troubled people break into a smile as they passed.

We learned to care about the little things.

Thank you.

He was given to us as a gift. I witnessed his previous life and wanted to improve it. I made sure he got the best health care, regular walks, play, and love. I've always felt that since dogs were domesticated by humans to give us unconditional love, it has since been our responsibility to return the favor and give that right back. That's the contract.

As he got older, we both played naïve to the fact that his various abilities were going. I figured he was just preparing us for taking care of the coming babies my wife is carrying. We believe he knew they were coming and wanted to get out of the way. When a pet grows old slowly and begins to lose senses and abilities, you constantly fear the day when you may have to say THIS is the day we put him to sleep. So are we lucky he died of cancer? No. Was it easier? Well, maybe a little. When they did the exploratory and found it had spread, he was already under sedation. That's when we said this would be the easiest on him.

I'll never forget the day before when

183

I knew it might be his last day. I spent all day with him. That night we took him for a long car ride with his head out the window. It was one thing I knew I could do for him that I could be sure he would enjoy.

I believe the pain is hard because we find it harder to communicate to a pet. We feel like no matter how hard we try we want them to know we love them and that they will be okay on their journey when they get there.

I'm forty-one and I think it was the first time I felt that pang that mature adults express when they've lost their spouse. I wanted to go with him. Part of me felt like I was being rejected by an exclusive club. My wife and I both re-examined our religions. We had to; we couldn't agree on a memorial service. I've always known that animals are different from humans but not in the traditional sense. My religion is a combination of the fundamentals of all religions and science. I think they all on hint at the enormous. Superstring theory or the water droplet falling into the ocean, we are all part of the great cosmos. What I don't understand about my pet today, I will discover tomorrow. Sebastian was love.

Sara Lee
by Terri Delebo of Minneapolis, Minnesota

To Everyone Who Knew Me, Me, Me, Sara Lee
(May 13, 1990 – August 20, 2007)

I was a Prima Donna.

I had nothing but subtly curled-lip disdain for other dogs.

Occasionally I would try to kill the ones who lived in my house.

All six of the other cockers with whom I lived over the years eventually learned to steer clear of me.

I loved the couch and my many dog beds.

Though in later years my breath could wipe out a small network of terrorists,

I was generally quite a pleasant, lovely, deserving, and accomplished dog.

Sara Lee

I searched neighborhood alleys for loose garbage and ate my way through Hefty bags at home,

extracting only the choicest grease wads.

Occasionally I napped on the dining room table with that one dog...

(I think her name was Cricket, though I never cared enough to be sure)

and once ate most of a chocolate cake I found up there.

It was delicious, and I deserved it.

One time I ate a dozen M&M cookies stored in the back of the Expedition,

and returned them to the car in a new form the next day.

Recently, just before my seventeenth birthday, I ate a bag of chocolate chips which I stole from the pantry;

I was up for forty-eight hours, running up and down stairs and doing figure eights,

but was really none the worse for wear — so it was worth it.

I often stuck my head in grocery bags and carefully removed what I wanted.

I once ate mouse poison and lived to tell about it — barely.

I once ate a lovely cheese dip brought by a guest, employing my delicately agile tongue from two feet away.

I loved mealtime, almost to my dying day.

I wagged my tail long past the age of seventeen (that's 119 for you all).

I loved simple attention and graciously accepted much-deserved praise about my beauty, my pleasant demeanor, my wavy ears, and my lovely coat.

I rather enjoyed it when the neighbors celebrated my seventeenth with champagne; I had a hamburger.

I loved my family, especially my boys, who arrived on Tarrymore Avenue after I paved the way for children.

My motto:
"Everybody doesn't like something, but nobody doesn't like Sara Lee." (stolen from me for those cheesecake ads).

My manifesto:
"There is no other dog in the world but Sara Lee. Sara Lee does not see other dogs, does not acknowledge them. Me, me, me. Sara Lee."

Everyone who met me thought I was "the nicest dog." It is true.

Now I occupy a large damask pillow in the Prima Donna section of Spaniel Heaven and eat cake and garbage whenever I want.

See you all, one of these days!   *—Sara Lee*

A Sappy Tale

by Julie Wiley of San Antonio, Texas

Sappy

I want to share a little about my personal journey with pet loss. My husband and I had to euthanize our precious pet on August 4, 2003. His name was Sappy. He was fourteen years old and weighed about six pounds; he was a longhaired, white-coat Chihuahua. He was actually a college graduation gift, a tender six weeks old when he came into my life. He was my sunshine.

Anyway, after a brief battle with bladder cancer, diagnosed in June of 2003, he passed away. Putting him to sleep was the hardest decision I'd ever made in my entire life. Losing Sappy turned my world inside out. After only a month and in search of a support group in our city and being unsuccessful in finding one, we were inspired by our boy to start one. So, in September of 2003, we started the SAPPY Pet Loss & Grief Support Group of San Antonio. We gathered every single Tuesday for three years. Today, we remain faithful to the call and memory of Sappy, although we're now gathering once a month — on the fourth Tuesday of the month — to better accommodate pet parents. We still receive phone calls almost every week and help comfort those grieving at support group gatherings and/or over the phone.

I just wanted to let you know that out of something terrible like losing our precious Sappy, something wonderful came to be ... something that is helping those who are stricken with that grief that cuts very deeply into the soul and heart. My grief was very painful and often went unvalidated by others, but thank God, we overcame the sorrow with the help of others at SAPPY Pet Loss & Grief Support Group. I know firsthand what it's like to lose a wonderful pet and how deeply it hurts when the time comes for them to leave this Earth. It can be very devastating, and it can take months to years before the healing comes full circle. I don't believe that our grief ever ends; however, I do believe that our broken hearts and spirits heal and we are changed individuals, never to be the same again. Our pets truly change our lives for the better! We'll always miss him, but we know without a doubt that he's in Heaven with God, his creator. And, we'll see him again!

We also host an annual Tribute to Tails Candlelight Vigil in December to honor the memory of ALL creatures who've crossed over to Heaven.

Our group gatherings are open to anyone coping with the loss of a pet; they are supportive in nature and not to be confused with "traditional therapy."

sappypetloss@sbcglobal.net
210-216-0920 Calls are returned within 24 hours.

Ripley

by A. Miller of Minneapolis, Minnesota

Bernese mountain dog like Ripley

Ripley, a Bernese mountain dog, was eight years old when he died. My mom had been very sick for a year. It was such a hard, sad time. Ripley was my shadow the entire time I had him. He never left my side and would go from room to room with me. He was such a comfort to me during my mom's illness. After spending the day at the hospital, I could hardly wait to get home and have him by my side. I would take him to visit my mom when she was in the nursing home. She loved him so much. One day I noticed Ripley wouldn't eat, no matter what I offered him. I called the vet and he told me to bring him in the next morning and just drop him off and they would watch him and do some tests. That next morning, I got a call from the nursing home that my mom was dying. As I was leaving to go there, I remembered Ripley's appointment. My husband said he would drop him off and then come and meet me.

My mom died that morning a few hours after I got there. I got home around 4 p.m. and called the vet. He has been my vet for over twenty years, so I consider him a friend, too. I didn't tell him what had happened, just that I really needed Ripley to come home. I said I would bring him back the next day if they still needed to do tests. There was a long pause and he asked if I could come in to talk at 6 p.m. They close the office at 5:30, so I knew then that Ripley wasn't coming home. My husband and I went to the office, and the vet told us Ripley was filled with cancer and was bleeding out internally and it was just a matter of hours before he would be gone. We made the decision not to let him suffer. I asked my husband to stay with him and I went outside. My husband told the vet that my mom had just died that morning; the vet started to cry and said no one should have to lose their mom and companion on the same day. It was much more than that. I lost my two best friends on the same day. I like to think that Ripley knew my mom had suffered for so long and needed him to go with her.

Ripley died in December. I waited until May to get another puppy. I can never have another Bernese Mountain dog; it would be too hard. So I got a Newfoundland. He is wonderful and has his own personality, but every once in awhile, I will look at him and find him staring at me and just for a brief moment, it seems like it's Ripley looking back at me. The puppy lies in all the funny spots that Ripley did, like now, squeezing in between my chair and the computer desk so I can rest my feet on him! I think Ripley is with my mom, but every once in awhile, he comes around to check in and let me know they are together.

Mattie

by Lisa, Joe, and Zoe of Hutcherson, Kentucky

Mattie

I want to share with all of you about this sweet adorable angel that came into our lives, our home, and our hearts and blessed us with love and joy. When we found Mattie, she had had a very difficult start at her young life. She was not well cared for; she was skin and bones, with bald patches on her skinny little body. When she fell asleep in my husband Joe's arms, we knew it was intended for her to be part of our lives and us a part of hers. The woman we got Mattie from is a person who cares nothing for these blessed gifts from the heavens. We did not see the conditions that Mattie and her other pug relatives had to endure, but we have been informed by those who have been a witness to these conditions and let's just say that Mattie was our own personal rescue mission.

When Mattie arrived at her new home on March 12, 2004, her toenails were so long, they were curled under, and some were pressing into her pads. She was so skinny, she ate three bowls of food in less than an hour! She was not only starved for food but for love and attention and a home.

We took Mattie to our vet the following day, where they determined her age to be around eight or nine weeks old. She weighed only about two pounds, and they went ahead and began her first round of puppy shots and cut her toenails. Everyone at the vet's office just adored her. Looking at her sweet face, how could you not just love her? We also had to give her lyme baths over a period of one month, which she did not like, but she handled it like a champ all the way.

Mattie was growing, gaining weight, playing, and just loving life. She and her pug sister, our oldest pug, Zoe, had begun to play regularly and would chase each other through the house. They loved to play "Pug-o-War" with a sock.

But the happy times weren't to last. It was probably late April or early May when Joe noticed Mattie was having a problem with her right hind leg. We took her to the vet and they did some X-rays, which confirmed their suspicions. Mattie was stricken with a genetic disease, known as Legg-Perthe's Disease, which is a degeneration of the hip joint. She underwent her first surgery on June 14, 2004, on her right leg, where they completely shave off the femoral head. Her recovery went very well. She was running around and doing more than she could before. However, her left leg was progressing quickly and we knew the time for the second surgery was fast approaching. She went in on July 19, 2004, for her second surgery. As they were finishing surgery and closing, Mattie's heart rate dropped, and despite their best efforts, she did not survive.

Losing Mattie has been very difficult for all of us because we never expected that she would not survive given how well she had done with her first surgery. But now we know this woman is breeding these innocent pugs that are stricken with this genetic disease and despite all our efforts, nothing or nobody has made any attempt to stop her, and so the cycle continues and more innocent pugs will suffer and could eventually lose their precious lives.

Our sweet little angel, Mattie, made her journey to the Rainbow Bridge on Monday, July 19, 2004. Mattie was a gift to us, and her life was cut too short. Through this dedication, we want to thank Mattie for coming into our lives and choosing us as her family. Mattie, you will be forever missed, forever remembered, forever loved, and forever you will always be in our hearts. You have left paw prints on our hearts that can never be erased.

Mattie, we will never forget all the times that you would bark at the TV for no reason, and how you loved your yellow squeaky bone so much that you would fall asleep with it in your mouth. Mattie, we will never forget your first time eating peanut butter and how it was stuck all over your whiskers. Mattie, we will never forget how you would tilt your head to the side and stick out your tongue when we would talk to you.

Mattie was our inspiration for joining Kentuckiana Pug Rescue (KPR). Through the passionate efforts of KPR, helping any pug that needs us, will help us to honor Mattie and all those sweet lil' angels who come to KPR in need of help. We want to thank each and every one of you for the kind words, prayers, and emails extending your condolences on our loss. Our deepest gratitude goes out to all of you!

THANK YOU, KPR!!! The work you do is truly the work of angels! Thank you for allowing us to be part of this wonderful and blessed KPR family! We love you all!

Letter from Your Pet in Heaven Author Unknown
Submitted by Pat Lively

To my dearest family,
some things I'd like to say.
But first of all, to let you know,
that I arrived okay.

I'm writing this from the Bridge.
Here I dwell with God above.
Here there's no more tears of sadness.
Here is just eternal love.

Please do not be unhappy
just because I'm out of sight.
Remember that I am with you
every morning, noon, and night.

That day I had to leave you
when my life on Earth was through,
God picked me up and hugged me,
and He said, "I welcome you.

"It's good to have you back again;
you were missed while you were gone.
As for your dearest family,
They'll be here later on."

God gave me a list of things,
that He wished for me to do.
And foremost on the list
was to watch and care for you.

And when you lie in bed at night,
the day's chores put to flight,
God and I are closest to you ...
in the middle of the night.

When you think of my life on Earth
and all those loving years,
because you are only human,
they are bound to bring you tears.

But do not be afraid to cry;
it does relieve the pain.
Remember there would be no flowers,
unless there was some rain.

I wish that I could tell you
all that God has planned.
If I were to tell you,
you wouldn't understand.

But one thing is for certain,
though my life on Earth is o'er.
I'm closer to you now,
than I ever was before.

There are rocky roads ahead of you
and many hills to climb;
But together we can do it
by taking one day at a time.

It was always my philosophy
and I'd like it for you, too;
That as you give unto the world,
the world will give to you.

If you can help somebody
who's in sorrow and pain;
Then you can say to God at night ...
"My day was not in vain."

And now I am contented ...
that my life was worthwhile.
Knowing as I passed along
I made somebody smile.

God says: "If you meet somebody
who is sad and feeling low;
Just lend a hand to pick him up,
as on your way you go.

"When you're walking down the street
with me on your mind;
I'm walking in your footsteps
only half a step behind.

"And when it's time for you to go ...
from that body to be free.
Remember you're not going ...
You're coming here to me."

Tabitha and Ysah

by Suzanne T. of Edmonton, Alberta, Canada

I moved from my hometown in Manitoba to Edmonton in 1995 —
packing up my kids, our cat J.J., and our lives and moving to a city
where I was hoping to make a fresh start — away from my
ex-husband but totally without family. The one thing I promised my
kids was that as soon as I started working (which was within two
weeks) and we settled in to our place, we would add a lovely addition
to our home — a kitten we named Tabitha. She, along with our new
home, represented a new life for my kids and me.

Tabitha, a.k.a. Tabby, Tabiwaas, Waa-Waas, was a longhaired,
dark tortoise-shell-colored cat; she was my baby. She always greeted

me at the door with her feathered tail held
high and would always carry on about her
day. She was quite chatty. She was my best
friend in the whole world—she would console me when I was having a bad day; she
would mother the kids, almost scolding
them at times when they were being too
loud. She would get so upset if I raised my
voice to the kids, she would jump on the
back of the couch and pull my hair right at
the root!

Tabitha

Tabitha developed cancer in 2006 and I made the decision that I
would not put her through surgeries, drug therapy, etc. that would
only prolong her untimely death. I ensured that she was eating properly, getting her rest, and staying as active as she could. The vet and all
the research indicated that when a cat displays tumors such as the size
of Tabby's, there really is only about a year or so before the animal will
have to be put down. She knew she was sick, but she still walked
around with her tail held high—her form of dignity. A couple of
months before Tabitha passed away; we adopted another kitten—
Ysah—to whom Tabitha quickly became attached.

When it was time to take Tabitha to the vet, it was very devastating for me. She was my hope of a new future—a new life—and now
it was ending. My world crashed. She was my confidant, my shoulder
to cry on, my children's sibling.

Tabitha was no longer able to breathe correctly, having to open
and close her mouth to gain air. Perhaps we left her too long, but she
had been okay (or better) the night before. I took her to the vet in her
kennel and was escorted to a room to spend time with her. I could not
stay with her when they euthanized her, as she was just a walk-in at
the time. When I let her out of her kennel, her tail was held high. She
had the curious but wonderment-filled look in her eyes, and I could
honestly say she hadn't looked healthier in a long time. I think she
knew what was happening and perhaps welcomed it. She was even
trying to purr, for which she was famous. That was March 3, 2007.

After a day or two, both Ysah and J.J. seemed to feel the loss.

They continually ran up and down the stairs, checking every room, looking for Tabitha. All my cats are kept indoors, but about a week after Tabitha passed away, J.J. got out and she disappeared. The only thing I could think was that she went looking for Tabby. Thank goodness, J.J. came home, unhurt, after two long agonizing weeks — tired, a little dirty, but unhurt.

Ysah

Meanwhile, Ysah had started adopting some of Tabitha's habits, such as drinking out of the sink — he had never done that before; he always drank out of a dish. He also started to "bury" his food by scratching the floor like Tabitha did; he never did that before either. Please note: Ysah was blind.

There were odd times when J.J. would meow and I would have to turn to look, as she sounded exactly like Tabitha, and once in awhile I swear I would see Tabby from the corner of my eye. I know she is here. I can feel her sometimes, and it brings me much comfort. I pray to my Spirit Guide every night to always protect my Tabiwaas.

Ysah, my baby boy, was a shorthaired domestic with the prettiest dark markings and his white chest and feet and his apricot face. It wasn't long after having Ysah that we found out he was blind, and it sure explained a lot as he ran into things, couldn't see things to play, etc. We did determine he could see shadows in bright light, so to help him out, we purchased nightlights so he could better make his way down the stairs to his litter box. We did everything in our power to ensure that things weren't left "lying around" so he could make his way through his home safely.

Sadly, Ysah was diagnosed with kidney failure, and I was told that no amount of medicine could help him and that it would be best to let him go. I took him home that night and prayed for him, and I prayed for Tabitha to care for him the way she did when she was on Earth with us. I cried for Tabby to be there for him and in the darkness, I saw the shadow of Tabby on my bed. I was calm, stopped crying, and said "thank you" as my heart was filled with joy, knowing Ysah would be okay. The next day, I took Ysah in.

Unlike Tabitha, I was with Ysah when he was euthanized. I

wanted to be there because he was blind and I wanted him to be calmed by my voice. He, unlike Tabitha, was terrified and that hurt my heart even more. He sat on the vet's table shivering, but when I picked him up, he snuggled into my hair and started purring; the shaking had stopped. The vet was amazing and so compassionate and was welling up with tears, too, as Ysah was "just a kid," as she put it. It was very devastating to not only lose one animal, but two within six months of each other. That was August 23, 2007. We have a video of Ysah on his last day and pictures to print and frame, which will be hung alongside Tabitha's picture in my room. Incidentally, since Ysah used to sleep on my shoulder, I now have to have a little teddy bear in his place just so I can sleep. It's interesting what we get accustomed to.

My family has been amazing with the losses, as they felt the loss in their own way. They had their own relationships with our pets and their own memories. We still talk about Tabitha a lot and of course Ysah because he is the most recent, and I still cry for both of them. My Spirit Guide now has two of my pets to watch over. I had no other avenue to express my grief until I came across Chance's Spot (www.chancesspot.org), and I am grateful to have run across this site. All those on it know exactly where I am coming from and understand that my loss was not just of my pets, but also of my family. I couldn't ask for better support.

There is no greater love than the unconditional love that our pets offer to us. I have to be content with knowing that my babies are with me all the time, and when their name slips between my lips when I mean to say something else, I know that they are there with me at that very moment. Bless all the animals of this world and thank them for allowing us to be a part of their lives. We are fooled into believing that we are taking care of them. It is only when we lose our pets that we realize they were really taking care of us.

Murphy

by Lisa Johnson Gates of Mill Valley, California

I got Murphy, my golden retriever, on April 9, 1999. He was two months old. I am a dog walker and I walk his dad, whose human parents offered me "pick of the litter" in appreciation of my being their dog walker. He was my best friend from day one. He was my everything. We were together twenty-four hours a day, seven days a week, and I figured out that in the eight years we had him, I'd only been apart from him for three weeks (one week for my husband's and my honeymoon and two weeks in Hawaii). The only time I would be without him during the day was for dinner or a movie, which lasted about three hours.

Three weeks after I had given birth to my twin boys (and of course, I insisted on my mom bringing Murphy to the hospital for me to see him everyday), I was throwing a ball for him when I noticed bleeding. I thought he had bitten his tongue. He was diagnosed with osteosarcoma of the lower jaw, which had to be removed. I was a wreck, but as time went on and we made plans for treatments and I started to have an inkling of hope of his beating this thing, I became stronger for Murphy.

He had the surgery, started chemo, did radiation treatment even, and then when the cancer metastasized to his lungs, we did an experimental study for inhalation chemotherapy, which did kill the cancer in his lungs. But the cancer in his jaw had spread to his neck, and that is what eventually got him. He was still very much wanting to eat, run, and play, but he couldn't because the tumors had turned his throat into stone. That was the hardest part—he was uncomfortable but still wanted to play, as opposed to dogs I've seen dying of cancer who are listless and ready to pass away.

We took him to an acupuncturist and herbalist vet. I hand-fed him and cooked meals that were recommended to fight cancer. It was time-consuming but worth every second. It wasn't work—it was taking care of my buddy.

I've had human obstacles for my grieving. I feel uncomfortable talking about my pain and grief to many people because it has been four-and-a-half months now, and I don't feel like many would understand the pain I still feel from the loss of Murphy. My husband was supportive for about a week, and now it's been hard for him to understand. He loved Murphy, but not like I did. I turn to friends and clients who have lost their dogs for comfort. One of my clients lost her Bernese mountain dog a month before I lost Murphy, and he was only seven. We

Murphy

have become close and share our pain everyday. Reading grief books has helped, too.

I had many metaphysical experiences for about a month or more after Murphy died. Every night at 7 p.m., when Murphy was alive, I would put one of the twins down to bed (my husband did the other one). I would rock one to sleep in a rocking chair and Murphy would always come poke his head in to see if I was done with the twin so I could take him on his evening walk around the block. I would hear him approaching the door—his nails on our hardwood floors. After he died, I heard it several times. I then began to look forward to putting Stuart, my son, to sleep because I would hope to hear the nails on the floor. I have not heard them for about two months now, but I had heard them loud and clear.

I also heard him growl. I was in my office and heard a low growl. I ran out and there was nothing there. He used to lie outside my home office, and if he heard another dog walk by our front door, he would growl.

I also felt him lie next to me on the bed. I saw blurs of yellow light, or orbs, and I just felt like it was Murphy. I did contact a psychic, but she could not reach Murphy.

I did memorialize Murphy in a tribute letter, and I started a fund in his name to raise money for canine cancer research, specifically for his inhalation chemo study. We have raised $5,000 to date. I am planning on doing a "Walk for Murphy" fundraiser in the spring to raise more money for canine cancer research at the University of California–Davis.

We will be getting a relative of Murphy's in February 2008. It will be another golden retriever puppy. I want the twins to grow up with a dog. This dog will be our "family" dog, as opposed to "my" dog. I know I can never replace Murphy. I did try to get another dog earlier, but it was a disaster for my emotions. It sent me into a major crying session. I went up to meet a couple of older goldens who needed homes, and I cried all the way home, missing Murphy. I am prepared that when the time comes to bring in another dog, it probably will bring back much of my grief, but I also think it will help me move forward in my life and allow me to love another dog again.

Jeremiah's Reassurance
by Mary Beth Alban of Piedmont, California

Jeremiah was a beautiful, kind parakeet. He was green with a yellow crown and yellow spot on his chest. I had gotten him from a pet store when I first moved back to San Francisco and was alone again. He was my buddy, and we talked to each other, comforting each other. For a time, I had to let my daughter have Jeremiah live at her apartment. He was happy there, too, with her flute students enjoying his singing along with their lessons.

Jeremiah

When my daughter moved to an apartment that allowed cats, I got Jeremiah back again. I had moved to a new apartment with my new partner. We got Jeremiah another parakeet to keep him company in a new large cage. Little Jacob looked up to Jeremiah as if he were his uncle and copied whatever he did. A couple years later, my daughter noticed that Jeremiah was sleeping more and Jacob was actively nudging him awake all the time, giving him no rest. So we moved Jeremiah back to his first, smaller cage. The cages were right next to each other, and they frequently got as close as they could, talking to each other and sometimes trying to feed each other. But Jeremiah was allowed to sleep whenever he wanted, which was good.

I was getting busier and not spending as much time with Jeremiah as I had at the beginning. My partner, who had raised many birds, noticed that Jeremiah was sleeping more and more even though he looked healthy otherwise, and she warned me that he might be nearing the end of his life.

One afternoon, my daughter came to see him and did her special greeting to him, a slow blinking of her eyes while looking at him, to which he always responded with the same slow blinking while looking at her. It was their "Goodbye." The next morning, I found him dead on the bottom of his cage. We all cried a lot that Friday, and I held him often during the day before I put him into a sealed plastic bag and into the freezer to await an appropriate place to bury him. That weekend, I kept remembering how I hadn't spent as much time with him as I used to and felt guilty about that. It weighed upon my heart as I mourned his death.

That Sunday at church, I was scheduled to be on the healing team ministry after Eucharist at our Episcopal church. When we walked up to the altar to stand during the Eucharist prayers, we were suddenly all stunned by a loud chatter of two little birds who had gotten into a very high window at the top of the wall behind the altar. They sounded so happy and frolicked about on the window ledge as many of us looked up there in amazement; then they suddenly were gone. I had never seen this happen there before and in thinking about an explanation, I thought that they must have been sent by Jeremiah to encourage me and let me know that he was happy and all was well and that I need not feel guilty about his death at all. I felt a surge of love and a release of pain as tears streamed down my cheeks. I was suddenly full of joy at the memory of this dear little bird and all he had meant to me and others. I was healed and grateful.

Oscar

by Danielle Clarke of Huntsville, Ontario, Canada

From the day he showed up on our doorstep, I felt an immediate bond with Oscar. He was like a big orange teddy bear, taking every opportunity to snuggle with me! He was the funniest cat I've ever known, always into something, and he made us laugh daily. He was like my little shadow; no matter where I was or what I was doing, he had

Oscar

to be around me. This would, unfortunately, lead to his death.

A tragic accident involving a falling bookcase took the life of my beloved Oscar. The accident took him immediately and there was nothing that my husband or I could do to save him. My husband buried him in the backyard, in a beautiful spot overlooking our home. We adorned the grave with a couple sentimental items — a rock with his name carved into it and his "Pookie," a toy that he loved to drag all around the house with him.

I am forever grateful that we have other pets that have helped us through this loss. They seemed to realize that Mommy and Daddy were very heartbroken, so they each, in their own little way, have adopted their own individual tributes to Oscar.

Normally, none of my other cats liked to snuggle that much, but now they each seem to take turns occupying my lap. Oscar refused to use the scratching post, preferring to use the door frame; now two of my cats, Casey and Abby, have taken to doing the same. And once in awhile, I see our dog Bud visiting Oscar's grave in our backyard. These little gestures make my heart melt a little bit each time to know that we're not the only ones who miss him. Of all our animals though, it was our youngest cat Abby who was closest to Oscar, and it is she who seems to have picked up most of Oscar's habits.

Oscar used to stand on his rear legs and lean against the window frame to gaze outside. He also used to sleep with me every night, and he was terrible for stealing food off the counter. Abby has picked up each of these habits now, as well as a few more!

Whether it was because the two were so close or simply because she was witness to most of his crazy antics, Abby has helped me the most in overcoming the heart-wrenching sadness of losing Oscar. Seeing her doing things that Oscar used to do so frequently makes me realize that although he isn't around in body, he is definitely here in spirit!

This tragic accident has made me appreciate my other pets so much more. I go out of my way even more now to spend time playing and cuddling with all of them. I know that each will pass in time, but until then, I don't want to take a single moment with them for granted.

Nvwati
by Amber O'Hara of Toronto, Ontario, Canada

"I dropped a tear in the ocean.
The day you find it is the day I will stop missing you."

Nvwati was born on April 1, 1997, the second of five pups born to Miko, a timberwolf. Miko came into my life two years earlier, gifted to me in the will of an elderly woman who passed away.

I am American Indian and belong to the wolf clan. This grandmother knew of my love for wolves, so when she passed away, she left Miko to me. I had no idea Miko was capable of having pups! I thought by that age she would have either been spayed or sterile.

Miko met Timber, a black and white Siberian Husky and they fell in love. They would both cry for hours after their play dates together. I had to be out of town for a week, and Miko went to spend that time with Timber and his human mom. When I returned home, I was told they had mated.

Sixty-three days to the day later, five pups were born. Nvwati was the largest, and the second one to make his appearance. He was born butt first and I had to help him come out.

Nvwati

Two weeks later, I was awakened one night to the sound of howling. Imagine my surprise when I went into the solarium and found Miko howling at the full moon with little Nvwati sitting beside her, his little head up high, howling along!

After his mother, Miko, died suddenly, Nvwati wiggled his way into my heart and remained with me, my constant companion.

Nvwati loved to sing and would sing along with me whenever I took up my drum. He competed in and came in second in an International Pet Singing Competition. He was on several TV shows, including "Breakfast Television," "Oprah," "The Erin Davis Show," etc.

Over the next ten and a half years, he lived up to his name, which is a Cherokee word for "good medicine." I am a person living with AIDS and have survived breast cancer. During times I was so ill I didn't know if I could go on any more, he would be there for me, loving me and showing me that I had better not leave him!

Time after time I told him how he better not die before me because I couldn't bear the loss. I told him this just the night before he passed away.

On Friday, September 28, 2007, while out for our afternoon trip to the park, I noticed he was walking slowly.

Jokingly, I said, "Hey Bubbs, you're slow today. What's wrong? Are you an old man now?" Upon our return from the park, he laid down at the doorway to my bedroom and let out a yelp. It was by far not the worst yelp I had heard from him over the years, but his beautiful eyes told me something was terribly wrong. I helped him to my bed and called the animal hospital. I was told to bring him right over.

Thinking it must have been something he ate, I put him on leash and began the three-block scoot to the animal hospital. Two blocks from home, my darling wobbled then sat down. He put his head down and died right there on the sidewalk, one block from our destination.

His autopsy showed he had pericarditis, a large bag of fluid around his precious heart, making it hard for it to beat. He died of a massive heart attack. It feels as though my heart will explode from grief.

As I left the animal hospital, I sat outside on my scooter (wheelchair type thing) and looked up at the sky. On the one side of the street where I was, the sky was blue and sunny. Directly across the street the sky was black and it was raining. It was as though the heavens had opened to welcome my beloved Nvwati home.

Nvwati's permanent memorial is online at http://www.immortalpets.com/Nvwati/About.aspx?MemorialID=374

Josh and Casey
by Nell Hall of Shepherdsville, Kentucky

I am a sixty-three-years-young retired school bus driver. I live on a ninety-acre family farm with thirty-three rescued cats (not all in the house), two spoiled dogs, six silly goats, four nosey mini donkeys, four beautiful llamas, and three paint horses. Oops, I almost forgot, my husband also lives with me even though he says he wishes he were one of the animals at times.

A Pekingese like Josh & Casey

My main story is about an old Pekingese I rescued named Josh. Driving a school bus as long as I had, there were always kids trying to give me kittens and puppies, and I did take quite a few. We had been on Christmas break, and I made my stop to pick up a couple of high school students in a very nice subdivision, and though it wasn't quite daylight, something made me look over at this doghouse that had not been there before. I couldn't see a dog, so I didn't think much of it till I did my elementary run through the same subdivision. That time, when I went by, there was a dog tied to the doghouse.

None of the high school students knew whom the dog belonged to. Every day I would go by, I would get so upset because the dog had a very short chain and, being a Pekingese, and an old one at that, it should be in the house, not outside in weather like we were having. So I called our county shelter; it took about ten calls before I ever got any response and finally was told that as long as the dog had food and water dishes, there wasn't anything they could do.

I couldn't let it go. By now it was spring, the weather was getting warm, and the dog had so much matted muddy fur. One cold rainy night, I persuaded my husband to take me over just to make sure he was okay, as I hadn't seen him out for a couple of days. It was May and school would soon be getting out. I knew I had to get this dog. I had finally gotten a name of who owned the dog and just by accident was telling this story to a bus driver friend when she said she knew the girl who owned it, as she had at one time ridden her bus. She called the girl, asking about the dog and was told the dog was fourteen. It had been an inside dog, but her mom didn't want him anymore, so she tied him outside. She said that if I wanted him to just come and pick him up. I was so happy; it was May 24, the day before my birthday. Josh was the best birthday present I had ever gotten.

I immediately got him groomed, then I took him to the vet, which I really dreaded. My vet friend didn't have good news. Josh had heartworm, was practically blind, and didn't have very much hearing. I didn't care; I just wanted to love him and make whatever time he had left the best of his life. You would never know he was fourteen, as he would play with a ball and chew on my hand. He wouldn't be around for a long time, but he still had spunk and a big old heart for loving me.

It wasn't very long after I got him that he began to have seizures. When he had them, I would hold him till they were over. Josh had special dog food and his treat was boiled chicken. The first year he didn't have the seizures very often, but then into the second year they were getting worse. Josh was so well housebroken, he always let me know when he needed to go out, but then I finally put down papers because his arthritis was getting so bad.

The vet put him on some medicine for the seizures that would make him sleep a lot. We fixed his bed in the TV room and I slept next to him, seldom leaving his side, and if I had to, my husband was with him. After a few days, he wasn't responding much and was having to be force-fed. Then he started having the seizures, and I couldn't stand to see him go through any more. I called my vet friend and she said I would know when the time was right and when I decided, she would come over. I called and got a casket for him for I knew he couldn't live much longer and I didn't want him to suffer. My precious Josh died July 16, 2002.

Never had I ever grieved so hard and long, and I still miss him so much. He gave me so much love those two years. He has a special place in my heart. Josh is buried in my flower garden and I see him every day; he has a beautiful tombstone.

When I lost Josh, I didn't want any dog but, I thought, perhaps if there were ever a Peke to come into my life some day, I would want him to look like Josh. Little did I know that exactly two years to the day after I got Josh, I would find out there was a Peke at the shelter. I got him sight unseen and he's a smaller version of Josh.

Casey had been found by the road with his name on duct tape around his neck and taken to the shelter. I know with all my heart Josh sent him to me. Little Casey was so sick, but thanks to my vet friend, he is a healthy, spoiled dog. I hope we both will have many more years to share our love.

I only know how to love all these beautiful creatures God has given me to care for while I'm on this Earth and know that I will see them some day, and we won't be sick and in pain. I do have a name for my rescue: Whisper of Hope, and that is what I give them all. I don't make it public, but all my animal friends know.

Max

by Chuck and Peggy Burns of Chanhassen, Minnesota

Max

We took in young Max (Westie male, age two) in 2002 when we heard he needed a place to live, as he was being abused and neglected where he was. Max was known to be a dominant, aggressive boy, so we worked with him and made much progress. Much of the time he was a darling, energetic, lively, mischievous, and happy Westie boy. But then, without warning or provocation, he would turn into a snarling, biting demon. After months of working with him, we realized he had more problems than dominance and aggression; he was a dangerous little dog. He was diagnosed with rage syndrome, a disorder for which there was no cure and no effective treatment available, that caused him to bite, unprovoked and unpredictably. He bit us more than once, but no one outside our house, thank goodness! For his own peace and the peace and safety of those around him, our only option was to euthanize him. We wrote the following to help us accept the situation and comfort us after this difficult and painful decision.

We will love him and miss him forever!

Max was a dog who was his own "person." His head was held high as he walked from the van to the clinic, up the stairs, and down the hall. He eagerly went to Dr. Dan, who carried him down the hall to the exam room and put him up on the table. He stood there on the table awaiting his unknown fate, not fighting or growling, but standing fast and watching all that was going an around him. In his mind, all was right and going to be all right in his world.

Dr. Dan took a syringe and filled it with pink fluid. Max neither made a sound nor moved when a blue muzzle was placed on his snout. They were all petting him and telling him they loved him. He felt something prick his leg, but he made no move or sound. He simply looked ahead with knowing eyes. Slowly, oh so slowly, it seemed, he grew sleepy and he felt a friendly hand hold his head and slowly lay his body on the table. And he felt at peace.

Oh, his heart was strong and beat in defiance of the end, but the end came. Then there was a brighter light, a peaceful light, and he felt whole and at peace.

Max looked down and saw his friends around a body that looked like he used to look. Strange, but he felt sad for the two friends that he had known such a short time but had loved. They were crying and talking about — him. Why, he wondered, would they cry when he felt so at peace? He was sorry for having caused them any problem or pain. They had been good to him, had loved him, and he had loved them back.

He took one last look down, barked "goodbye,'"and trotted off, to the Rainbow Bridge into a new and calmer world that awaited him.

Goodbye, dear Max. We will miss you and hope to see you again someday. We hope that when you meet Burney, you'll say "hello" to him for us. Goodbye, dear Max.

Delilah

by Jennifer Graham of Chattanooga, Tennessee

Delilah

I am sure my story is one you have heard many many times, but I would like to think Delilah was special. My ex-hubby and I found Delilah's mom in 1993. We lived in an apartment complex, and her mom (who we named Blossom) was playing basketball (yes ... really chasing and trying to catch the ball) with the neighborhood kids. She was very skinny, covered in fleas, and had matted hair. We could not have a dog in our complex, so we cleaned her up and took her to my mother-in-law's. A trip to the vet told us she was preggers. She had five pups a few months afterwards.

The only golden pup (and only female) fell into the water dish a few weeks after they were born, and Blossom would not have anything to do with her. Long story trying to be short, my ex and I kept the soggy blond female, whom we named Delilah. We had bought our first house by this time, and Delilah made herself at home. She was automatically potty-trained (don't ask me how) and was the most loving and docile pet I have ever owned. I could take her into PetSmart, Lowe's, Ketner's Mill, etc. and never have to have her on a leash. She always wanted to be right next to me.

Through my divorce, living in an apartment again, building a home ... she was never over five feet away from me. She went to work with me for a while when I was running an auto parts store in a small town, and she never walked around the counter unless I walked there with her. She sat in the recliner with me for hours watching the NFL, not flinching when I would jump up and cheer when my team finally did something right. She accepted my new hubby perfectly and would cuddle and walk with him like she did with me.

When my new hubby brought a Jack Russell (named Max) into the home, she played all the time with him. When we had to have her put down at sixteen years old, my hubby and I knew it was coming, but we were crushed. We still have not spread her ashes and have kept her collar, food dish, tags, etc. She was the most amazing friend I have ever had. She was there through my first husband, my divorce, all of my job transfers, building a house, new hubby, new dog ... and so much more I could mention. She was the only thing constant in my life. It has been over eight months and I still cry. Everyone who met her loved her.

If I could paint a picture of a perfect dog, it was Delilah, my golden girl.

Spunky and Samson
by Dave Spagenski of San Diego, California

We picked the runt of the sheltie litter because we just wanted a companion, not a show dog. His name was Samson, and we'd had him eight years when we came home to see not one but two same-colored shelties on our porch up the stairs, side by side! Some neighbor saw the second one and believed him to be our Samson because they looked so much alike and dropped him off in our backyard. When our attempts to find his owner failed, we knew we were meant to keep him. We named him Spunky.

Spunky & Samson

Many years went by and our curiosity was killing us as to whose pet he was, etc., so we contacted an animal psychic and she told us the amazing story of his past, that he had been on the streets for many weeks and had survived by street smarts, eating trash food, and so on.

She warned us of his medical problems as well, saying that he was fighting off liver or kidney problems and what to start treating him for in order to help. Unfortunately, since he had earned fully his name "Spunky," I paid it no mind and was skeptical. I started to go over the conversation in my mind and wondered if I'd somehow fed this "psychic" just enough information to have her fill in the blanks in a plausible way.

To our dismay, six months later, Spunky was dying of kidney failure and we were told that, had we caught it sooner, he might have survived with treatment. When he was unable to go to the bathroom without our holding him up for support, we had no choice but to let him go and put an end to our poor boy's suffering. I stayed with him till the end, and I know he understood and forgave me.

It was one of the toughest things I've ever had to do, but nothing as bad as the hindsight-based knowledge that I could have saved him. Many months later, I worked up the courage to call the psychic and tell her my story and apologize for having disbelieved her. She said she has that happen a lot (i.e., people doubting the validity of what she reports) and was very sorry for our loss.

To any and all that don't believe in spirits and outside powers, please open your minds to the possibilities at least.

When Samson was around thirteen years old, he was showing signs of medical problems. Having recently lost Spunky, this time we heeded the warnings and took him to specialists of all kinds. They all said he had little to no chance because his liver and kidneys were too far gone, and it was their belief that those organs can't replenish or heal themselves.

Having once suffered the consequences of our own skepticism, we recognized the same closed minds among those in American medicine fields. So we contacted a holistic vet and the psychic I'd spoken to before, and on their instructions began boiling chicken livers and smashing it up and feeding him, even by force at first because he was ill and weak and refused to eat. Several days later, they proved to us that treating liver with liver and vitamins had helped him make an eighty-percent recovery. We took him back to the specialists (Ha ha!) and they even responded that they wouldn't have believed it if they hadn't seen it, and one even said, "This is one for my medical journals!"

So, please have an open mind and don't give up.

Sad as nature is, Samson did pass away years later from heart problems, but we enjoyed those years together as a result of trusting alternative medicine to take up where Western medicine failed him.

Lestat

by Leigh Anne Marshall of Houston, Texas

Lestat

I lost my baby, my dog Lestat, this past Monday, in the wee hours of the morning. He suffered congestive heart failure, and I had to make the decision to put him to sleep. I am an extremely intuitive person. At this point in my life, spiritual experiences are commonplace ... and I start to think something's off with me if I don't have them.

But the intuitive knowing a week or so before my little boy was to move into Spirit was not a welcome one. I kept waking up every morning and immediately going to where he slept. I would stare at him to make sure he was still breathing and would feel so relieved when he finally popped his head up and looked at me.

Lestat loved French fries and tater tots. He could smell them coming from a mile away. For three weeks before he passed, I could not get over the need to cook tater tots. I would eat them for dinner and share them with him. One tater tot for me ... one for Lestat ... and so on. He would sit as he always did, hunched down a bit and staring at the tater tots with heated intensity. If I did not respond to him quickly enough, he would ever so gently touch my leg with his paw, as if to say ... "Hey, that was *my* tater tot you just ate."

On his last day with me, I had an intense desire to eat ice cream. Besides French fries and tater tots, his favorite thing was to lick my ice cream bowl. I'd always leave a couple bites of ice cream in the bottom and he'd lick away until he'd gotten every last drop. Well, I knew I could not come home that day without ice cream, so I stopped at the grocery store and bought some. That dog was so happy with that ice cream bowl.

I tell you these things, because I am certain that Spirit was leading me to do this ... both for him and for me, for us to have bonding moments in our last weeks together, and when he did pass on, for me to have good memories to help me through the grieving process.

When he started to pant, and it became clear to me that he was not getting enough oxygen, we had a moment together. I sat with him on the floor and he stared directly into my eyes. Normally, he would have looked away after a few seconds. But this time he did not break my gaze. I understand now, that he was telling me that he was going to be going home. And he was asking me to help him.

I took him to the emergency vet and left in him their care, planning to pick him up in the morning and get him to my regular vet. I went home, and after tossing around in my bed, finally went into a fitful sleep. At 2:30 in the morning, I shot straight up in my bed, knowing that something was terribly wrong.

Seconds later, my phone rang.

It was the emergency clinic calling to tell me that Lestat had gone into labored breathing and that he was not responding to treatment.

He was dying, and I knew it. I asked the vet if he felt that I should let my baby go to sleep, and he told me, "yes." I threw on my clothes and drove as quickly as I could to the clinic. When I arrived, I held Lestat's paw and gently petted him while the doctor gave him the medicine. It was very peaceful and gentle, and I know he did not suffer. And when it was over, I felt such a resounding sense of peace that I knew I had done the right thing. I had honored the wish my dog had communicated to me earlier with his eyes.

One of the most extraordinary experiences I had with Lestat was that I actually heard him speak to me one day. I rarely tell this story because most people would think I was crazy. But I know that it was real.

This happened several years ago. I was playing with Lestat in the living room of my apartment. We had finally worn each other out, and he was lying on the floor on his side. I laid beside him and lazily petted him across his little body. It was a very quiet, content exchange between human and animal. I noticed him watching me and when I looked in his eyes, I was startled to hear a voice that rang both inside my head and just outside of my ear. This was not an unusual experience for me, as I'd been spoken to by spirits before. But it was the source of the voice that shook me up. It came from the dog. He said, "I love you so much and I'm so glad we're together." The voice was not at all what I had expected it to sound like. It was a high tenor voice, clear as a bell, and resounding with the innocence, purity, and love of a small child.

I did not hear that voice again, until after he passed into Spirit. And immediately after I felt him leave his little body, I heard him telling me not to be sad and how much he loved me. I saw a vision of my mother (who passed away ten years ago) holding him. I had felt my mother's spirit with me the entire night and literally felt her walking beside me as I went into the emergency clinic to help my baby pass on.

I know without a doubt that when it is time for me to go home to Heaven, my buddy, Lestat, will be waiting to welcome me.

In the days since his passing, I have continued to hear his voice. When my house has been very still and quiet, I have heard the tags on his collar clink together. He is with me still, helping me to grieve. And most interestingly, I have heard his little tenor voice encouraging me that it was okay to get another puppy. And that he wanted me to have that companionship again.

He was literally my angel on Earth. He was a constant companion, always there, loving me unconditionally. I will miss his physical presence, but he is not gone. I feel his spirit with me. He is part of me.

Kokitty

by Angela Lloyd of Zurich, Switzerland

Kokitty

I received Kokitty from my ex-boyfriend, to whom she always went to eat. She was the cat everyone knew in the neighborhood, but nobody wanted to let her inside. So I took her. As I had just lost one of my two cats, I thought she could be Archie's new companion. She had been traumatized. The vet noticed most of her teeth were missing and she wouldn't let herself be touched for too long. But she was always at home, waiting for me when I arrived. When I showered, she watched, and when I went to bed, she wouldn't even let Archie jump onto the bed without a fight. Everyone fell in love with Kokitty because she had the prettiest eyes and was really small and adorable.

After two years of living with me, she disappeared. I knew something was wrong because she never left the house. I ran around the house late at night calling her name, looked everywhere and after three weeks eventually gave up hope that I'd find her. After approximately four months, I had to call the police because my neighbor, who landed in a psychiatric clinic, had broken into my house

and pretty much moved his things in while I was gone one weekend. There were skulls of some sort of animals on my sofa, piano, and table.

The police also discovered Kokitty in a box in my neighbor's cellar.

The hardest part was identifying her and watching them wrap her up in a plastic bag. This is quite unresolved for me. I feel angry and also guilty in some ways, and I miss her. My other cat Archie is fine and I still have him. I just wonder sometimes if *he* knows more.

The Gift – A Story of Death and Rebirth

(An excerpt taken from *Paws & Listen to the Voices of the Animals*)
by Jenny Shone, of Kyalami, Midrand, Gauteng, South Africa

Make no mistake, I dearly love all my animal companions, but my Jack Russell terrier Smurfie and I developed a very special bond; she, I felt, was indeed my soul mate in doggy form. Smurfie was always at my side, keeping me company, protecting me, being there for me when I was down. We grew closer and closer.

Smurfie

One day I noticed a lump on Smurfie's leg, so off we went to the vet. They decided to remove the lump and in doing so discovered it was a cancerous growth. I was devastated. But Smurfie came out fighting and made a full recovery. We played ball, went swimming (her favorite activity), and went for long walks.

Two years later, my gardener was away on leave and my husband was working in Oman. I was at home alone, Smurfie and I were playing in the garden with the hosepipe, when the phone rang, and I dropped the hose and went to the phone. When I went back outside, Smurfie was in the water-playing medley. I turned off the tap and we went inside. I later noticed that my little dog was very bloated and thought it must be the water she drank while playing. Later when she wouldn't eat, I decided to take her to the vet for a checkup.

The vet said to me she would be okay, and he gave me some tablets to give her. That night, I eventually fell asleep with Smurfie's head on my pillow next to mine. When I awoke much later, she was gone, I sat up in a panic and saw her lying on the floor in the corner of the room. I jumped up and ran to her; she was unconscious. I picked up her little body and raced to the phone. I managed to find a vet that worked from home and a neighbor that would take us to this vet. I sat with her and held her while the vet worked on her, but sadly Smurfie passed away at 3 a.m. on Good Friday.

I felt as if the bottom had fallen out of my world; the pain was unbearable. I felt nauseous and just wanted to die. My little light had gone out. Whereas before I gave thanks every day for my life, the animals in it, the beautiful sunsets, now all I could see was grey. My parents came from Natal, Brazil to look after me. I was going downhill fast, and there was nothing I could do — there was nothing I wanted to do. My girl was gone, and all I wanted was to be with her. The other pets in my life gave me lots of support and love, but I was feeling too numb to notice.

Eventually, just when I thought I was reaching my breaking point, a friend gave me the phone number of a psychic. I had never been to a psychic before, but I was desperate so I made an appointment.

As I walked into the psychic's room, she started talking to me. After awhile, she suddenly stopped and asked me who the little black and white dog was that was at my feet, and the more I talked the more she yapped. It was Smurfie, my little girl!

She told me that Smurfie was going to come back to me in this lifetime. I was thrilled. There was a shimmer of light at the end of the tunnel, at last.

I started reading books, trying to develop my own psychic abilities. I did various courses in Reiki, ESP healing, pet reflexology, anything and everything that would help me understand and help other animals in need and their humans.

Shortly after the loss of my little Smurfie, I sent her photograph off to Amelia Kinkade, an animal communicator in the United States of America. I asked Amelia to contact Smurfie for me. I had a list of questions for her. She told me Smurfie would be back in this lifetime, just as I had been told by a psychic I had gone to see two weeks previously.

How would I know her? What if I missed her? What if I got the wrong dog? What should I do?

Years passed, then one day I picked up the *Animal Talk* magazine. The article on the cover was all about Siberian Huskies. I had an urgent desire to go and see them. I wasn't planning to get a puppy, just to go and see them.

I got to the breeder. There were puppies running everywhere. They were all very cute. While I was sitting in the lounge enjoying the puppies, the owner brought in some puppies that were only ten days old. I looked at them, when, suddenly, it was like a bolt of lightning hitting me in the chest. There she was — Smurfie — I just knew it was her. All my old feelings for her came flooding back. I picked her up and held her tightly, she licked my face all over. My little dog had come back to me. I bought her on the spot and visited her three times a week until the day came when I could take her home.

I arrived on that sunny day, picked up my little dog, which I had now named Candy (pictured at right), and drove home with her sitting on my lap. When we got home, I took her inside, she already knew exactly where she was. She knew the house and garden; she had been here before. She had come home.

Candy

All the other dogs got on well with her. By the end of the first day, I had noticed Candy had diarrhea. I decided to take her for a checkup. My vet at that time treated her for a tummy bug and sent her home. The next day, I took her back for the same problem, we got more antibiotics, and home we came. After the fourth day with no success, I decided to get a second opinion and went to my present vet who diagnosed parvovirus and put her straight onto an IV drip. I was distraught.

My sister Linda and I went to visit Candy in hospital that night. She looked up at me, and we connected on a deep level. I saw straight into her soul and she into mine. We looked at each other without uttering a word for what seemed like an eternity.

The next morning I arrived at the surgery to visit her. The vet came out to meet me only to tell me. Candy had passed away minutes ago. I was devastated. I picked her up and took her home to bury her in my cemetery at home. I have no memory of how I got home that day. I felt ill. Why had Smurfie come back just to go again after only a few weeks? I thought life was cruel. What had I done to deserve this? How was I going to go on?

Then one day out of the blue came a very clear message from Smurfie (Candy). She said there was another dog out there that needed my love and would give me great enjoyment. I should stop waiting for HER. This is what she had come back to tell me. That same day, I noticed an advert about puppies for sale. I felt drawn to them, so that night Linda and I went off to Kempton Park to see the puppies. The puppies were Siberian Huskies. One of them came running up to me to play. He was beautiful dark gray and white with a dot on the tip of his nose. Riff-Raff (Raphael, pictured below) had arrived, my gift from Smurfie. Linda drove home while I sat with Riff-Raff on my lap where I could admire him all the way home.

My little Smurfie had given me the greatest gift anyone could get. Although I still miss her terribly, I know she is with me, and I thank her for her sacrifice and her gift.

I love you, Smurfie, you are the light in the bottom of my soul. I am honored to have shared your life with you. Until we meet again, you will always be my shining star.

Jenny & Riff-Raff

Jasper

by Klio Grice of Antwerp, Belgium

I lost my dear cat Jasper to a cancer tumour 24 August 2007. He got very sick and lost so much weight in a very short space of time.

That morning, he was very weak and he was beginning to smell. He was hiding behind the TV. I knew then that he would most likely have to be put to sleep. I went to the vet's with him alone. My partner was at work. The vet immediately felt Jasper's abdomen and told me that it was a cancer tumour and it was best that he was put to sleep. The poor little guy was still purring when I kissed his head and told him that I loved him very much. I could not stay in the room when the vet gave the injection, so I left in floods of tears. I paid the bill and ran out of the door.

Jasper was a very special cat who was very sensitive, and he used to sleep close to me when I was sick, or he would come and sit on my knee when I was down and tell me in his catty language that everything would be okay. He was eleven years old when he died. He was a cute black cat with huge yellow eyes. I could never tell whether he was frowning or smiling, as he always held the same expression.

I believe in the Spirit World. Two days after Jasper passed, I had the strangest dream. In it, I was sitting in the living room on the sofa and he came to me looking really well, as if to say, "I am okay again." His sister was in the room, but she could not see him and she was hissing because she felt a strange presence.

I said, "Jasmine, it's your brother. He is there. Can't you see him?"

That week, I won two ten-Euro notes on the Belgian lottery. The following week, I went in to the news agent's to collect my lottery winnings. As I passed the door, there were many greeting cards on a stand. Staring right at me was a card with a photo of a black cat that was the spitting image of Jasper. I thought to myself that is a sign that he is okay and also he was now my Guardian Angel, watching over me and, I am sure, his twin sister Jasmine.

Another two days later, I was buying cat litter in the supermarket. I took the sack home and when I put it on the table, I noticed on the back was a photo of a black cat on this lady's shoulders. Again, it was almost like Jasper. Maybe this is wishful thinking; I do not know. All I know is that it gave me some comfort in those dark days. I still get down, and I still miss the little guy very much. I lived alone for many years with just the two cats before I met my partner two years ago. We went through some very tough times together.

I shall also tell you another strange story. About six years ago, when I was living in London, I had some financial difficulties. I remember that one week I did not even have money for a tin of cat food, let alone a loaf of bread. I was in despair as to what to do in order to get food for my two cats.

I just prayed and asked my angels for some help. That same afternoon, I went down to collect my mail from my mailbox when I saw my neighbour coming up the staircase. She said that there was a large parcel hanging out of my box. To my great astonishment, it was some free food samples of Whiskas cat food from the supermarket where I had a points card. For every ten pounds you spent, you got points that you could eventually use towards your shopping. I thought, yes, there are angels out there. And my cats happily got fed for the week.

Trapper
by Barbara Stevens of Bloomington, Minnesota

I remember a friend's words of condolence: "It is far better to have loved and lost than never to have loved at all." Seven years later, I still hear those words echo in my head, often as I run.

Trapper was not only my dog but also my running partner. We trained together for everything from 10K races to marathons. The distance never mattered to him. It was the time he got to spend with me that mattered. He quickly became my confidant … someone I could trust with my innermost thoughts. He listened intently to me as I talked about how my day went, what we needed for groceries, my frustrations, and anything and everything that came to my mind, without ever speaking a word.

After six years of running, suddenly and without warning, on

December 28th (a day that is forever engraved in my head), he couldn't muster up enough energy to walk down a flight of steps. Cancer had consumed his body. He was given a few months to live. After a spleen surgery and a round of medications, he slowly regained his strength and his eagerness to run. For the next few weeks we ran gentle short runs.

One morning in March he didn't greet me in his usual way of holding my running shoes in his mouth. My heart became heavy, as I feared the worst. I decided that if I could just get him in the car and to our usual running place that he'd be fine. I helped him in and out of the car. Though I began talking as I usually did on our runs, something was very different. He was running slowly, but instead of running at my side as he always had, he was now a few steps behind me. I was afraid to turn around to look at him. When I did, I could see it in his eyes. He stopped, first sitting, then lying down. I laid next to him with tears welling in my eyes as I stroked his head. His eyes and the movement of his brows spoke to me. He was tired and had run his last run. I carried him back to the car. I talked to him as we drove home, trying to convince him, but mainly me, that with some water, a special treat, and rest, he'd feel better tomorrow. In my heart, I knew that would not be the case. I spent the night lying next to him on the floor, afraid to go to sleep, afraid he'd pass during the night. I wasn't ready for him to go. The next day, I lay with him as he took his last breath.

Though I continue to run and train, it has never been the same. I feel his presence as I run, many times on the paths we once ran together. It gives me comfort.

I miss you dearly, my friend. May you forever run free.

Trapper (in 1999)
April 1990 – March 2000

My Girl Jazz

by Pam Snell of Minneapolis, Minnesota

A stray who'd wandered into my mom's backyard, she was offered up by a few neighborhood kids who were playing with her and claimed she didn't belong to them, asking, "Do you want her?" Despite my mom's protests, I took her home to meet my kids and our other dog at the time, a sheepdog named Genii. After watching this energetic, destructive ball of fur, I named her Jazz. She was black with tan points, small-tipped ears, and a tail that

Jazz

curled up above her back. What breeds were intermingled within her, I have no clue, but I figured husky was a good portion of her heritage due to the fact that she had a thick undercoat in the winter and would make the most gosh-awful noises when out walking, due to her excitability.

Jazz slept on my feet every night. When I was in the backyard weeding, she would join in, taking whatever plant I was pulling from the ground in her mouth and yanking it out for me.

Who knew that bright April morning, as I patted her goodbye as I left for work and noticed a depression on one side of her head, would be the start of her slow decline down the hill of life.

The vet said it was very unusual, this sunken defect, but her aunt's Irish wolfhound had the same thing for over three years and was fine. I looked at the vet and said, "She's going to lose her eye, isn't she?" I was assured everything would be fine, including her eye. Unfortunately, after several months and many eyedrop applications later, Jazz had surgery for removal of her left eye. She was never the same. When she went back for the post-eye-surgery checkup, I said to the vet, "She doesn't have much longer, does she?" The vet said she would be fine.

A few months later, my Jazz repeatedly fell off the bed at night. I trained myself to catch her between my legs with the covers when I would feel her stir at night. Several nights, I looked at her to see her panting heavily and looking at me with her one good eye. "Help me," she seemed to be saying. Then one night, she fell off the bed so hard I had to banish her from the bedroom to protect her from hurting herself seriously. I was very sad because I knew it was time. It is really hard to come out of your denial and face the truth about the quality of life currently endured by your best friend.

The next few days, I watched as Jazz could only walk in a clockwise circle, falling every now and then getting up and continuing in her route. Sleeping on the couch the last night with her so I could be close, she circled practically the whole night. It was now time.

Don't you ever wonder where all of the tears come from when you are grieving? It doesn't seem possible that the human body can contain that many tears and then lose all of that liquid without suffering severe consequences.

Jazz is still at my bedside, in a box, shrouded in purple velvet with the embroidered words, "Rainbow Bridge." I give her a pat every now and then and thank her for all the good times, protection, unconditional love, and support she gave to me for eleven years. I think about her when our new small terrier mix Teva sleeps beside me every night. She loves fuzzy tennis balls, going for walks, giving kisses, and devouring blankets and bed spreads! I thank Jazz for sending Teva to me when I was in need.

Lately, I have been astounded by the number of people who express surprise over the fact that more and more people seem to be concerned with animal welfare rather than with people welfare. Supposedly, humans are the most intelligent creatures on Earth and some like to think, at the top of the food chain. Yet humans abuse, neglect, and exploit not only animals but other human beings as well. You don't see dogs starting wars, killing bike riders for the sheer excitement of it, or taking advantage of vulnerable adults. That is the human factor.

Personally, I don't see anything human about those things, and many times I find myself feeling ashamed to be a part of the "human race." That is when I cuddle with my furry best friends and happily receive their kisses and bright-eyed looks of love. That is when I realize I am a human being and these little guys are in my care—and I am thankful for them.

Jake the Retiring Hero
by Mary Flood of Utah

Jake

Here's an email I sent to one of the people that helped me with Jake when I first rescued him. Actually, it was written by Jake. At the time, I figured he had another month or so to live, but it was just nine days.

Sent: Saturday, July 14, 2007 8:17 p.m.

Hi,

You might think this is a message from Mary but actually it is me, Jake, writing. As you know, I have many skills and sometimes while Mary is outside I get hold of the computer and send the occasional email and surf the Web for tasty treats that I can charge to her AmEx and have delivered to a secret spot that she has not discovered.

It was so awesome of you to come visit us yesterday. Your kindness to me and to Mary early on was something she has treasured over the years. We've talked about it pretty regularly. I had a tough time healing that first year but finally got well. Then after we lost Lottie, Mary gave me a chance to show that I'd been watching all along. She was difficult to train and convince, but I'm pretty convincing when I want something, so eventually she realized that a slightly gimpy male Lab was way better than a German shepherd.

I've continued to train Mary over the years and think I've made some progress. Sage worked with me on the project for a while, too. Rex showed her a lot but we could never convince him what fun it

Jake & Tracker

was to walk through rubble to find people. He sure did keep us organized though until he finally convinced Mary to let him do his thing.

I've been enjoying retirement and hoping Mary would get a dog that I could give her a hand with. She found the right dog in January—Tracker. I let her know as best I could that I was all for the choice. Humans can be so obtuse though, so it was decided that he really wasn't the right dog. Fortunately, she decided to give him another try. Since he came back, I've been working to show him how to handle Mary and what it is we try to accomplish.

The last few weeks, I pretty much just watch. Some days I feel pretty lousy but my cup continues to be almost full. I don't believe in half full. I've adjusted to watching Tracker do the running and I just tug a bit and play gentle catch. Mary is taking time to make sure I get a swim at least once a day. I get to hang out in the yard and watch the passersby, smell the world as it makes its way through each day—the myriad scents from early morning, slightly damp and cool from way up the canyon, to the grass drying as the morning progresses, to all the various people and animals that make their way around our property. I'm also enjoying the ease of being off my diet.

I enjoyed the time with you in the shade of the tree and then out in the field along the creek. You are always welcome here. I will be around some time longer and will try to see you in Salt Lake.

Thanks again for all you have done for me and for Mary.

Oh, one more thing. Mary told me she was going to send you a CD with some pix of me. Here's one taken in New York at the World Trade Center. Actually, I was quite popular!

Mary & Jake on a post-9/11 rescue mission

Poem to Beau

And now he's dead and there are nights when I think I feel
Him climb upon our bed and lay between us and I'd pet his head,
And there are nights when I think I feel that stare and
I reach out my hand to stroke his hair,
And he's not there.
Oh how I wish it wasn't true.

— *actor Jimmy Stewart*

Christopher, My Seven Months Without You
by Georgeann McKee of Sacramento, California

My Dearest Christopher:

It is 6:30 on October 20th, the time seven months ago when you left me here and went to Rainbow Bridge. My world is shattered and my heart is broken. I have cried a river of tears and felt pain only God can understand.

Each day, I see so many people who loved you for so many years; they have moved on and do not talk about you anymore. I am frozen in time and cannot move forward. I still remember holding you in my arms and feeling your lifeless body slowly slipping away from me, leaving for Rainbow Bridge.

I was in the nursery looking for something special to put by your memorial in the yard. As I walked into the flower area I saw this beautiful sparkling angel looking at me. She had a beautiful, comforting smile on her face and the word JOY written across her gown. JOY is what you were in my life and the JOY is now what is gone. The beautiful angel is now sitting behind your memorial, watching over you to make sure that, when I am not around, you are always safe.

I have been sitting and thinking about what it will be like when I arrive at Rainbow Bridge. As I close my eyes, I can see you in a beautiful green field with flowers everywhere. You are playing with Sammy, Beethoven, Missy, Pasha, Chancey, Digby, Squirt, Milly, Morgan, Peanut, Luiz, Paco, Shadow, Nike, Arthur, Moses, Sadie, and many other pet loss babies. Flying over your heads is a beautiful rainbow.

Christopher

This journey has been a long and painful one but not in vain. I have learned so much from your loss, my sweet angel. You taught me that life is too short, that money cannot buy anything that is really important, and that unconditional love and true friendship are rare and last for eternity. I have learned the importance of giving as much as I can to those animals whose parents cannot afford to save them and to give as much as I can to those who can help others in pain just as I am. I have learned that nothing can replace a hole in your heart or the moments so precious that you share with your loved ones. I have learned that health and family are all that really matters in this world. I have learned how much true love really means and how much it is missed once it is gone. I have learned to cherish each precious moment we experience on this Earth, as none of us knows when our time will end.

On November 2nd I will be going to attend a church service in San Francisco. I will leave your picture along with others in front of a beautiful Rainbow Candle at the altar. Please listen for my prayers to you. Hopefully, I will be able to feel your presence when I am there so I can share my prayer with your spirit. Maybe God will let you visit at least for a moment.

Dude's Story
by Vicki Skognes of Grapevine, Texas

Dude

In the spring of 1991, our fourteen-year-old daughter was molested by a police officer. She began a path of self-destruction for the next four years, which included drugs, sex, and constantly running away. At one point, I hadn't known where she was or even if she was alive for nine months. My life became absorbed with trying to find her and trying to help her. Nothing I did worked! Hence, the next four years were sad and dark days and sometimes almost unbearable.

My husband, Jim, talked me into buying a puppy for our youngest daughter, who was eleven years old. He thought a puppy would help her cope with the turmoil our lives were filled with.

When I handed her the puppy, I heard the words, "I don't want a puppy!"

My first thought: I don't, either! But the first words out of my mouth were: "Okay, he'll be mine and I'll call him Dude!"

Little did I know, Dude was my "gift." Dude may not have known what was happening, but he always sensed something was wrong. When I cried, Dude licked away my tears. When I was staring into space, Dude would bring a toy/ball and make me laugh. When I would sit in my daughter's room and pray for her safety, Dude was right by my side. When nights were dark and long and I couldn't sleep, Dude was with me. He became my constant companion, loyal friend, and someone that had pure love for me. Always giving and asking little in return. I think people should learn lessons from their animal companions!

I always thought Jim would be with me to share in the grief of Dude's death but unfortunately, he passed away in 2001. In January 2007, I noticed Dude was drinking excessive amounts of water, so I took him to the vet. The test results confirmed; he was a diabetic. I had to give him two shots of insulin, daily. He also had arthritis in his lower back and back legs. In February, he went blind and was almost deaf. He only got worse and, at times, his back legs wouldn't hold him up. It was my honor to be his nurse and give him twenty-four-hour care. I cherished every moment with him.

On April 27 at 10:30 p.m. he began to cry very loudly. I rushed him to the emergency clinic, where they said he was having side effects from the insulin. They regulated it and I took him home. I requested that they leave the needle in his leg in case I had to bring him back. On April 28 at 4:30 a.m. he began to cry again. The cries were almost human, and I knew it was time to let him go. At 5:30 a.m. I chose to end his suffering. At 5:31, my suffering began!

Popcorn
by Leanne Ashley of Chanhassen, Minnesota

Dear Friends,

I am sending sad news that our darling West Highland white terrier, Popcorn, was given wings on Friday, April 3, 2009, at 2:30 p.m. and is with Grandma Donna and Blue in Heaven. She died from complications of IBD (inflammatory bowel disease), which she fought all the twelve years of her life.

Popcorn was born December 10, 1996, in Manley, Iowa. It was the year I lost my sister to suicide in October. We brought Popcorn home in March of 1997. Popcorn became my healing comforter and gave of herself during my most difficult time.

Popcorn grew up with Anika, who was nine when she came to live with us. Popcorn became the star of "show and tell" at school and was the main attraction when friends came to play. Popcorn quickly became Grandma Donna's "baby," as the two of them fell in love and had a strong bond. In 1998, Popcorn moved over without any hesitation or jealousy for a rescued Westie named Blue. Blue and Popcorn got along well. But within a year, Blue died. In 2004, we felt loss again when Grandma Donna died at age eighty-three. Popcorn never forgot her name! Any mention of Grandma Donna sent Popcorn running to the window to see if she was here to visit! Popcorn often went to Lakewood Cemetery to help put flowers on her grave. A picture is attached.

**Popcorn with flowers
for Grandma Donna**

In 2006, Popcorn felt the devastation of our divorce from a twenty-nine-year marriage. She stayed in the family home with Anika and me, giving us unconditional love and support for the two years it took to settle our case. In 2007, Popcorn saw her papa, Frank, for the last time. She sat in his lap as he said his good-byes and left for Oregon. She fre-

quently peered through the stairway rails looking for her papa or would head for the back
door thinking she heard he was home.

Popcorn had many friends. She took to people who would let her occupy their laps. She
was loving to everyone she met. When it came
to other dogs, she was cautious of female
Westies but otherwise was happy to warm up to
all the others. Popcorn loved to be outside with

Anika & Popcorn

the wind blowing across her pretty face or watching rabbits and squirrels. She learned not to dig and not to bark too much. She loved the
gardens that her mom tended and was often by her side in the shade.
She loved finding raspberries in my patch and figured out how to get
them right off the vine! She loved swinging next to Anika outside in
Popcorn's very own baby swing! In recent years, Popcorn sat by Anika's
side every time Anika was ill, which was often. She always "knew"
when Anika needed her soft, white, quiet presence.

Popcorn loved the Bandenmiere Park in Chanhassen, where she
frequently took walks and never wanted to leave. For many years,
Popcorn walked in the Wayzata Westie Walkers Parade. She loved the
attention and seeing dogs that looked just like her. Popcorn also was
a therapy dog who visited all the grandmas at the Auburn Manor
nursing home in Chaska. She was fond of the memory care residents
and the once-a-month birthday parties where she found cake crumbs
to eat! Her illness caused her to discontinue the visits.

After she passed, I chose to bring her body home. The vet put her
in a nice small cardboard coffin, and she is on my screen porch with
her bowl, harness, ball, and flowers. Morbid as this may sound, my
daughter and I wrapped her in heavy yard plastic and put her back in,
covering her with a pink blanket. We go out often to "touch" her, running in a still-motion body. We will bury her when the ground is ready.

We will miss her darling presence, her tip-tapping paws on the
floor, her original fragrance that was toxic to us. We will miss her
hugs. I will miss holding her the few times I did while driving the car,
not to mention the attention she got at the bank and McDonald's.
Our home is too quiet and empty without her. But our hearts are full

of many great memories of a perfect Westie we absolutely LOVED! God bless her memory and thanks for twelve years of joy! Our lives were enriched just because Popcorn was in them.

Duane

by Beth Cluck of Benton, Kentucky

Duane

I had not been a foster mom for too long when I saw Duane. Duane was one shot away from being euthanized at a local shelter due to aggression. There were times with that little guy when I wondered what I was doing and didn't know if I could handle him. For instance, I was sleeping soundly and awoke in the middle of the night to an odd rustling and crunching sound. I stumbled into the laundry room to find the back end of a twelve-pound min pin hanging out of a bag of dog food ... eating his way to the bottom. He was still very aggressive and protective of food at this point, and I had to fend him off with a flip-flop when I approached him.

Duane taught me a lot in a year and a half. He taught me that I had more strength than I realized to deal with his aggression, and underneath it all, found a friend like no other I had ever had. He knew what I was saying, knew what I felt, and could comfort me with one look out of those beautiful brown eyes. Once the rough times passed, I was amazed at the transformation in us both.

My favorite story to tell of Duane happened when I was remodeling my kitchen and it was a disaster area. I made sure I had picked everything up to keep Duane safe ... but being the ever-smart boy he was, he escaped his crate and decided to venture out. He managed to climb a small step-stool and get on the countertop. He then weaseled into the cabinet and got a jar of peanut butter. These are all deductions of the scenario from one picture I cannot remove from my mind. That dog had gotten the peanut butter jar open, devoured half of it and passed out, belly up, on the sofa. This is what I saw when I walked through the door after work. I was worried, then mad, and finally, laughed so hard I cried.

Duane

Duane escaped one night and was hit by a car. I found him and rushed him to the vet. They kept him overnight and the next morning I was there when they opened. They could not do anything to save him. He was going to die. I held him in my arms and told him I was sorry. My friend and vet tech, Shawna, came in the room and told me it was the right decision to let him go. I held him as the shots to end his life were administered and sat there until I was numb. I felt drunk, dizzy, sick, and I didn't care about anything ... I just wanted him back.

I called in to work the day I had to let him go. Most people thought I was crazy, although no one said anything to me. I could feel it. I was known as the "dog lady" at work. I was asked to take any stray someone wanted to dump because their kid didn't want to feed it. I hated all of them for not understanding that this was like the loss of a child. I do have to give credit to those who did tell me they were sorry and didn't roll their eyes at me randomly sobbing on the work-room floor—Lisa, Marti, and many others.

There was an upcoming shelter benefit, and I told my friends that I wanted to speak at the event. I started the "Campaign for Duane" at work and sent emails to everyone I knew. I made flyers and cried, distributed flyers and cried, talked about Duane to anyone who would listen and cried some more. If anyone I had ever worked with or met had thought I was crazy, they were now sure that I was. Because of Duane, I didn't care what anyone thought anymore—another strength he awarded me, even after he was gone.

The night of the benefit, I got dressed up and slapped my make-up on and told the story of how I had saved him and he had saved me. I bawled like a baby and felt comfort to look up and see other people crying with me. I had found others who understood. I raised about $200 in three days with my little campaign.

I always bring my babies home and bury them in the back yard. I plant a flower for them and hope that I will see them slinking underneath or around it one day. I decided to have Duane cremated. I had never done this before and for some reason chose this. I picked him up from the funeral home and put him in the glove compartment. He LOVED to go for rides, and this was my way of trying to make it up to him. He rode there for over two months and I still pondered as to what I should do with his ashes. Buy a pretty vase? Sprinkle them in his favorite spots in the yard? I couldn't come to a decision.

Almost three months to the day after Duane has crossed the Rainbow Bridge, I received a phone call. My ex-fiance Luke had been killed in a car accident. I couldn't breathe. I mustered the nerve to ask Luke's family if I could lay Duane to rest with his Daddy. Thank God Luke's uncle understood what that dog had meant to the both of us and gave me permission. I knew that this was where Duane was meant to be.

Katze

by Pat Cumbie of Minneapolis, Minnesota

Katze had been my kitty since I was a college student in Madison, Wisconsin. I'd insisted on having him as a condition of my move-in relationship with my husband.

The early years with Katze were like living with a hurricane. Every time we left the house for class he'd ruin something—plants,

Katze

posters, furniture, pottery. He scratched and clawed and knocked things over. Once when I was out of town, Sean took him to his mother's house. In a twenty-four-hour period, he'd ruined her drapes, permanently scratched her furniture, and run away.

None of that mattered to me. I loved his verve, his sense of entitlement, his insistent naughtiness, the way he looked and felt and smelled. I could hold him with my right hand under his chest, his body tucked into my armpit, and he'd allow me to carry him around anywhere like that. He always sat on my lap after meals or when I was writing. He'd lie on my chest as I read and purr, his paws draped over my shoulder. He loved to be beloved, and I was in love with him.

The year Katze turned twenty-one, I watched my beloved kitty slip away. I found his personal charm had been swapped for irritated insistence, although friends and family assure me he'd always been that way.

I had to lock him out of my office at home because he wouldn't sit in my lap and sleep peacefully like he used to. He jumped up and down, up and down, from me to the floor and back to me again because he wanted to be fed or pet or amused. He'd taken to cater-wauling at all hours, and in the middle of the night I'd get up and soothe him. I fed him every two hours, small meals of terrible commercial wet cat food just so he'd eat. His arthritis hadn't stopped him from having an active life, but he was thin and his haunches were caved. It hurt him to be handled in nearly any way.

When our dog Madra died, over a decade earlier, we were completely taken by surprise. She'd been so vital up until she'd had a stroke and we had to put her down. We cried a lot for many months afterward. The shock was so great.

As Katze aged, we lived with death's quiet, panting insistence everyday, but mostly I pretended not to hear it. The moment I realized I had to let him go, no matter how much time he gave me to "get used to it," was still devastating.

The grief is different this time in nearly every way. Katze's death was planned for and we had him cremated. Friends and family acknowledged his passing as a member of the family, something Sean and I longed for when Madra died. Yet losing Katze feels quieter, deeply private. I know people always say they'll never get another pet again after losing such a special friend, but if I do, I know for certain it won't be the same. Katze and I grew up together and loved each other with the fierce abandon of youth. As the years went on, he showed me the joys and travails of aging, and, at the end, how to let go. As much as I yearn for Katze, my grief is tempered by gratitude. I understand that there are some things in life you are lucky to experience because they are by nature one of a kind.

Chelsey

by Wanda Andrews of Bellefonte, Pennsylvania

(See also her story in the Animals and the Afterlife section.)

Chelsey

Christmas morning, 1988, in a small town in Central Pennsylvania, I got in my little red Chevette and drove to an Amish farm, nestled in what was called Penns Valley. I'd learned of an Amish family who had some rat terrier pups for sale. Black and white, with the most adorable little "deer-like" face and body, was Chelsey.

Through the years, she was there to comfort me when my daughter, Darbie, went off to junior college and when my son, Dusty, left the nest for college as well. She enjoyed good health most of her life, but she began to develop cataracts at age sixteen, and by the time she turned seventeen, she'd lost most of her sight. By the time she approached her eighteenth year, she'd slowed down quite a bit and developed arthritis. She began having a series of collapses and experienced congestive heart failure from which she was unable to recover. I made the decision to help her end her struggle and made an appointment on a Friday in March with a "mobile" vet to come to the house to help her cross over. However, as fate would have it, we got a big snowstorm that day and the vet could not make it.

That Sunday morning, Chelsey barked exactly three times and then was silent. I suddenly got a very strong feeling that made me jump up out of bed and go downstairs. I ran to the kitchen and found her lying on her side (a position I had never, never seen her in before). I picked her up and found she was barely breathing. I tried blowing some air into her mouth, all the time crying out her name. She seemed to try so very hard to "come around" but just couldn't. I watched her take a few more strained breaths, and then her body went limp. She was gone.

My daughter, who was working as a vet tech, came by to collect my sweet little Chelsey's body and take it to the clinic where she works. Chelsey's body would be frozen until she could be picked up for cremation.

The following week was torture for me. I kept seeing her little body lying on the floor. I beat myself up for not going downstairs sooner, even knowing that it probably would not have made any difference. I couldn't go to work. I lost interest in eating and couldn't stop crying. My little pal of eighteen-plus years was gone. Though I knew it was a blessing for her to leave that weak and crippled little body, my grief lingered.

To this day, I can't help but think Chelsey somehow sensed what was to happen that Friday and, knowing it would have been too much for me to handle a decision like that, decided to relieve me of what would have been an awful guilt trip. So she spared me the torturous decision and went home on her own.

In the six months after she crossed, I found that all I wanted to do was talk about her to anyone who would listen. I felt lost and alone in my grief. Yet I knew there had to be others out there who could understand what I was feeling. I gravitated to books on the afterlife of animals. I even contacted two psychics in the hope they could contact my little girl so as to let me know she was safe and sound—once again young and vital. I did receive some relief from that, though not as much as I would have liked.

I made a memorial for Chelsey with a shelving unit I purchased. On it, I placed her precious ashes, now in a beautiful wooden "dog house," some pictures of her, some of her dog tags, and a couple of angels. I have a picture of her in a frame with the well-known poem "The Rainbow Bridge." I wear a necklace that has her picture in a tiny frame and a doggy angel pin in her honor. I continue to sleep with a little blue doggy Chelsey used to play with, which now wears Chelsey's red collar.

My life with Chelsey opened my heart towards animals even more than it had originally been. I also now have such unbridled compassion for others who have, or are about to, lose their precious animal friends, whatever breed or species they happen to be. I have added to my prayers those who have, or are, experiencing the loss of their animal companions, in hopes that they will be comforted and find strength to deal with the loss and terrible grief that come with this kind of experience.

CHELSEY

Celestial being, my little angel. You truly graced my life, filling my

Heart with tenderness, wonder, and happy smiles. You discovered a way to

Enter the very core of my being, and for so many years granted me unconditional

Love, companionship and loyalty, while asking so little in return.

Sadly, the time came for you to go. Softly and silently, you made your way back to

Eternity—your true home in Spirit. Until the appointed time when I can be with

You and once again hold you in my arms, I will be holding you forever in my heart.

— by Wanda Andrews

Chase

by Shelly Brander of Dayton, Ohio

We got our Samoyed, Chase, when we lived in Lincoln, Nebraska. He was only twelve weeks old or so when we got him. We lived in a town house at the time and he was just the right size to fit on top of the air conditioning vent. That's where he slept.

When he was two years old, he moved with us to Rochester, New York. I remember he was such a great traveler during the twenty-hour drive. He just sat there and looked out the window. He loved the cold weather there. The winter before we moved to Ohio, it snowed fifty-three inches in three days!! The snow was so deep I had to shovel the yard so he could get through to take care of his business. Even though the snow piles were bigger than he was, he still tried to run through them and would take his nose and toss the snow up in the air and try to catch it.

We moved to Ohio seven years ago. A year or so later, he was diagnosed with diabetes. Until the day

Chase

he was no longer with us, we'd give him insulin shots twice a day. He was now on a strict diet and a routine that he didn't seem to mind. When it was time for his shot, he'd just turn his head and look at you. Once it was done, he'd hop up for his "big cookie," as we called them, and he'd head for the backyard.

The following year, Chase was out in the cold weather (it was just a few days before Christmas, and we were getting ready to go back to Nebraska to visit our families). When I called him in, he had trouble getting up and he whimpered. I finally got him inside, thinking he was maybe he was too cold or he was just a little stiff. That night, I sat next to him on the floor and gently massaged his back leg for three hours. The next day it was off to the vet and were told Chase had torn his ACL (anterior cruciate ligament). Needless to say, Chase couldn't travel with us that Christmas. He stayed with the vet for X-rays and had surgery to repair the ACL the first week of January. He had to be kept at a minimal activity level for eight to twelve weeks. The only thing we had going for us was that it was the middle of winter — not a great time to take walks anyway. When we showed people the pictures of his stapled leg and talked about the surgery, many people raised their brows that we had spent over $2,000 to do this. There was no doubt in our minds that this is what we had to do. We don't have any human kids, so Chase was our child. When spring came, we began walking and he was like a new dog with a new spring in his step. Life went on.

In April of this year (2007), Chase had to have a couple of teeth removed. He was high risk because of his age and diabetes. It was difficult to talk to the doctor about what should be done if he didn't come through the surgery. Did we want a DNR (do-not-resuscitate order)? It was difficult for me to say, but I didn't want him to suffer if he was struggling to get through the surgery. He'd make it if it was meant to be. And it was. He came through with flying colors.

The summer heat was here and we could tell Chase was having trouble. His breathing was becoming labored. He slept quite a bit. When he did get up, he really struggled to stand. His legs were very weak. Over the next several weeks, he eventually couldn't do it any more. When we awoke on Saturday, August 25, we knew it was time.

With heavy, heavy hearts, we put Chase to rest that morning. He was at peace now — in a place where his legs were strong and his body was healthy again. Even knowing that, our hearts are broken.

Over this last week, we received many cards, thoughts, and prayers from our vet, our friends, and our families. It made each day a little more tolerable.

It had been five emotional days when I received a sign that God was trying to heal my broken heart and Chase was right there with Him. You see, my company contributes to the United Way. During the first week of September, we are having our second annual Extreme Community Makeover, where our employees volunteer their time to go to various United Way organizations to help with projects, clean up, do yard work, etc. When I opened my email, my mouth dropped. I had been assigned to go to the Humane Society. It was a sign. It was meant to be. It was God's way and Chase's way to let me know it would be okay, and even though Chase wasn't here with us physically anymore, he will always be with us in our hearts.

In two days, I'll be going to the Humane Society. I know it will be emotional, but Chase will be with me in spirit. And that will make it all worthwhile.

Chancey and Digby

by Helen Sloan of Milton-Freewater, Oregon

Digby & Chancey

Chancey was a dachshund-terrier mix, and we had her for just over eighteen years. We got her from the shelter in Portland, Oregon. Digby was a poodle-terrier mix, and he lived to be fourteen. We saved him from a private breeder. These two were the closest of friends from the moment they met until the day they died together.

Chancey and Digby were our once-in-a-lifetime dogs. Chancey came first, as a small brown package of pure joy and love. She was ours from the second we saw her, our perfect little girl.

She never cried once and slept between our pillows the very first night. She would snuggle in one neck or the other and snuffle in our ears. That is the way we slept together for the rest of her life.

Digby was the little brother Chancey wanted so much. So we brought Digby home and we became a whole and complete family. Chancey proceeded to teach Digby the ways of our lives. He learned quickly and well. He always wanted to do everything she did and be loved as much as she was, and he did and he was. They were both loved beyond measure.

But as with all things it had to come to an end. Chancey and Digby both developed health problems that just could not be healed, and with their age we did not want to subject them to invasive operations. I think Chancey decided to stay around until Digby was ready and then they decided that the time was right and they would go together. As in life, they would not be separated in death. We gave them the gift of being together in death forever. They would not have survived without one another. That, of course, was the hardest thing we have ever done.

We have done all the things we can think of to memorialize them, although we really don't need "things" to memorialize them, as they are always with us in everything we do, everywhere we go, and in all we plan for our future.

We have mugs (which we don't use) with their pictures and names. We have their pictures wherever we need them to be to make us feel safe. I have written volumes about their lives with us and I have created a web page about them.

Buster Southpaw's Story
by Sherry Nemmers of New York City

Buster Southpaw

My Maine Coon tuxedo cat, Buster Southpaw, and I found each other on August 10, 1997, at an ASPCA adoption center. Though I'd looked at seventy cats that day, and have had many pets before him, Buster Southpaw was the love of my life.

Always a robust Maine Coon, at twenty pounds, he loved to eat and loved me, but he was terrified of everything else. Because of his shyness and terrible fears, whenever the doorbell rang, Buster always took off for the highest closet shelf to hide.

Buster got sick suddenly, on May 20, 2007. He vomited, and I took him to an exclusive, feline-only veterinary clinic in New York City, where I'd taken all my cats for twenty years. He was put on an IV, but they starved him for eight days, and then due to further incompetence, starved him for another five days, waiting for a sonogram doctor to show up over Memorial Day Weekend.

Buster was finally diagnosed with abdominal cancer, and came home for only four days before he died an agonizing death on my bedroom floor, gasping for breath. It seems during hospice care he was given cortisone to reduce the cancer, but because they'd ignored the fluid on his lungs, he suffocated and "drowned" in front of me, for a

Buster Southpaw

horrendous twelve hours from night until morning.

From the onset of signs of illness to his horrifying, unexpected death was only two weeks. I have forgiven neither myself nor those horrible vets. Buster was traumatized at the vets', couldn't sleep, or rest, or eat, couldn't blink, so terrified was he, though other cats were oblivious.

Buster did not die from cancer. Buster's killer was medical incompetence.

Despite my rage and guilt, I have received some comfort from surprising places. For four weeks I had excruciating back pain, until a stranger on a plane said I was carrying the grief; the truth hit me, and three days later, I released it.

In the bathroom of the Metropolitan Opera, a stranger told me Buster was now very social, no longer afraid, and pulled two tarot cards from her purse (!), the Three of Cups and the Ten of Cups, which she said were cause to celebrate.

I "dreamed" (had a vision) that Buster was sitting in his favorite chair, and I saw him. I knew he was dead, but instead of my being sad at this, Buster let me know he was fine.

A woman I barely knew emailed me, randomly, and I impulsively responded by telling her that Buster had died (she didn't even know I had a cat), and she wrote to say, odd as it might seem, she knew Buster had brought us together because her cat Five had died of cancer as well a year before (and I didn't know she had a cat!)

I have honored Buster with eight picture albums and framed photos, a song written by a songwriter, and a poem written by my husband. Buster's ashes are beside my bed, near a picture of Buster drawn by a friend.

Yogi

by J.P. of Canada

Yogi, Yorkshire Terrier
April 2, 1993 – March 25, 2007

Ever since I was a little girl, the only thing I wanted more than anything in the whole world was a dog, someone I could call my own — all mine. My parents would not hear of it because we lived in an apartment. My father always said, "When you get married, you can get a dog."

Years passed, I got a job and met the man of my dreams. Life was good, but something was missing. Out of the blue, I started getting panic/anxiety attacks. For almost a year, I became afraid to come out of the house. I had to quit my job. I felt dead inside. My husband saw an ad for someone who was selling Yorkies.

Though afraid to venture out, I made it to the breeder and picked the one I wanted. I had to send my husband to the store for his accessories because I couldn't go in the store. But I was overjoyed to have my new baby. We named him Yogi, and he changed my life for the next fourteen years. Yogi did for me what no human could. He made me whole again, made me live again.

Slowly, I started to come out of the house. I had to take him for walks. We would venture further and further from the house, until one day we reached the park. We went out three times a day, and soon I'd gone from 147 pounds to 115. My fears abated over the first five years with him, and I eventually got a part-time job. Ten years later, I'm still at the same job.

As the years went by, Yogi slowed down and showed health problems common to old age. When Yogi started going downhill, I searched the Internet for a support group for owners with aging pets. I found Chance's Spot, a pet loss site. I read others' postings about their loss and cried almost daily. A couple of times, I asked for prayers and they worked. Yogi would recover for a while. Reading other people's books on pet loss helped, too.

The week before his passing on, we had gone to the park. He ran just like a puppy again. The next morning upon awaking, I noticed he was not himself. He was walking unsteadily. The vet said it was most likely he'd had some kind of brain tumor and that it was time for us to think of putting him down.

My parents and brother came over to see him, too. They knew Yogi was leaving us. My dad, who never wanted dogs, loved him so much. Yogi would sleep with him when my parents dog-sat. As if Yogi knew what was ahead, that night, he walked to all of the rooms of the house, just looking around his home for the last time.

That last night, we slept together. Many times during the night I saw him looking up, like someone was there up above, telling him it's okay, his job here on Earth was done. It was time to come home, to rest his aching body. I knew his time had come.

We reached the vet's office and, just before we went in, I found a penny. He and I had been finding a lot of pennies in our last few months of walking. That would turn out to be our sign from him. (Every time we find a penny, we know it's pennies from Heaven, Yogi telling us it's okay, he's okay.)

My husband held him and I kissed Yogi, told him I loved him, not to forget us, and to come and see us in our dreams. His passing was quick and painless. We went home to our quiet, empty house.

That night as we crawled in bed, I heard the sound of him jumping on the foot of our bed.

When I lost Yogi, I lost myself again. Fear and panic returned. I spent each and every day crying, avoiding the outside world, avoiding friends for months.

Now, six months later, I'm up at our favorite getaway. Last year, Yogi and I were sitting at our favorite rock, looking out at the lake. And now I'm here to throw in some of his ashes in honor of his life.

At home, I've put up a shelf. On it are his ashes in an urn, a baby picture/adult picture at our favorite vacation spot, a jar that holds all our found pennies, his collar and tag, and a pouch holding his fur and baby teeth. A candle has burned there every night since his passing.

I still say, "Good night, sweet dreams, sleep tight," except for now it's to his picture.

No human could ever have done for me what this little six-pound furry dog did. No medicine could have healed me, but he did. He was my angel.

I love you, Yogi. Till we meet again, you'll be forever in our hearts.

I have adopted another Yorkie. His name is Mini and he's eight months old. He's not Yogi, nor will he ever be. He's managed to take away some of the pain, but I will never forget Yogi. I'm afraid to let myself feel all that love again. I'm afraid because I know how fast the years go by and that one day this guy's death will be another heartbreaker for me. But I'm already falling in love with him in these last couple of months. How can you not? I'm allowing myself to love again, slowly giving of myself again.

Bruzer

by Elaine Pederson of Andover, Minnesota

(See also his story and photo in The All-Important Grieving Process section.)

When we lost our West Highland white terrier, Bruzer, I cannot describe to you how devastated we were. That day coming home without him was so, so hard. We cried for days and woke up in the night because one or both of us were crying. I could not go to work and instead dragged out every single picture we had of Bruzer and started putting together albums of pictures and also a memory box that had all the albums of his pictures, his paw print taken on the day we lost him, his two collars and special Christmas scarf that had his name inscribed on it, and all of the cards that I received from people. I had a lock of his hair that I took home with me on that awful day. I also kept a very special book and the card they sent that was signed by everyone at the vet's office.

We then went to Hallmark and bought a very nice memory book and started writing everything we could think of about Bruzer's life with our family, all his nicknames and funny things he did. That book is so precious to me, but it is really hard to read, and when I do I always start crying. Another thing we did was take our favorite pictures and some I had enlarged. We bought frames for them and put pictures of him in our family room and in our bedroom. They are still there and always will be. It has been over two years, and I still have his memory book, his memory box, his ashes, and a picture in a frame on my sofa table, which is the first thing you see when you walk into my living room.

I think that losing Bruzer was more devastating to us than even losing our parents will be. Bruzer lived with us every day for sixteen years, and I only see my parents once in awhile. He was a dear member of our family.

P.S. We grieved for six months and had said we were not going to get another dog, but after that long we just could not stand life without a dog. We were very unhappy and depressed without a dog. We now have two Westies, Cody (boy) and Charlotte (girl). We love them dearly and know that someday we will have to go through this again, but we decided for all that a dog gives you in happiness, it is worth the pain you have to go through when you lose them.

Brandy

by Amy Romer

We had to put our precious orange tabby cat Brandy to sleep in May of 2006; she was twenty-six years old. She adopted me in 1986 when I got her from my aunt, and the loss still upsets me to this day. She had diabetes the last four years of her life, and we gave her shots every day. Letting her go was the hardest thing I've ever had to do. Thankfully, my husband was home and was with me at the vet's the day we let her go. I held her and cried, and he was crying just as hard as I was. He had known her since 1998, and she had a special place in his heart.

Some people say they could never hold their pet while it's put to sleep, but I could not leave her, surrounded by strangers. I needed her to know that I was there, holding her in her last moments on this

Earth. I still cannot think or talk about it without getting emotional. She was such a huge part of my life for so long and I miss her dearly.

Brandy

My husband built her a box, screwed it together, and sealed it with caulk. He placed a piece of tin on the lid so I could write on it. We buried her in the flowerbed under the bay window; she used to love to lie in the bay window and soak in the sun. For the longest time, I was angry and hated the fact that she was in a hole in the ground, and I wanted her out of there. I cried for weeks and lost eleven pounds because this loss was so great and very difficult for me to accept.

She was chosen for the Page-A-Day cat calendar two years in a row: 2006 and 2007. The day I received the free calendar and letter in 2007, after her death, I stood at the mailbox and cried ... such a bittersweet moment that brought all of the memories flooding back to me. After her picture appeared in the calendar on April 23, 2007, I received several phone calls, cards, and letters from pet lovers as far away as California, telling me how hopeful they were about their pets living long, healthy lives because they had read that Brandy was twenty-six. It tore my heart out to tell them that we had lost her in 2006, but they were very sympathetic.

She was a beautiful, long-haired orange tabby with strikingly beautiful green eyes. One kind gentleman remarked how regal and wise she looked in the photo. I was her third owner, and we still aren't sure of her true age, so twenty-six was just our best guess. She could have been a few years older than that. After our loss, our house seemed so empty and she wasn't there to greet me when I got home. It was such a hollow feeling, and I would find myself looking around for her to be there, standing up to reach out to me for affection.

We adopted a kitten and an older cat a week later because our house was just so empty and we wanted to save lives. I have loved on them and held them and cried, feeling guilty about filling our home with more babies, but now I know that Brandy is watching over us, happy that we've saved lives and are giving them the best loving, happy home we possibly can. Toby is our fourteen-pound orange tabby, and Patches is our beautiful twelve-pound calico. Still, I will never forget Brandy, her unconditional love, and all of the joy she brought to my life.

> "Cats invented self-esteem"
>
> –Erma Bombeck

Sweety Pie
by Ava of Minnesota

I was living in Eugene Oregon in 1996 when my beloved Maine Coon Sweety Pie died of kidney cancer. Our veterinarian is an extraordinary person. By following her advice, and with assistance from two other friends, I found great solace and closure after she passed away.

The vet suggested that I light a candle for a week and dowse the areas of the house that were her favorites with sage while saying, "Go to the light." Another friend of mine made me the finest flower essence I've ever been given, a grief-healing flower essence. I took that for a few weeks. Yet a third friend came over and added some new pictures to my walls and moved a few pieces of furniture.

I was amazed at how quickly the pain lifted. One month later, a handsome black-and-white tuxedo cat—George—entered my life! He is million volts of energy, which seemed to be the final panacea.

> "Who would believe such pleasure from a wee ball o' fur?"
>
> –Irish Saying

Hurricane Aili

by Mike Jowdry of Portland, Maine

(submitted by Mike's sister, Melissa)

Hello all,

I wanted you all to know our beloved Aili said goodbye to us on Thursday, July 5th, at 7 a.m. She passed away peacefully on one of her favorite pieces of furniture, our bed. She meant the world to us, and we will never forget her and always cherish the time we had together. Thanks to all of you who treated her so great over the years.

Heartbroken,
Mike & Andi

Hurricane Aili (pronounced "I-lee")

Born March 16, 1997, you came into our life at eight weeks old, and you were the first present I ever bought for Andrea. I'll never forget the way you howled in my ear as I held you and drove you away from your brothers and sisters to deliver you to Andrea for her eighteenth birthday—a risky idea since Andrea and I had been dating less than a year. The risk paid off in a big way, and you gave us both ten years and five months of every possible emotion—most of all happiness.

Your list of credentials grew every day:

- Mountain biking partner (Bar Harbor, Acadia, Evergreen to name a few)

- Roller blading partner (Dallas, Arlington Stadium)
- Couch and bed warmer (you loved your furniture and never met a floor you'd even consider lying on)
- Exercise companion (without you I'd weigh 300 pounds)
- Amazing car rider (three trips to and/or from Dallas—one in a single cab U-haul, curled up between Andi and me)
- Great hiker (Tumbledown, New Mexico, Acadia, Gulf Hagus)
- Iron stomach (two pounds of raw chicken in ten seconds, candy bars with wrappers)
- Escape artist (no matter what barricades, leashes, seat belts, etc. we used to contain you, you could always figure out a way to get in or out if you wanted to)
- Dog trainer and great big sister (you have set the bar for our future dogs to achieve; without you, Lucy would've never turned out to be the good dog she has become)
- No leash necessary (every dog owner should be so lucky)
- Facial expressions (we've never seen a dog smile, but you literally smiled every time we came home)
- Snob-like abilities (you could act very stuck-up toward some people, and for some reason I liked it)
- Stuffed-animal protector (you always took such great care of your babies)
- Gentle giant (you were the softest and nicest dog to all kids)
- Best ears (your velvety soft ears flapping in the wind were unforgettable)
- Best co-worker, especially for work breaks (I'll never forget our numerous coffee break trips and walks at Baxter)
- So many more but easily summed up by this credential— "Best Dog Evah."

It was just the three of us for so long. You gave us so much joy, and we'll always treasure those years. I'm so grateful we were able to bring you back to Maine for the last few years of your life. You'll be in our hearts forever, and you're truly the reason why we love each other

251

so much, and we'll continue to give our dogs and our kids the amount of love we gave you and you gave us.

We love you so much, Aili.

An Emailed Personal Note

Sid,

My sister likes to do things "for me" without my knowledge. Aili was a Weimaraner. I was sitting here watching the Red Sox, contemplating drinking a beer, when I opened this email. It's been thirty minutes of crying and looking at pics of her, and I had to send you a few. Consider yourself lucky—I almost sent you forty or so pics.

You really must enjoy beating yourself up emotionally to write a book like this, but I'm glad you're doin' it. If dogs ran the world, it would be a peaceful planet. They deserve the recognish.

In all seriousness, dogs are such superb companions to grow older with that when they pass, you do not only mourn the loss of your dog, you mourn the loss of a chapter of your life you cannot get back—and both suck.

Good luck with the book,
Mike Jowdry

Passion Emerges from the Ashes of Grief
by Marilou Chanrasmi of St. Paul, Minnesota

Our eleven-year old collie/shepherd mix, Shen, is in surgery at the University of Minnesota's small-animal hospital. An ultrasound confirms that Shen has a mass in her spleen. The doctors suspect cancer. I am thrown into the hellish vortex of cancer. The only way we can confirm cancer, and the extent of how far it has spread, is through surgery. No guarantees. In fact, I am told, "She's dying. Any surgery would be palliative. You may get a couple more weeks with her, maybe three, if you're lucky."

My head is spinning; my heart is burning. I am not ready to say goodbye. Just days ago she was acting like her usual self. Today, life has been drained from her like a tornado ripping through a town, demolishing and flattening what was once a living, breathing community. Today, there's heaviness in my heart—an all-consuming tightness. It's as if tentacles of an octopus have latched onto my heart, with their suction cups working tirelessly to drain the remaining life out of me.

I prepare to say goodbye to a family member, to a spiritual companion, to my best friend. I opt for surgery. The vet assures me she is not suffering. If we discover the cancer has spread, we can make the decision to humanely let her go while she is still "sleeping."

I pace the hallways, waiting and hoping. Outside the hospital, it's sunny and feels like spring. Is today the day? Is the sun shining brightly in preparation for welcoming Shen into Heaven? I pray for strength, wisdom, and courage to do what is best for Shen, not what's easy or comforting to me.

The doctor comes out. She's wearing blue scrubs; her face carrying a somber look. With empathy, she says, "The cancer has spread. Shen is losing a lot of blood. We have done one blood transfusion. She is stable now. We need to remove a large tumor that has formed in and around her liver." Since it will be awhile, the vet recommends we go home. They will call when the surgery is over and we can come back to visit her.

The phone rings. Our caller ID indicates it's the University of Minnesota vet school. It's way too soon for them to be calling.

"Is this Marilou?" the voice on the other end asks.

"Yes." I'm afraid to ask any questions, to say anything more.

"Shen's condition is far worse than we anticipated. The cancer has spread. She's losing blood. We need your permission to do another blood transfusion."

At that moment, in my head, someone hit the pause button on

the DVD player. The frame freezes: "She's losing blood; we need your permission…. She's losing blood, we need your permission…." plays over and over again. In the background, the rhythmic, powerful beats of bachi sticks on taiko drums vibrate and beat the message, "It's time, Marilou. It's time."

I return to the phone conversation. With sadness and acceptance, I say, "No more transfusions. It's time to let her go."

I make it back to the University of Minnesota in time to hold her, as her spirit, wrapped in mine, is set free. I wrap my hands around Shen's paw as the doctor inserts the needle into her vein. There's a deep sadness in my heart, yet a sense of relief for her.

Her chest rises, and she takes one last breath. I close my eyes and breathe in her spirit, as tears of both denial and acceptance roll down my cheeks.

In the weeks that follow, I immerse myself in ways to relieve myself of the pain in my heart. I cry in the arms of my partner. I hold our second dog, Shadow. I take walks with Shadow, feeling Shen's presence in the wind that blows gently on my face. I write. I doodle. I make home movies of Shen. I share my grief with friends. As days pass, the tentacles holding my heart hostage loosen their grip, one suction cup at a time, till one day I innocently search Petfinder. Shen's Spirit Guides me to a dog rescued by Pet Haven, a foster-based animal rescue. Not quite ready to adopt, we offer to foster.

In search of an outlet for the floodgates of grief, I throw myself into volunteering and helping the homeless, abused, and abandoned dogs. I begin by fostering Missy, a two-year-old Lab/pit/rottweiler mix, only to "fail" within hours. (In the animal rescue world, the term "foster failure" is an affectionate term for someone who ends up adopting the dog they are fostering.)

Next, as an intake phone volunteer, I return calls from people finding strays or surrendering their own dogs for one reason or another. In a month, I move into the role of volunteer director. Seven months later, with surprise and gratitude, I am asked to take on the role of president of a fifty-five-year-old animal-rescue organization.

The pain of losing Shen pushed me forward to live my passion. I had always wanted to do something with animals. I guess I didn't know how to "make it happen," or maybe I was too afraid to follow my heart. What emerged from Shen's ashes was a new Marilou.

Out of the ashes and tears came conviction and passion to be a voice for the animals. Out of the ashes came defiance for standing on the sidelines of life. I found myself, and I found purpose by volunteering for a cause I believe in. As I held Shen in my arms on the afternoon of September 15, 2006, unbeknownst to me, I was on stage in the prologue for a play that was yet to unfold. Of the many possible roads leading from grief, she led me to the following:

"Spirit of Shen—
Finding your voice,
Living your passion,
Transforming the world."

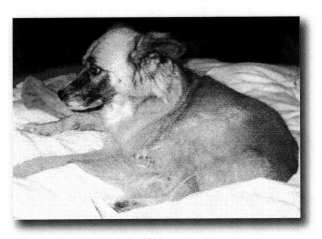

Shen

Marilou is currently serving as president of Pet Haven. Marilou embraces creativity and passion through writing and storytelling. By day, she is an academic program manager for a software company and shares her home in St. Paul, Minnesota with her partner, their three rescued dogs and one cat, all adopted through Pet Haven. She has been volunteering with Pet Haven since October 2006.

My Dog Cricket

by Jack Delebo of Minneapolis, Minnesota

I loved my dog Cricket.

I loved the way she would attack the door.

I loved the way she would chase the other dog across the floor.

I loved the way she snarfed down her food.

She would always lick me and put me in a good mood.

I loved the way she wagged her tail.

At being the best dog, she'd never fail.

I loved her bright eyes and her silky jet-black fur.

When a dog was by her while she was eating, she would say grrrrrr!

But then she got cancer when she was only six.

And the vet said, "This is something that we cannot fix."

My dog Cricket was in great pain,

So we decided it was time to cut her loose from this chain.

All of us could not help but cry.

And then the time came that we had to say goodbye.

We are all so sad that Cricket had to die.

I loved my dog Cricket.

Cricket

Keisha's Gifts

by Laurie Crawford Stone of Cedar Rapids, Iowa

Keisha, Keesies, Keesies Marie. She was an independent cat. A friend called her "small but mighty." I adopted Keisha, Teddy, and Coco on Valentine's Day 1997. The moment I saw her, I knew I was destined to have a gray cat. She had a croaky meow. She looked like a potato on short toothpick legs. I adopted her,

Keisha

overlooking the fact that she ignored me at the shelter, preferring instead to sit on a pile of newspapers, purring loudly.

Keisha always found my lap, where she never quit purring. The stillness, without her constant loud purr, was the first thing I noticed after she died unexpectedly exactly ten years and five months after I'd brought her home. Keisha bit me almost every day. She was a challenging, strong-willed, yet wildly affectionate cat. Her death left a gaping hole in my life.

I had taken Keisha to the emergency clinic because she was having trouble breathing. She rallied at the clinic, but as a precaution, the veterinarian recommended she spend two hours in the oxygen tank. He called an hour later and said Keisha had died. Necropsy revealed congestive heart failure and early stage lung cancer. I believe Keisha gave me the gift of not having to deal with the same disease and prolonged dying process that Teddy went through with lung cancer four years earlier.

I rushed to the clinic where I held Keisha's still-warm body, stroked her, talked to her, prayed, and wept. I had lost other cats, but none so unexpectedly. I needed to hold her the way I had held my other cats when they died. I hated to leave. I asked the vet for some of her fur. I requested plaster impressions of her tiny paws and private cremation. I had moved after burying two other cats, and I didn't want to leave another grave. My ashes will someday be co-mingled with those of Keisha's and all my cats.

When I got home, I started writing about Keisha. I knew my memories would fade over time. I wanted to remember everything about her and keep her close in the days following her shocking death. The next morning, I was aware of Keisha's hot little body pressed against mine as I awakened. Then the horror of the previous day slammed into my consciousness and I wrote more memories. Mostly I noticed the deathly quiet. None of my other five cats purred loudly. The quiet screamed of Keisha's death. I wrote about her yowling at night and playing by herself, rolling down the stairs, of her being a lap hog. She loved food. These memories made me laugh out loud and comforted me.

I shared my memories with friends. I wrote Keisha a letter and read my memories during a private service for just Keisha and me. I performed a Native American ceremony with sweet grass. I celebrated her life and thanked her for sharing mine.

A year later, Keisha sent me a stray calico cat—another potato on short toothpick legs with a loud purr and a croaky meow. She bites me, too.

Teddy

by Charlene M. Bellville of Rising Fawn, Georgia

In 1998, my husband and I made the decision to downsize, leave suburban Atlanta, and relocate to the country. We found a log home that backed up to Lookout Mountain in Rising Fawn, Georgia. We moved there and

Teddy

did not know a single person. My husband, Evan, traveled extensively and I was quite lonely. I began looking for a companion, a dog — female, short-haired, small build. A neighbor told me about a friend of hers that had "rescued" a dog that had been pitched into a creek by someone in a passing pickup truck. She already had three dogs of her own. I went to look at "Teddy." I sat on her front porch in a rocking chair, and Teddy put his head in my lap and looked up as if to say, "Will you take me home?" At six months, Teddy was already sixty-eight pounds, longhaired, and a male. He was part chow, part golden retriever, and he was going to get bigger (eventually reaching 128 pounds)! Teddy went home with us on a trial basis — a trial that lasted eight glorious years.

From day one, he was the best dog ever. He would not use the bathroom anywhere except in the woods — never in the yard, even though we had six acres. He never messed in the house, never chewed anything, and was in his glory if we were walking. Teddy decided early on that my truck was his truck, and if it were leaving the house, he was going with us. My husband had a custom tag made for the front of the truck with Teddy's picture and it said, "Teddy's Truck." Everyone in our community recognized Teddy and loved him.

One night in January of 2006, Teddy became sick — his first illness ever. He was uncomfortable and making whining noises. His stomach started to swell and we rushed him to the vet. Teddy had stomach distortion, very serious for larger dogs, and the vet was not sure if Teddy would survive, but he was willing to try and save him. Anyone who has read *Marley and Me* knows about stomach distortion and what can happen. Teddy's stomach could not be turned, and the vet advised that surgery was the only way to correct the stomach's position. During surgery, the vet told us that complications had arisen. Teddy's stomach had been severely damaged and the only way to possibly save him would be to remove one-quarter to half of his stomach. We agreed to the procedure and prayed that Teddy would survive.

Well, Teddy was not ready to leave us yet. The vet asked me to bring Teddy something he liked to start him eating once he was out of intensive care. He was partial to bacon and bologna — he was a country dog, after all. He began eating and recovering. The vet told us Teddy had more visitors than any dog that had been there.

Within a month, Teddy was his old self again, walking the mountain roads with me and riding in his truck. We were all so grateful and, even though we didn't think it possible, we loved Teddy even more.

On August 15, 2006, eight months after his surgery, Teddy started to throw up and I could tell his stomach was swelling again. We called the emergency vet center, and by the time we were dressed, Teddy could no longer walk and we had to carry him to the truck. The emergency vet told us Teddy's stomach had compartmentalized and was cutting off circulation to his legs. He would not survive, and we had to make a decision regarding what was best for Teddy. My husband was a Force Recon Marine who served in Vietnam, but he crumbled that night as we tried to console one another and say goodbye to our beloved Teddy. We did not want him to suffer anymore. He had had a great last day. We had gone for a mountain walk, he had gone to McDonald's for his favorite double cheeseburger, and he had had a ride in the truck. (As long as I have this truck, it will always be Teddy's Truck.)

I would like to say we recovered quickly, but to this day my arms ache to hold that big guy, and tears still come even one year later.

Teddy's life with us was not particularly unique or remarkable, but he gave us eight years of unwavering love, devotion, and companionship that will stay with us until we leave this world. I asked our pastor if I would see Teddy again, and he told me that he believes God gives us whatever we need in Heaven to be happy. I know in my heart that Teddy will be waiting on the Rainbow Bridge for my husband and me.

Ripley

by Gretchen Anderson of Minneapolis, Minnesota

Ripley lounging. A hound enjoying her leisure time!

My husband Clint and I are both dog people. We bought a house so that we could have a dog. Then, after much searching, I adopted (that is, brought home) an adorable eight-week-old puppy. She was from a farm in Elmwood, Wisconsin — home of UFO Days. I was told she was a border collie mix. Never believe what you are told. She turned into a tall, leggy hound dog. I took her to obedience school. Note: I had previously trained an almost perfect obedience dog. Let me tell you, the hound/shepherd mix is deadly. The shep half gets what is wanted, learns all of the words, and smiles a lot. The coonhound looks sweetly at you and stubbornly does whatever she pleases. Now if we *ask* rather than demand, that's another matter.

She possesses the hunter's olfactory sense, yet interestingly enough, she ignores squirrels as if they are beneath her. Once when we were camping on the Echo Trail in Ely, Minnesota, she even made friends with the chipmunk who ate her food!

At this time [2007] we, my husband and I, are facing the imminent loss of our first dog together. She is not the first for either of us — we both grew up with a slew of dogs (and other animals). But she is the first that we shared together, raised together. That alone makes her special.

She is the most empathic dog I know. She can read our moods in a second — I can always tell what kind of day my husband has had by the way Ripley greets me when I come home! The joys we three have shared, the walks in the woods, the romps and play dates. She is a very independent dog — very much knows what she wants. I admire that.

She is now fourteen and has been having serious health problems

for about a year now. It is wrenching to see her stumble — she who
was so agile and graceful such a
short time ago. She loved her hikes.
She and Clint used to go out on
serious two-hour hikes in the
Mississippi River gorge three to
four times per week. They would
tease each other, racing up and
down cliffs. One day, we all went

Ripley

down the dog park by the river ... the hound nose took over and she
took off. Clint tore after her. (I do not run, *ever*, so I just walked
along.)

Pretty soon she was racing towards me, with my husband behind
shouting for me not to touch her. She got to the beach and just stood
in all of her glory — reeking beyond anything imaginable — she had
scented a long-dead muskrat. It was puffed up and bloated. Clint was
close enough to see her flip in midair, at a dead run, and land on her
back, full force on the carrion! It burst open, spraying all of the rot-
ting juices around. She was the queen of the beach that day — all the
dogs wanted to sniff her; all the people backed away!

Her idea of being top dog (with the other dogs in the park) was to
outrun them. She would challenge other dogs to a race and tear off
around the field or along the beach. Generally she would win.
However, one time, we were at the park with a standard poodle and a
Rhodesian ridgeback. Ripley and the poodle were in a race, and it
was magnificent to watch — the poodle prancing along neck to neck
with Ripley, who was long and low to the ground. They were eating
up the ground and well matched speed-wise. Simba, the Rhodesian
could not keep up. Simba stopped and watched the two speed
demons jockeying for position. She then trotted deliberately over to
a spot and positioned herself — then, as the other two rounded a corner, Simba launched herself at them in one burst of speed. She
knocked Ripley on the shoulder. Rip careened into Jocko (the poodle), and the next thing we saw was a blur of legs and bodies rolling
around. Ripley and Jocko staggered to their feet looking very bewil-

dered. And Simba just sat there grinning! Their human companions were laughing so hard we could not stand up!

To see her now, not able to walk for more than a quarter of a block saddens me beyond description. We know it will not be long. We got ready to put her down a week ago, then she rallied, now she is slipping again. She is by nature a robust dog, and to see her so frail, struggling to keep up, is wrenching.

For the past fourteen years, she has been friend, therapist, and companion. In her younger days, she could slip into the bed under the covers without waking us up! I have never been able to figure out how she could do that—she weighed sixty-five pounds.

Ripley

I wrote the previous piece three months ago. Ripley rallied again and is still with us. She was strong enough to go to the North Shore over Thanksgiving weekend. The weather was perfect. We did some great hikes along the Cascade River and Superior Trail. It was not like before, but we were out there as a family again, one last time. We have enjoyed every moment and thrilled to see her walking slowly along, nose to the ground. It looks like we will share Christmas with her. Every day that we get to spend with her is special. The day is not far off when we know we will lose her. The hole in our lives will be huge, but she will always be there.

Excerpt from
"Goodbye, Old Girl (A Eulogy to Ripley)"
by Clint Hoover

On Friday, March 6, 2009, Gretchen and I had our beautiful, ancient dog Ripley put down. She was almost sixteen years old. Ripley had a long, rich, wonderful life, but it was time for her to go —time for us to let go.

Words cannot express or explain the depth of bond I had with her. She was my constant companion and brought an amazing amount of joy to our lives. She was a great comfort in hard times and made me laugh. It's possible that I spent more time with her than anyone else I know. In some crazy yet very real way, she was my best friend. With her, I was never alone or lonely.

Some people have wondered at her "title," The Serpent Dog. Although she could sometimes be a devil, it had nothing to do with her personality. It was about how she moved. In her prime out in the wild, she would cast about in the undergrowth, her nose attached to an invisible wire. She weaved through the flora with a graceful, undulating, serpentine motion.

On the next page is the poem I wrote for her:

Dream of The Serpent Dog
by Clint Hoover

for Ripley

The Serpent Dog sleeps
  and dreams the dream
  of the good life:
The scent of spring rebirth —
Padding down wooded shade trails
  through fields light with prairie grass,
Toe claws sink deep in cool velvet
   moss,
Ears cock to the quiet voice of the
   swamp,
Scrabble scratch over rocks slick with
   creek water,
Tongue on root, bark, and stem.
But best of all —
Wanton rolling in the
  thick, fecund dead.

It was my hope that we could have one last spring together.
But it was not to be. Here is a postscript to the poem:

The Serpent Dog sleeps,
Now forever,
In the dream of spring rebirth.
Goodbye, old girl.
I'll never forget you.
Sleep well.

Caesar

by Marie Michaeloff of St. Anthony Village, Minnesota

Caesar was a gorgeous white German shepherd I had from the early 1960s through 1978. He was amazingly gentle, patient, and tolerant with children. We called him "the babysitter" because kids could get really rough with him and he'd never hurt them. One toddler poked a toy up Caesar's nose, making it bleed, and he just docilely accepted the abuse. It was not at all uncommon for kids to use him as a big

Marie & Caesar, 1967

pillow. He would even use his body to block the top of the stairs if a child came too close and might have fallen.

But this same gentle giant had an uncanny sixth sense when it came to people's character. Once, when a female family member who was staying with my husband and me invited a fellow she'd just met into our house, the usually unflappable Caesar attacked him, barking and nipping until the man fled.

We discovered in the newspaper a month later that this man had been apprehended for a string of home burglaries, wherein his M.O. (method of operation) was to pick up a young lady, get invited to her residence, case the joint, and return later to burgle it. Caesar had him pegged from the moment he saw him.

My husband and I had a general contracting business, and one day one of our subcontractors let himself into the house without our knowledge. We came downstairs to discover Caesar had jumped on the guy, apparently head-butting out one of the man's teeth in the process and knocking him into a closet, where he stayed hidden until we came to let him out. We found out later that this same subcontractor had been stealing refrigerators and other appliances from some of our job sites.

Caesar was a phenomenal protector and one of the dearest beings I've ever had in my life. Though many decades have passed, I miss him anew each time he comes to mind. I'll always love my white knight.

Part Five:
All Things Considered
Seldom-Discussed Issues Surrounding Pet Loss

The following section discusses important, albeit out-of-the-ordinary, pet loss scenarios.

When the Loss Is Reversed

My dear friend Mavis Vitums was in hospice when I began collecting stories for this book back in 2007. I knew she'd had myriad animals in her sixty-eight years of life—from award-winning bantam chickens to horses to a crow to dogs and cats to doves and even a fox. I expected to hear several stories about this menagerie gone by, but what she chose to tell me zeroed in on another poignant aspect of coping with pet loss I hadn't yet considered.

"You assume you'll outlive them," she said stoically, looking at her faithful companion, her Pekingese Zeke, who lay at her side in her hospital bed. "How are you supposed to handle the grief when you have to say goodbye when you face death? That's my big question."

She went on to explain that she'd had to put a great deal of effort into being careful of what emotion she showed around Zeke, often swallowing her own guilt and fear for her dog's sake. "I have to make sure he understands it's not his fault I'm leaving."

Like a child of divorcing parents, our pets can internalize the emotional atmosphere in unanticipated ways.

"Zeke's become very clingy. He needs to see absolute joy when we come together after we've been apart for a while. He needs to see it from me. What

Zeke & Mavis

good it'll do [sparing him her darker emotions] I don't know, but he's been asking for it."

Mavis told me she would sometimes set her "pity party" timer for one hour and one hour only, during which time, she said, "I grieve for all the things I have no control over. I allow myself that when things build up."

Zeke would often lie between her legs so she couldn't go anywhere without his knowing it. "So he's not worried and can sleep more soundly," she explained.

The time came when Zeke refused to eat and had to be carried outside to go potty, growling the whole way, because he couldn't bear to be separated from his mama for a minute. Though there was no lack of willing candidates for adopting him, it nevertheless wasn't until Mavis had made her decision to have her foster daughter Crystal take Zeke into her home on a farm in southern Minnesota after Mavis' passing—and had clearly explained this to Zeke himself—that she felt she could relinquish her grasp on life on this side of the veil.

Once his mama was gone, physically, Zeke fairly quickly overcame his despondency, accepted food and water that was offered him, and seemed almost light-hearted walking on his leash with his new yet well-known-by-him mistress. Perhaps it was because the agonizing wait was over and he could relinquish his nonstop job as her protector; perhaps it was because he perceived/saw/felt Mavis' loving spirit was now pain-free and surrounding him; perhaps it was because he approved of her choice of caregivers and accepted his life was to continue without her—we cannot know what caused Zeke such relief. I only know that he was a changed dog as soon as his human mama died; he seemed downright happy for her and accepting of her new state of being as well as his new circumstances.

His accompanying Crystal home most certainly helped her heart handle the loss of her mother, too. It was like they both shared a little bit of Mavis when they were together.

〰〰〰
〰〰〰

Mavis' story drives home the point of how important it is for us to have health directives and/or wills that clearly state our wishes about our companion animals should we die before them, be it suddenly, as in an accident, or after a protracted illness. If there is a family member or friend who is willing and/or equipped to give your pet(s) a home, specify that in writing.

If not, research ahead of time a no-kill animal adoption agency to be contacted to pick up your pet(s) and work to find him/her/them a new loving home, or, as in the case of Home for Life Animal Shelter near Star Prairie, Wisconsin, provide a home there for the rest of their lives (see sidebar). Do not leave their fates to chance. Your peace of mind regarding their future will lessen your and/or your family's worries at a deeply trying time of grief.

Christopher J. Burns, an estate-planning attorney at Henson & Efron, P.A., advised in his LIFE: PLANNING column in *Minnesota Good Age* (August 2008) to check your state's laws regarding trusts benefitting pets. For instance, New York and a number of other states allow these; my state, Minnesota, does not. His clients who have wished to plan for their pets' future have generally followed one of the following four options:

1) They made an outright gift of the pet to a child, friend, or other loved one;

2) They made a gift of the pet, together with a gift of cash, to a child, friend, or other loved one;

3) They created a trust for a "custodian" of their pet(s); or

4) They made a gift of the pet to a "no-kill" animal shelter or similar organization. (For a comprehensive list of no-kill shelters, go to the Resources section of this book.)

Burns says some of his clients who leave their pets to a friend or neighbor choose to include a monetary gift in their wills so as to avoid creating for that person an undue burden of caring for their pet without the funds to do so. The amount they leave, he explains, "often depends on the type of animal and its historic needs and projected future needs. Some clients I have worked with have consulted with their veterinarian to determine an appropriate amount for what might be the future care needs for their dog, cat, or other pet. For clients with horses and more expensive animals, the gift might be rather large, but in my experience, clients with dogs, cats, and similar common household pets have left a separate gift between a few thousand dollars and $50,000."

Still others of his clients have money set aside for their companion animal in a trust-like entity. In these instances, he says he prepares a "trust named for the benefit of their pet with a trustee and a 'custodian' or caretaker for the pet. The custodian has the legal right to request money, and the trust specifies the client's hope that those funds be used by the custodian for the benefit of their pet."

Whether you go a formal route and use an estate planner or simply write out your wishes and have them witnessed and keep them with your important papers, the vital thing is that you do take steps to secure your pet's future.

The Home For Life® Vision

http://www.homeforlife.org/vision.htm

Home For Life® is an expression of a new kind of animal shelter—the long-term animal sanctuary. We provide animals with loving care, a nurturing environment that is safe and stable, a place to belong ... a home for life.

We provide lifetime care for cats and dogs with special needs who cannot find a home but who can still lead a quality life.

Most shelters offer two options for animals: adoption or euthanasia. A typical family home is not appropriate for every animal. Those who are old or who have disabilities, health, or temperament problems may do better in another setting. Home For Life® believes that these special animals deserve an alternative that will meet their needs. Hence, we created "Door Number Three." The Home for Life® animals enjoy a quality life, where they can be themselves, run and play, and be loved and cherished for as long as they live.

What Happens Behind Animal Shelter Doors

In an impassioned letter written by an anonymous animal shelter manager, we are offered these sobering, tragic facts:

- **There is a ninety-percent chance the animal you turn in to a shelter will not walk out alive.** "Purebred or not! About fifty percent of all the dogs that are 'owner surrenders' or 'strays' that come into my shelter are purebred dogs."

- **"Odds are your pet won't get adopted. . . .** Your pet has seventy-two hours to find a new family from the time you drop it off. Sometimes a little longer if the shelter isn't full and your dog manages to stay completely healthy. If it sniffles, it dies."

- **If your dog is big, black, or any of the "bully" breeds, (pit bulls, rotties, mastiffs, etc.) "It's pretty much dead when you walked it through the front door.** Those dogs just don't get adopted."

She closes the letter by saying, "I hate my job. I hate that it exists.... Between 9 MILLION and 11 MILLION animals die every year in shelters, and only you can stop it. My point to all of this: **DON'T BREED OR BUY [FROM PUPPY MILLS/PET STORES] WHILE SHELTER PETS DIE!** PLEASE PRAY FOR THE STRAYS ABANDONED BY PEOPLE AROUND THE WORLD; AND PRAY FOR THOSE PRECIOUS FUR BABIES LEFT IN SHELTERS ACROSS THE COUNTRY BECAUSE THEY ARE NO LONGER WANTED."

Musings on Terminology
by Corene Johnston

Hello,

I'm a nurse practitioner currently doing some online coursework to be certified as a grief counselor. I read about your plan to write a book about pet loss and agree wholeheartedly about the need for such. I'm gonna tell you about a couple of my "pet" peeves, though.

First is the use of the term "pet." That indicates a hierarchical relationship in which one member (always the human) is superior, the other (always the animal) subordinate. As one in whose kitchen a pygmy goat is presently napping by the stove, I want to tell you that my critter roommates—big, sweet black dog Charley; four wise and complex cats; Adelina the rescued goat; and a yardful of chickens—are often my teachers. They all learn to understand "human" so much faster than we learn to speak "canine" or "caprine" [goat]. I'd love to see our culture moving away from the "pet" image and terminology of interspecies relationships and toward the "companion" concept.

I also bristle when I hear people refer to themselves as "Momma" or "Daddy" to their furred or feathered "kids." I'll tell you what— I'm not the mother of a dog, cat, or goat! And except when they are puppies, kittens, or kids, they are not children. Again the terminology implies a hierarchical relationship, rather than one of equals. These guys are full-fledged, adult members of their species, deserving of the appropriate respect.

My Counterpoint

Hello Corene,

Thanks much for your input! I do address the "pet" issue in my book, but as I am including people's stories in their own words, I cannot control how they themselves viewed their companion animals, nor can I dictate how they grieve their passing. For instance, if they feel like they've lost a child when a companion animal dies, that's their right.

I do appreciate you bringing up your views on the "children" title aspect, too. However, I don't necessarily agree that viewing them as children is inherently a "power-over" stance. Even adult human children will always be seen as beloved, cherished, and ones to be cared for by most parents, particularly mothers whose maternal instinct thrives long past their kids' age of majority.

I think it more conveys the deep heart connection many people feel toward the animals in their lives. To say they are your children often implies they are in the person's heart in an indelible way. And, until these domesticated animals develop opposable thumbs and can open their own food cans/doors and clean their own litter boxes, kennels, or cages and thus be totally independent, we ARE responsible for their care and well-being. (One could take this to a ridiculous extreme and accuse the animals of viewing us as their slaves or servants. That'd be just as hierarchical, right?)

How we refer to companion animals may indicate some people's less-than-equals viewpoints, to be sure, but for a great many of us, it doesn't mean we don't inherently respect their uniqueness, importance, and/or gifts they bring us. If anything, I, for instance, elevate animals above most humans because of their ability to unconditionally love and their lack of the dark motives of some people.

Best,
Sid Korpi

When the Companion Animal Is Not and Never Should Be a Pet

There are innumerable animals that Nature has not intended for domestication. Case in point, the "pet" baby alligator my own mother, as a young girl, used to let sleep under her hair and across her shoulders, until, of course, it grew, and her father flushed it down the toilet, thus breaking his daughter's heart—and helping to feed that unfortunate urban legend about giant sewer-dwelling 'gators, too.

That does not mean, however, these creatures cannot be described aptly as "companions" to us humans in a very meaningful sense when treated with their deserved reverence and respect for their inherent wildness. Unforgettable lessons in forgiveness, trust, and living in the joyous moment that only animals can teach are poignantly illustrated by my friend Susan Timmerman in her story of Meme, the Bengal tiger that was rescued by Tammy Quist and the wonderful staff of The Wildcat Sanctuary in Sandstone, Minnesota.* (See sidebar after this submitted story.)

SUBMITTED STORY

It's All About Meme
by Susan Timmerman of Minneapolis, Minnesota

This tiger I knew, Meme, came to The Wildcat Sanctuary on a sultry June day in 2001. For over twenty years, she'd lived as an indentured servant, producing litter after litter until her body was now ravaged and weak. Her home for all those years had been a small ten-by-ten-foot dark shed filled with waste and carcasses over a foot deep. We estimated that in those twenty years she could have mothered over 100 cubs—all sold in the pet market by her owner/breeder. No one, including our resident vet, expected her to live long, so transporting her across the country to another sanctuary was out of the question. We had to make quick accommodations for what we thought would be a temporary resident.

Within her small, dark, and warped world, Meme never experienced the warmth of sunshine on her fur or the feel of earth beneath her feet. Now, at the Sanctuary, there were many "firsts" to experience: a fresh and constant source of untainted food; a clean drinking bowl; a den with straw to sleep on — instead of a pile of bones; and a spacious enclosure in which she would soon discover a whole new world with sky and trees and grass and birds and kind people with gentle voices. Basking in the sun, high above the ground on her new "throne," soon became a favorite passtime. From here, she could watch over the entire sanctuary, where she soon became either the envy or fear of all the other residents.

In July of her first year with us, we installed a twelve-foot-diameter, two-foot-deep galvanized watering tank and filled it with water. In nature, she would have visited a local watering hole regularly for a cool swim on a hot summer day. Meme didn't know what to do with this huge "drinking bowl." It took thirty minutes for her to realize that she could actually climb in and submerse herself in the cool waters. If a tiger can get "pruney" toes, she definitely had them that day. We watched for hours as she jumped in and out of the pool and flew around the enclosure like a young dog unleashed for the first time.

Each day, each month, each year that passed, we all marveled that she was alive, and we watched how she had mastered the "joy of being." The injustices of her prior life faded away as she exuded the epitome of forgiveness for everyone to observe. She had an air of dignity about her in the purest and most deserving way. She knew she was the queen of the sanctuary and we were all her subjects. Feeding time became a ritual where her highness would chuff from across the way, announcing that "Yes, I will dine tonight." Each specially cut piece was handfed with tongs, one at a time, through her food opening. She would take each piece with such gentleness and care. A connection was made between her and her feeder—trust now lived on both sides of the fence.

For over four years, our darling queen reigned in pure bliss. In the wild, she would have died of natural causes by the age of fifteen years. Now, well over twenty-six and riddled with cancer, we knew that her

time was near. We got the
call the first day of March
2006 at 8:00 p.m. that her
health was rapidly declining.
Sanctuary vets came to the
conclusion that the time had
come. When we got there, we
knew it was true. Her breathing labored, her eyes unfo-
cused, she laid in an
unnatural position for a
queen. I held her tail as we
gave her the last gift we could
offer—the gift of peace and
freedom. She left our lives as

Meme

quickly as she came, but I felt confident that we have vindicated the
wrongs [done to her] and shown her the compassion she so deserved.
I kissed her good-bye and thanked her for coming into our lives. For
two days after her passing I could still smell her sweet, peppery musk.
She had gone on now to reign over yet another kingdom and here I
am, the lucky one, blessed with precious memories and the honor of
telling her story for the rest of my life. The story begins with "This
tiger I knew …"

*ADDENDUM—A word from The Wildcat Sanctuary (excerpted,
with permission, from their website):

The Wildcat Sanctuary (TWS) is a 501(c)3 nonprofit, no-kill rescue
facility located in Sandstone, Minnesota. TWS provides for the humane rescue and sheltering of unwanted, mistreated, and neglected
privately owned wildcats that pose a risk to public safety.

At TWS, animals are never bought, sold, bred, traded, or mistreated in any way. Each resident is given every opportunity to behave
naturally in a wonderfully humane environment for life.

Hundreds to thousands of exotic cats are sold to roadside zoos and
to individuals as pets. A surprising number of people are buying these

wild animals as cubs, without understanding the difficulties involved in caring for and containing them properly as they mature into adults. The results can be tragic for the owner, the public, and the animal. The exotic pet trade causes more suffering for big cats than poaching and loss of habitat combined.

The captive wildcat crisis is no secret. It is in the news almost weekly. In Illinois, a man was mauled to death by two tigers he kept in his backyard. A "pet" leopard attacked a woman in Louisiana. In North Carolina, a ten-year-old boy was killed by his aunt's tiger, which pulled the boy under a fence and into its cage. Near Little Falls, Minnesota, ten-year-old Russell Lala fought for his life after being attacked by a lion and tiger. The boy's spinal cord was severed and the injury left him paralyzed from the neck down. He sustained a brain injury and several facial fractures and is dependent upon a respirator.

The Humane Society of the United States estimates there are as many as 10,000 large wildcats in private ownership across this country. Ron Tilson, conservation director for the Minnesota Zoo, states unequivocally that there are more tigers in backyards across the U.S. than in all of the zoos put together.

In a CNN report, Humane Society President Wayne Pacelle said, "The exotic animal trade is second only to the drug trade in raw dollars. It's literally billions of dollars exchanged in the exotic animal trade." On Internet sites you can point, click, and buy lions and tigers. The motive is profit. Unfortunately, in the end it is the cats who pay the highest price. They often live in cramped, filthy conditions. Many are fed improperly and receive no veterinary care. And most pose a very real threat to public safety.

As much-needed legislation is passed and greater control is brought to the largely unregulated practice of importing, breeding, buying, and selling wild animals as pets, there are likely to be confiscated or abandoned exotic animals in increasing numbers. Critical to this will be the provision of accredited and secure facilities like The Wildcat Sanctuary to provide appropriate lifelong care for all these animals.

For further information or to offer your much-needed support, go to www.wildcatsanctuary.org.

Animals as Teachers

I look around at my slumbering trio of West Highland white terriers: Mortimer snoozes under my desk, cushioned no doubt by the dust bunnies there (they're not actual pets, mind you); Blanche is sacked out on my lap, putting my leg to sleep; and Keely, our newly adopted puppy, is happily chasing squirrels in her dreams.

To me, this is absolute bliss. Being an unabashed animal lover, my seven companion animals (three dogs, two cats, and two finches) bring an effortless fullness to my existence no human relationship can (though my hubby magnanimously accepts that he ranks a close second in my heart).

But, lurking just behind the heart-swell of love I feel for these four-legged children of mine is that chilling reminder that they won't be with me forever, no matter how devoted I am to them or they to me, no matter how great my "pet debt" at the vet's office. For instance, my sweet fella Mortimer's degenerative arthritis, progressive deafness, and cataracts are daily reminders that he won't live forever. But at least thunderstorms have lost much of their power to frighten him because he seldom hears them anymore. That's a small blessing.

Philosophically, I can and do accept this as the necessary balancing act of the Universe, the circle of life. What's more, I do believe that all souls live on in another form after their corporeal experience of life on Earth, so they're not really "gone" other than physically. But, as is human nature, there will always be a primal part of me that tortures myself by fast-forwarding to the endings, the inevitable loss, thinking, I suppose, that I'll hurt less if I'm prepared through much mental rehearsal. And there may be a bit of truth to that.

However, if I let it, that dread can take on a life of its own, siphoning off much of my joy as I look at these pleasantly pooped-out pooches and worry

Mortimer, sacked out

about the time when they must leave me— or I them.

Keely, Blanche, & Xander

It's when we are most fearful of unwelcome change that we must attend most closely to the lessons our beloved animal companions have to teach us. We all need reminders from time to time that in order to be our happiest, most fearless, and most content, we have to try to live a little more like animals—and, no, I don't mean excavating buried treasure from the cat's litter box for a snack. Our animals / teachers show us the value of living our lives in the moment.

When I feel my worry wart-ism growing, I remember the poignant message in Gary Larsen's charming "Far Side" cartoon depicting an excitedly happy mutt in front of a page-a-day calendar for dogs, each page reading "Now."

Fear is inextricably linked to thoughts of a future we cannot control. Guilt is attached to a past we cannot alter. Now is all we have. Like our very own "Doggy Lamas," animals are master teachers of that philosophy.

Celebrate Them While They're with Us!

As our companions age, slow down, or face health problems, it can be extremely difficult not to focus on the ever-shortening span of time we have ahead of us to share with them. But such is truly the path of misery. Better to focus on each moment we spend mutually adoring each other. In other words, find some small way to celebrate every day you have with your beloved pet. Reach out to your fellow-animal-lover friends to help you if you'd like.

Celebrating Simon

by Lisa and Adam Mauer-Elliott of Minneapolis, Minnesota

(This was an email sent out to their friends regarding Simon, their greyhound.)

Today is Simon's thirteenth birthday (November 1, 2007). To celebrate the day, we took a lovely walk in the morning sun by the Minnehaha Creek, had some extra treats, and just got back from a wonderful nighttime walk with Simon's very good doggy friend, Milo. We are so grateful for this beauty who's been sharing the better part of eleven years with us—a gift with endless depth and grace. In honor of his birthday, we'd love to gather your words about Simon—how you see him, who he is to you, stories you love, or just a word or two. Thank you for being such an important part of his life and ours.

Giles & Simon

My response:

Simon is stunning.

Simon is gentle.

Simon is a darling.

Simon is photogenic.

Simon is loving.

Simon likes my fraidy-cat Giles … a lot.

Giles even took a liking (of sorts) to this "giant" creature.

That's a miracle in itself.

Happy birthday, beautiful dog!!

Love, Sid, Anthony, Mortimer, Xander, and Giles

Simon

Editor's note: Simon suddenly passed away from heart failure in his human dad's arms in the winter of 2008 at age fourteen. His was such a beautiful presence, much loved by all who met him. He will be greatly missed.

281

Part Six:
The Roles of Philosophy, Religion, and Spirituality in Healing

"Those who believe in an afterlife and [in] being reunited with their loved ones probably find acceptance and peace sooner and more easily [when that loved one dies] than do people without such beliefs.... Like human immortality, animal immortality cannot be proven, but many believe devotedly that it is so."

— Joan Coleman, *Forever Friends*

Speaking for myself, I know I wouldn't have come out on the other side of the maelstrom of loss I experienced were it not for my faith that all those I'd lost in a physical sense were still near me and still exist, albeit in a form that takes a particular kind of openness to access.

I, too, have noticed that people who have a strong sense of spirituality (which may or may not be connected to identification with a particular world religion) have a somewhat smoother time coming to accept death and heal following the loss of a beloved person or pet. The belief that once a being dies it is simply gone and ceases to exist in any form or on any spiritual plane, while a valid choice, may leave one bereft of any comfort that comes from a faith-based (read: not necessarily intellectually sustained) certainty that those we loved and lost are transformed and capable of some sort of continued communication and/or await an eventual reunion with us when we, too, are similarly transformed after death.

There is something uniquely human about wanting and perhaps needing to feel/believe/know there is something larger than ourselves out there that cares for and sustains us in times of sorrow. Whether you're most comfortable envisioning this presence as "God" (straight out of the Old Testament, complete with Michaelangelo's white-haired-man depiction), or you're drawn to the abstract and resonate with the concept of an amorphous loving energy/light that exists within all things, chances are you can heal your heart more quickly if you tap into those beliefs. Perceiving ourselves as absolutely alone in how we feel about losing our beloved companions is bound to re-double the pain we experience in grieving for them.

The following section will give you a wide range of viewpoints regarding issues surrounding death, loss, and the afterlife, both in general and as pertains to companion animals. Consider this a sort of roundtable discussion, without the table. Give each perspective some thought and take from it only what gives you comfort and/or helps you make better sense of your pet's passing. You may find bits and pieces appealing to you, you may choose to disregard a perspective altogether, or you may be so intrigued by a heretofore unexamined school of thought that you investigate it further on your own. As with everything in this book, take what you need and leave the rest.

A Psychological/Philosophical Perspective
from Carl Jung's Interview "Jung Speaks About Death"

Carl Jung, a Swiss psychiatrist and founder of analytical psychology, studied Eastern and Western philosophies, as well as dreams, art, mythology, and religion, to understand the human psyche—also known as the spirit or soul. He explained in an interview (http://www.youtube.com/view_play_list?p=FAE7F234A9D51A24&search _query=Carl+Jung+Interview+Jung+Speaks+About+Death) that death is "largely disregarded by life," saying, "Life behaves as if it were going on." He recommended we anticipate death as simply the "adventure that lies ahead … the next stage of life." It's when we fear death and spend our time looking back that we die before our time.

With this perspective in mind, we can have some control over the amount of suffering to which we will subject ourselves. He said, "When you think a certain way, you may feel considerably better. When you think along the lines of Nature, then you think properly."

Jung believed there are parts of the psyche that are "not confined by space and time," such as dreams or visions of the future. He said the psyche is not under the obligation to exist solely in this plane, leading to his belief in the continuance of life beyond the present time and space.

Below, he describes three types of rebirth:*

1) Metempsychosis — transmigration of souls. The life force lives on through different physical incarnations — human, animal, plant, etc. Individual personality doesn't continue, and past lives aren't recalled. Karma (the Hindu and Buddhist philosophy that states the quality of one's current and future lives is determined by his or her behavior in this and previous lives) accumulated can affect future incarnations.

2) Reincarnation — Continuity of personality with life force that can be accessed by memory. Same ego-form in previous/present life can be recalled.

3) Resurrection — from ancient Egyptian and Christian religions. Egyptians believed in the end of physical life; the astral body functioned only if the physical body remained uncorrupted. Early Christians believed the physical body lives again.

> * This section was excerpted from
> *Pet Loss — A Spiritual Guide*
> by Eleanor L. Harris

"If there are no dogs in Heaven,
then when I die, I want to go where they went."
– Will Rogers

For many, finding evidence in their sacred texts, be it the Bible, Torah, etc. that supports their belief that animals share an afterlife experience is key to their being able to carry on. The following section cites various passages/examples that may prove helpful to those in search of such support.

1) In his book, *All Creatures Do Go to Heaven*, author Bernard J. Coombs makes the biblical-text-supported argument for animals going to Heaven when he quotes Luke 12:7 "And all flesh will see the saving means of God" (New World Translation). "All" is translated in other verses as: every one, every thing, any thing, every creature, whatsoever, every branch, all manner of, and others.

2) In the book of Matthew, verse 29, Jesus says, "Are not two sparrows sold for a cent? And yet not one of them will fall to the ground apart from your Father." Wallace Sife, Ph.D., author of *The Loss of a Pet—A Guide to Coping with the Grieving Process When a Pet Dies* posits with this passage that if a sparrow dies and this is heeded by God, then certainly all other creatures, including our beloved pets, are blessed as well.

3) "For the fate of the sons of men and the fate of beasts is the same; as one dies, so dies the other. They all have the same breath, and a man has no advantage over the beasts; for all is vanity. All go to one place; all are from the dust, and all turn to dust again." Ecclesiastes 3:19–21

4) Thirteenth-century Christian monk St. Francis of Assisi called all living creatures brother and sister because their Source and Creator were the same as his. He preached the word of God to flocks of birds, who, when he asked them to be silent, stopped their singing while he prayed aloud to them. There are many stories of his uncanny way with wild animals and his belief in their souls, attested to by eyewitnesses during his lifetime.

〰 〰 〰
〰 〰 〰

SUBMITTED STORY

Grace

by Alexandra Safchuk of Bethesda, Maryland

I can put words together in a sentence, combine the ingredients for tuna casserole, and plant chrysanthemums in pots, but I cannot make a cat. It takes God to make a cat. God created the animals (including the cats) before he created man (Genesis 1:20–25) and He gave man dominion over them, in fact giving man the opportunity and the obligation to name the animals. It is an honor to name something. When we name our child or

Grace

an animal (or for some of us even our car, uh-hum), we put our mark on them. We show possession, but we also show personalization.

Later in Genesis (6:19–20), God shows His concern for the animals. He asks Noah to preserve the animals, sheltering them in the Ark so that they can continue to survive. Time and time again, we hear how man and animals live in harmony. And today, we harbor some animals so close to us that we call them domesticated. For over seventeen years, we had one of those animals, our cat Grace, who lived with us and helped us to balance our lives, giving us both the opportunity to give and receive affection and an obligation to care for her as she aged and journeyed away from us.

She was a good friend to me and I will miss her, but crushed as I was by her death, I am even more joyful that I had her in my life and that after she came to us as a too-young stray who had been battered and left for dead, she seemed grateful to take up her abode with us and make our couch a depository for her fur.

Daniel in the Lion's Den, St. Seraphim and the bear, St. Kevin and the birds, St. Francis and all manner of animals — there are lots of instances where harmony with animals is blessed by God. And God blessed our life with Grace, for although she had some nasty, unbreakable habits and could charm the milk right out of your cereal bowl with that cute way that she would put her paw on the edge, it is good to have known her, and we are more patient for it. And having known Grace and been saddened by her death, I feel more able to understand this incredible bond we all develop with our animals. We name them and care for them, but they enrich us. Their death is yet another time when we must give up, trusting God that He will continue to care for these precious creatures.

SUBMITTED STORY

Brittany
by Beverley J. Matthie

Through the years, I discovered many scripture verses that proclaimed that "all creation" will be with the Lord, especially in the resurrection chapter in Corinthians, wherein it mentions the flesh of humans, fish, land animals, etc. I needed to know she was with the Lord and prayed deeply about it. One night, when I was in bed, not asleep, but lying on my back, grieving for my cat Brittany, she appeared right above me. She looked, with her gold eyes, deep into my eyes, with a searching, intent look. I could make out her colour (a tabby), her whiskers, and the fact that she was now healthy and youthful in appearance. I truly felt that God sent her to let me know that she was safe and happy with Him. After that, I slowly began to heal.

A Prayer for Animals
Hear our humble prayer, O God,
For our friends the animals,
Especially for animals who are suffering,
For any that are hunted or lost or deserted or
Frightened or hungry,
For all that must be put to death.
We entreat for them all Thy mercy and pity,
And for those who deal with them we ask
A heart of compassion and gentle hands and kindly words.
Make us, ourselves, to be true friends to animals,
And so to share the blessings of the merciful.
– Albert Schweitzer

Sunday, 18 September, 2005 – www.worldfaiths.org

In a spirit of reverence for what American Unitarian Universalists call "the interdependent web of all existence of which we are a part" and British Unitarians affirm as "respect for all creation," Golders Green Unitarians hosted on 18 September what World Congress of Faiths (WCF) President Rev. Dr. Marcus Braybrooke called "a beautiful and inspiring occasion": the second **WCF Interfaith Celebration of Animals.**

A packed meeting house saw Jackie Ballard, director general of the RSPCA, light a candle for all the world's animals and heard adherents of the major religious traditions, Brahmo Samaj, Buddhist, Christian, Hindu, Jain, Jewish, Muslim, and Sikh, affirm the central importance of compassion for all sentient beings and respect for the living Earth, our common home.

Representatives of leading animal welfare organisations, including the RSPCA, IFAW, International Primate Protection League, and Compassion in World Farming, affirmed the importance of their vital work in raising consciousness and helping prevent the unnecessary suffering of billions of vulnerable nonhuman animals at our mercy. In a practical expression of compassion, over £300 was donated for humane medical research to help save human and animal lives.

Understanding Other Spiritual Perspectives

The human/animal relationship is noted to varying degrees in many, if not all, world religions. The following is a quick snapshot of some of the ways animals are regarded in a wide array of religions.

Native American Perspectives

"If all the beasts were gone, man would die from loneliness of the spirit, for whatever happens to the beast happens to man. All things are connected. Whatever befalls the Earth befalls the son of Earth."

–Chief Seattle

"There are different levels of consciousness with which we have no contact. The unconscious is one. Consciousness is found in animals, plants, and everything in nature. We must learn to recognize these consciousnesses and to honor them."   — Mad Bear of the Iroquois

"All animals are expressions of the Great Creator. Would He limit them? Would He only exist in man?"   — Louis Flying Cloud

Unitarian-Universalist Perspective*

"We affirm the inherent worth and dignity of every person, and the interdependent web of existence of which we are a part ... [When someone loses a pet] we can participate in acknowledging the reality of the loss, affirming the feelings of bereavement, of emptiness, in remembering the happy moments, and in learning to say goodbye. Bless and honor our animal brothers and sisters."

— Rev. Dr. Tracy Robinson
Harris Unitarian Universalist Community Church
New York

Zen Buddhist Perspective*

"Impermanence is a natural law or truth of the Universe. Animals accept these changes. Suffering comes through attachment. When grief arises, if we can recognize it in our mind, then when the crushing wave of feeling has eased, we can let it go and return to the present moment — the place where our own life is taking place.

Bear witness to feelings without being overwhelmed by them. With time, they will soften and fade. It creates unnecessary misery to hold too tightly to the memory or feeling.... In holding on to feelings of sadness, we trap both them and ourselves

Let go of the deceased so they can be free in death. Let go of our feelings of loss so we can be free in life."

— Geoffrey Shurgen Arnold
Zen Mountain Monastery
Mount Tremper, New York

The Wiccan Perspective*

"In religions such as Wicca, rituals bid farewell, give blessings, and assist deceased loved ones to the spiritual plane.... The beauty of pagan spirituality is that it allows people to discuss, study, and recognize death as a natural stage of life. Religions such as Wicca teach the dark side of the Goddess, the Crone, who is not dark as in evil, but is considered dark in her reign of death and the gift of rebirth.... In Wicca, the soul is ageless and nonphysical; it contains the essence of the Gods and Goddesses, the Creator....The soul returns for renewal and revitalization to the Divine Source from which it originated."

* These sections were excerpted from
Pet Loss—A Spiritual Guide
by Eleanor L. Harris

Islamic/Moslem (Muslim) Perspectives

"Islam, to its credit, respects the souls of all living things. But you will never see a pet in the home of a fundamentalist. The Koran, like the Old Testament, makes no reference at all to pets. A strong general concern for the humane treatment of all animals is emphasized instead."

−Wallace Sife, Ph.D.,
*The Loss of a Pet—A Guide to Coping
with the Grieving Process When a Pet Dies*

"The animals are a people like ourselves and shall, when released from earthly pain, share the joys of Heaven with man."

−Mohammed, the Moslem prophet

Religious Leaders' Viewpoints

In writing this book, I invited learned representatives of about a dozen world religions to share their beliefs in response to the following survey questions:

1) How would you summarize your faith's formal teachings about the relationship/bond between human beings and companion animals?

2) Does your religious/spiritual belief system account for animals and humans each having souls/energy that exist even after physical death?

3) When counseling bereaved parishioners/members during their grieving process, what words of wisdom or comfort would you give them if the loss were of a human being?

4) How would that be different if they were grieving the loss of a companion animal?

5) Have you ever performed (or would you ever consider performing) a private memorial service for a pet?

6) If so, what might that service entail? If not, why would that be unacceptable to you/your faith community?

Any further observations you'd care to include may be stated here.

I received the following three responses from leaders of Christian, Jewish, and Eckankar faiths. My eternal gratitude is given to each of these spiritual teachers for taking the time to share their perspectives with all of us. While not every member of a particular religion may agree with their portrayal of their respective scriptures—that would be impossible—every attempt was made to be true to the teachings of their faith. Their candid answers are presented here with the aforementioned survey questions removed. They are listed in the order in which their responses were received.

The Christian Perspective

by Pastor Dale Christiansen, Crane Community Chapel
Austin, Minnesota

We see in the Bible that God created all the animals and brought them to Adam and Eve, giving them stewardship over these fellow inhabitants of this planet. There was to be some kind of mutual benefit to their living together.

The Bible doesn't seem to refer to animals having an afterlife, but its silence does not rule out that possibility. However, mankind is unique in the creation account in that it is only into humanity that God breathes in "the breath of life."

We have the Bible's clear assurance that Jesus gives eternal life to those who trust in Him. "He who has the Son has life" (1 John 5:12), and so, when we grieve over the loss of a loved one, it is the sorrow of being apart for the remainder of our earthly life, not forever.

Animals matter to God and to us, but the Bible does not give us the same assurance that we will be reunited with them as we expect to be with our loved ones. I certainly do not minimize the pain of losing a beloved pet, but I have no Scriptural grounds for promising someone that their pet will someday be with them again, though that could happen. It fits all that we know of the heart of God to believe that He means only to bring us good, and He would only be pleased that we value the gift of a pet that He has given. But I can't say for sure whether or not that pet will be in Heaven.

[Regarding performing a memorial service for a companion animal that has passed,] I think I would do something privately with the person/family.

I do think it honors God as our Creator and Father when we treasure the pets He has provided for us. They bring us gladness and comfort in unique ways and sometimes meet needs that no one else does. As with anything God gives, we must beware of taking pets beyond what God intends; for example, perhaps in elevating them to the same importance and giving them the same devotion as we do to humans. With that caution established, [I would] encourage people to love deeply and to enjoy fully the unique gifts God gives. When we do, it will be a profound heartache to lose that gift and we can expect the One who first provided this gift to share in our pain and to comfort us in it.

The Jewish Perspective
by Rabbi Avraham Ettedgui, Sharei Chesed Congregation, Minnetonka, Minnesota

The Torah teaches us to be kind to the animals. In fact, one is not supposed to sit to dinner until he [or] she had fed his [or] her animals first.

There is a sage in the Talmud that says, "Who knows whose soul is more elevated? The soul of the animal might have better in the world to come than the soul of humans."

Obviously, this is not the opinion of the majority, but it goes to show that our sages had a tremendous respect for the animals.

We always speak of the memories left behind, of our gratitude for having known that person even for a brief period, and how the bonds of love will always be there.

We have a strong empathy for people who have lost a companion animal, especially one that has been with the individual or family for a long time. The loss is real, and we try to give words of comfort to that person.

I have not and I probably would not [perform a service for a pet's passing]. My emphasis would be to comfort the person rather than pray for the soul of the animal. Humans need memorial services and the prayers for their souls, as they stand in judgment for their actions in this world. I don't believe that animals will be called to account for their behavior in this world.

The loss of a pet is a real trauma to the family and especially to young children. Every situation is different and the rabbi/clergy need to find a way to bring comfort for the loss.

The Eckankar Perspective

by Linda C. Anderson, Member of ECK Clergy
Eckankar World Headquarters, Chanhassen, Minnesota

Sri Harold Klemp, the spiritual leader of Eckankar, writes in his book *Animals Are Soul Too!* (Eckankar, 2005): "Animals are Soul, too. Every variety of pet—cat, dog, or whatever—is an embodiment of Soul, just like you and me.

"Each is individual and each can act as a channel or instrument for divine love…. Our relationship with animals is often defined by what we most need to learn. Pets can teach us a great many things—patience, flexibility, how to live in the moment, how to laugh at ourselves. But most of all they can teach us how to give and receive unconditional love."

This statement by Sri Harold is right in line with my personal experiences and beliefs. I have observed that animals are great teachers, and I'm always learning more about God's unconditional love from them.

In *Animals Are Soul Too!* Sri Harold says, "Many people love their pets very much and feel a deep sense of loss when they pass over. And they often worry, 'Is that the end? Does my dear friend simply cease to be?'

"Soul is eternal. Soul lives on in the next world, just as It did in this one."

There are many aspects of the Eckankar teachings that bring comfort to grieving people. Below are a few of them.

- You will meet loved ones on the other side so there is no need to fear death.

- Even though you know that it's only the physical body that is gone and the Soul lives on and continues to love, it's natural to feel pain at the loss and to miss loved ones who have passed into the other worlds.

- The love you and this person have for each other endures, and eventually you must let yourself heal. Tears can help the healing.

- One way to move through a sorrowful time of grieving is to let your love flow into giving a gift of love to others. Offering to assist someone in need or volunteering for a charity takes you out of your own pain and gives you time to heal.

The words of comfort would be similar [if they were grieving the loss of a companion animal]. The bond of love between the person and the pet will endure. It's natural to grieve the loss of someone who has been important to you. And volunteering to help animals or people offers a pathway and time for healing to occur.

Sri Harold also mentions in *Animals Are Soul Too!* about reincarnation as another aspect of Soul's eternal nature that can bring comfort to those who grieve the loss of a pet or other loved one. He writes about animals as Soul reincarnating:

"And if it is right for that Soul, It can come back to Earth in another body, sometimes to the same family It was with before."

Eckankar doesn't have a pet memorial service, so I couldn't perform one officially as a member of the ECK clergy. Privately, though, I can join with friends and family members who want to honor the memory of a pet with a service that is not an Eckankar ceremony.

In a private remembrance to honor the life and passing of a pet it would be helpful to sing the holy name for God taught in Eckankar, which is HU (pronounced like the word hue). In his 2007 talk at the ECK Springtime Seminar, Sri Harold said, "HU opens the heart to healing."

In *Animals Are Soul Too!* he states, "Some human beings think animals are so low on the scale of life that they could not possibly provide a suitable embodiment for Soul. But in Eckankar we know that animals are Soul.

"And since they are Soul, they too need the love that HU can bring."

Animals are here to gain spiritual experience, too. When a pet comes into a home, the people and the animal help each grow in their ability to give and receive love. The Holy Spirit will often use animals as vehicles for us to learn more about ourselves or life and to touch our hearts with God's love.

Part Seven
Moving On After Loss

Many people I interviewed on the topic maintained that it was awareness of the anguish that follows experiencing the shattering loss of so deep a loving relationship that prevented them from getting another pet. "Losing my pet broke my heart. I never want to go through that kind of pain again," was a common sentiment.

While I thoroughly understand the impulse to avoid undergoing this devastating pain a second, third, fourth … time, I really don't think hermetically sealing our hearts was what our dear companions wanted for us when they died. Mourning following a loss is inevitable, appropriate, even necessary, but suffering interminable misery is a choice we make.

Though having differing approaches to the topic of an afterlife, the numerous animal communicators I contacted agreed on one thing: Animals do not fear death as we humans do. But they do feel both their own physical pain and their human companions' subsequent emotional fears and sorrow. Some companion animals may will themselves to stay alive longer solely for their human's sake, masking their own suffering in order to make us happy, until they just can no longer stay within their physical bodies. Oftentimes, this requires we make the selfless decision to put the dear ones to sleep, sparing our closest friends more pain because they cannot take their own lives to end their suffering.

Once freed of their own pain, they'd certainly wish the same for the hearts of their cherished human caregivers. They'd recognize our need for the healing effects of love — love stemming from the memory that will never leave us of the departed pet who is now at peace, as well as love for and from the next in a possibly long line of animal companions that are meant to enter our lives.

As William Sife writes in *The Loss of a Pet — A Guide to Coping with the Grieving Process When a Pet Dies*, "If your pet could send you a message, it would tell you to take better care of yourself since he or she is not there any longer to protect you."

Animals also lack the pettier human frailties. They carry no resentments or grudges against those who have loved them well. They cannot revel in another's suffering, as some of our fellow bipeds can. So, once we have processed our grief and are emotionally ready to move on, we are actually honoring our departed pet's wish for us to be happy, not "betraying their memory" or "replacing them" as so many of us fear. We are simply fulfilling one of our purposes in this life—allowing love to flow fully through us to our fellow beings.

Sometimes, daring to risk again brings with it unexpected healing for us. Such was the case with my beautiful cat Xander.

Xander—In Sickness and In Health

In the mid-1990s, my two fifteen-year-old Siamese cats, Dudley and Genevieve, had both passed away within months of each other. Then came the news that my mother had colon cancer, which was surgically removed only to be replaced by inoperable lung cancer a year later. All around me, those I loved so dearly were wasting away. (My subconscious mind apparently equated "skinny" with "dying" so, subsequently, I packed on the pounds around then, seeking to protect myself.)

Many months after my previous cats' passing, when we had found and adopted Giles (see his story in the Animals and the Afterlife section), I continued to search for his soon-to-be housemate Xander. (As I've said, I often know my pets' names before I meet them in the flesh.) We went to numerous pet-adoption events, but although every cat we saw was lovely and most assuredly lovable, I kept feeling restrained by the knowledge that none of them was Xander.

One afternoon, my first husband and I had gone to a Pet Haven cat-adoption event at a local veterinarian's clinic. Once again, I was feeling downhearted because I still hadn't made the right connection with any of the cats, and we were about to leave when something made me turn around and notice a small green cat carrier set well behind the woman volunteer. It was sideways to me, so I couldn't even tell if there was a cat inside or not, but something made me say, "Who's in that carrier?"

"Oh, that's a little girl we just took in. She's too sick to be out for adoption just now," the woman answered.

Something compelled me to press on. "Could I see her, please?"

The volunteer gingerly lifted a small furry ball of what we all supposed was a young adult tabby cat.

I took this full-grown creature into my arms and was appalled to find she'd been starved to the point of emaciation, every rib and vertebrae articulated. She weighed, at most, four pounds. Her ears were scratched bald due to a persistent mite infection. All in all, she wasn't the most attractive feline I'd ever seen. Part of me shuddered, reminded of my recently lost cats' bony bodies before they died.

What came out of my mouth then, unbidden by my brain, was my Spirit Guides' explanation of why I had to adopt this poor kitty: *"I have to prove to myself that something can get well."*

I knew I'd found my Xander.

The foster mom said she'd have to keep this little girl for another week while she was being treated for her infection. I gave her our money and took her number, vowing to call and check on her every night, which I did.

When I finally brought her home and opened the cat carrier, I fleetingly worried about all these new animals accepting one another. Giles and Ludwig, my male Westie, were relatively new adoptees, and my female Westie, Tuppence, was the longtime queen of the household.

But I needn't have worried. After thirty seconds of cautious sniffing, everyone was getting along like old friends. Once again, they'd simply "recognized" each other's spirits and harmoniously formed a new family.

Xander did, indeed, get well. She has grown into a beautiful little lady, maintaining a healthy eight pounds weight and sporting a luxurious pelt. She enjoys sleeping on top of the birds' cage and is quite happy to have become Daddy's Girl.

Ludwig & Tuppence greet their new housemate, Xander

Giles & Xander share a cat nap

"He's mine—all mine!" Xander seems to say of her human daddy

~~~ ~~~ ~~~
~~~ ~~~ ~~~

Sometimes we open our hearts and homes for the sake of our other companion animals' happiness and longevity and find the fresh presence of yet a new creature to love lengthens, deepens, and broadens our own as well. Enter our most recent addition to our very-full family, Keely.

Keely's Story–The Joy Continues

"Talk me out of this!" I begged my husband as we looked at the Pet Haven website photo of a six-month-old Westie puppy. "We already have six pets—you have to talk me out of this!"

His response: "Do you want help with the application?"

My *War and Peace*-length paperwork, illustrating that ours is a Westie-Wise Household (we're on numbers three and four), apparently won the hearts (or at least numbed the minds) of the volunteers in charge of screening adoptive parents because, though they said they'd been drowning in applications for this little girl, then named Kiwi, we and one other family were the only ones to make the cut.

Now fully committed, I admit I stacked the deck for the home visit, presenting my sister Diane (whose yard happens to be Puppy Club Med and who baby-sits our dogs when we have to be out of town) and our friend Cathy Menard, owner of The Urban Dog, a dog-walking/pet-sitting business, who often tends to our four-legged kids, as members of the "village that would be raising this dog-child."

But the real ace in the hole was Blanche, our then nearly three-year-old rescued Westie. She was the actual impetus for our getting another dog because her older brother, Mortimer (our North Dakotan rescued Westie), was ten-ish at the time and had arthritis, so his play-time was pretty limited, and Blanche has a ton of puppy still in her that was going to waste. She and Keely (the pup's new moniker, named for jazz vocalist Keely Smith) raced around the house like Keystone Cops, sliding into walls as they rounded corners because they couldn't stop on the wooden floors. They'd made their choice to be together quite clear.

Taking the pup to visit the other runner-up household just after ours supported the decision, as their older dog wanted nothing to do with her.

From the moment we picked up Keely from her foster mom, Robin, our three dogs were mellow and perfectly adjusted to one another—when they weren't busy wrestling and playing their hearts out, that is.

(See all our babies in action on Keely's first day with us on YouTube: http://www.youtube.com/watch?v=241S2n8wj5w).

Again, it was as though they were being reunited rather than newly introduced. Even our eleven-year-old cats, Giles and Xander, accepted Keely immediately. It feels as though the family became truly complete once this bundle of white light and energy joined us.

At the time, this then-teething maniac ate everything—from buried treasure in the cat box to my yet-to-bloom bulbs in the garden to the trunk of our thirty-foot-tall tree.

And although Keely was wily enough to know to "fake" going potty outside to get a treat, housetraining was still a challenge. When she first made it forty-eight hours without an indoor accident, we thought of naming a national holiday to commemorate the milestone.

The joy with this darling imp continues as she employs her unusual habit of licking walls, floors, cabinets, and so on. We often say to her things like, "How was that floorboard, Keely?" expecting her to answer, "Tastes like porch."

Keely at six months

Epilogue—Courtesy of a Dear, Dear Dog

As you might imagine, the process of writing, researching, and editing stories for this book has been, to say the least, emotionally taxing at times. In the saddest bit of irony I've ever known, I suddenly lost my precious Mortimer just as the pages of this pet loss book were being laid out for publication. He'd developed what had seemed a run-of-the-mill eye infection on Monday, June 8, 2009. The infection, however, would not respond to antibiotic treatment and progressed frighteningly fast, rendering him blind and causing him intense pain. By the following Sunday, June 14, we knew we had to end his suffering.

All through the week, I told my boy that, while I would obviously prefer that his medicine work and he be allowed to continue his life with us, if that couldn't happen, if he couldn't be happy and healthy again, it was okay for him to go to the Other Side. Although I knew what agony I'd be facing without him, I couldn't put my needs ahead of his. Knowing his deep devotion to me, I was aware he'd keep fighting to stay here unless I assured him I would be all right and that he shouldn't hang on just for me.

The only uncertain thing for me was wondering about our differing definitions of a happy life. For me, being deaf and blind would be my cue to exit right there. But I realize that dogs are zen masters and he might just accept those limitations as long as he still enjoyed his food, lying in the sun, being stroked and kissed by his human mama, etc. I didn't want to project my ideals on him, but when he awoke shivering uncontrollably on Saturday, I knew he was in pain, which was absolutely unacceptable, and unless a new medication could effect a miracle cure, I'd be having to say goodbye to my darling boy.

I was in the backyard with him, crying softly, when I said, "I wish you'd met your Gamma Lu while she was alive. She'd have loved you so much." I then said aloud to the heavens, "Who's going to meet my Mortimer when he crosses over?"

No sooner had I said this than a beautiful red cardinal swooped in, landed in our tree directly above us, and proceeded to sing his little heart out. "Thank you, Mom!!!" I cried, reassured that my darling boy would be in wonderful, loving hands. Considering all our pet losses over just the last several years, I told her, "You're starting to hog all the best dogs that have ever been, you know!"

That Sunday, I'd received an early-morning call from my friend Liz, who practices animal communication. I'd asked her to check in with my baby so we'd be certain we were doing what he wanted and needed us to do. She got straight to the point, saying, "Sid, how's Mortimer's breathing? Is he panting?" He was, I confirmed, my heart sinking. "Oh, Sweetie, I'm sorry, but he's in a lot of pain. I think it's time to let him go.... He's mostly worried about you."

She suggested I get a second opinion, but I already had that—my own.

My husband and I called a few people we knew loved Mortimer and at least needed to know what would be happening that day so they could send their love and prayers and tell him goodbye in their hearts. To be honest, we needed to hear their comforting words, too.

We tried to explain things to our other pets, as well. Little Keely seemed the most sensitive and sniffed her big brother gently.

Giles showed us life must go on and demanded we feed him.

We settled our baby, Mortimer, on his blanket on my lap in the car and left for the emergency clinic. While he'd been hurting, he'd kept his ears back. Now, his ears were erect and he was alert and appeared happy and calm, glad we'd gotten his message. I sang some old Beatles songs to him, choked with tears, of course, to reenact for us both the trip home from the Jamestown, North Dakota, Humane Society where we'd first met a mere three years and four months before. I knew he couldn't hear me anymore, but I hoped the vibrations from my body as I hugged him would feel comforting.

We were on Highway 62 West, a.k.a. Crosstown, heading to the Eden Prairie Emergency Animal Hospital. The day was beautiful, sunny with fluffy individual clouds overhead. My focus was on my dog, my husband's divided between Mortimer and the road, yet both of us suddenly looked up and to our left and said almost simultaneously, "Do you see that cloud over there? It looks just like a Westie that's facing away from us, looking down the road!"

I squeezed Mortimer tightly and said through a new batch of tears, "See, baby boy, your cloud is ready for you to be our angel!"

Then we turned onto Flying Cloud Drive to reach the clinic. (See my sworn affidavit about this.)

GENERAL AFFIDAVIT
BEFORE NOTARY

I, *C. Sid Korpi* ("Declarant"), am a resident of *Minneapolis*, County of *Hennepin*, State of *Minnesota*, and do hereby certify, swear or affirm, and declare that I am competent to give the following declaration based on my personal knowledge, unless otherwise stated, and that the following facts and things are true and correct to the best of my knowledge (insert facts): *On Sunday, June 14, 2009, my husband, Anthony Kaczor, and I were taking our beloved West Highland white terrier, Mortimer, to the Eden Prairie Emergency Animal Hospital (located adjacent to Flying Cloud Drive) to be put to sleep. Minutes before our arrival, we both happened to look up at the same time & notice a singular, stand-alone cloud formation. This cloud looked exactly like a Westie's head as seen from slightly behind and to the side. It gave the appearance of a dog looking off along its path. We did not have a camera with us, but I am re-creating below exactly what we saw:*

Signature: C. Sid Korpi
Signature of Declarant

State of *MN*
County of *Hennepin*
On *June 16* (date), 20*09*, *Cynthia Lu Korpi* (Declarant) personally came before me and, being duly sworn, did state that he or she is the person described in this document.

Viktoria Zempel
Print or type name of Notary Public

Viktoria Zempel
Signature of Notary Public

VIKTORIA ZEMPEL
NOTARY PUBLIC
MINNESOTA
MY COMMISSION EXPIRES JAN 31, 2012

Mortimer remained calm even before he'd received his sedative. We had the vet tech turn off the harsh overhead lights and put on the X-ray viewing box for subtler illumination. The vet was very compassionate as he administered the final shot. Mortimer was lying on my lap, being petted by his human parents. He had held up his head until the drug took its effect. Then his head gently fell to the blanket, as if a deep sleep had suddenly overcome him.

I remember whispering, in awe over the beauty of his last peaceful moment, "Yes!"—tenderly urging him to go to the light, my mother's waiting arms, Heaven, all of the above.

We got a lovely paw print made of his polar-bear-cub-sized footsie and took a small clipping of the fur at his ear, in memory of his Horatio Hornblower hairstyle when we first picked him up at the shelter. His ashes will be next to Ludwig's and amid all the Westie photos and paraphernalia I keep in my home office. We brought home his blanket to let the other animals get a clear picture of what had happened. Blanche sniffed it, tail wagging happily for her brother.

Giles promptly took a nap on it.

That night, I sent out an announcement of Mortimer's passing to all our friends, family members, and even those fine folks who'd contributed stories to this book. In it, I wrote, "As you may know, I'm in the process of publishing a book I've written called *Good Grief: Finding Peace After Pet Loss*. I believe Mortimer timed his departure from this life precisely so he could give a poignant sense of closure to this book. I'm certainly being compelled to practice all I've "preached" about coping with such loss, and I can promise that what I've learned in researching and writing this book IS helping me and Anthony both stay strong and at peace even as we openly weep over Mortimer's death.

"Please hold our boy and us in your thoughts for a moment, wishing us all gentle passage into the next transformation in our lives."

The following morning, I had to spend three solid hours responding to the hundreds of messages of condolence and support—from people we knew personally, those I knew only via emails and their submitted stories, and from absolute strangers (via a Westie-lovers group that was notified by a friend), all of whom showered us with empathy, sympathy, and loving energy.

I'm sure I nearly short-circuited my keyboard a few times from crying so hard.

I've saved every one of those messages in a file called "Mortimer's Send-off." I told folks this unprecedented outpouring of love and compassion was commensurate with Mortimer's wonderfulness and that it was doing wonders to help our hearts, seeing his passing made so meaningful by all these kind human beings' acknowledgement.

The second day, I was still occasionally doubling over with sobs as I moved through the house with my eyes continually drawn to places he should still be. Though I knew he was all right, living on in another form, I was greedy for him. I wanted my dog and to free him, too.

Just then that canny canine worked a miracle of healing in my heart.

I had walked into my husband's office, which also houses my clothes closet, a dozen or so times since Mortimer had left us. Nothing was out of the ordinary on any of those visits. This time, however, I was overcome by the smell of ... Could it be? ... Oh my God, it was! .... Mortimer's marking!!!

What can I say? He'd had a hard life and sometimes needed to mark in the house to have a sense of security. We accepted that rescued dogs can have issues. We'd just groan and grab the paper towels and odor-eliminator spray.

I checked everywhere in the room to see if there were any fresh urine spots from one of the girls. There was nothing fresh, nothing old, even. The most recent "spritzing" had long since been cleaned up. Yet the pungent odor now accosting my discerning nose was unmistakably Mortimer's signature scent!

I said to him through laughter and grateful tears, "While I can think of a lot of your smells I'd prefer to remember you by, Sweetheart, I have to tell you you are *brilliant!* There's no way I could mistake the fact that you'd come by for a visit. Thank you, thank you, my magnificent marking Mortimer!!!"

My sister appreciated the story when I called and told her. "Isn't it funny how what was the worst of his behaviors is now such a comfort?" she said.

Just hours later, I went back into the office for another sniff. Nothing remained of that pungent "doggy dew." My heart was lightened immeasurably, and I felt I had turned a major corner in my grieving process. Not that I'm finished crying for my loss, not by a long shot, but I had undeniable (by me) evidence that my dear boy is only gone physically. What's more, I can be certain he is receiving the endless waves of love and gratitude I send him, too.

The smell and a huge chunk of anguish disappeared, but what did remain was my certainty that every word I've personally shared in this book is gospel, capital-T True. My Mortimer made sure to lend final credence to the fact that our beloved pets (and people) continue to live on and surround us with their love whenever we need them most. And communications of love work both ways.

If this book has helped you heal in any way, and I sincerely hope it has, whisper a little thank you to Mortimer. His uncannily timed sacrifice was meant to help us all glimpse the eternal nature of the human-animal bond.

Mortimer, honey boy, we will always love you!

Mortimer, with post-nap bed head

Bibliography/Suggested Reading

Anderson, Allen and Linda Anderson. *Angel Animals—Exploring Our Spiritual Connection with Animals.* Plume Penguin Group, 1999. ISBN 0-452-28072-9.

Anderson, Moira, M.Ed. *Coping with Sorrow on the Loss of Your Pet,* 2nd Edition. Alpine Blue Ribbon Books, 1996. ISBN 0-931866-97-9.

Andrews, Ted. *Animal Speak—The Spiritual and Magical Powers of Creatures Great and Small.* Llewellyn Publishing, 2002. ISBN 0-87542-028-1.

Coleman, Joan. *Forever Friends—Resolving Grief After the Loss of a Beloved Animal.* Las Vegas, Nevada: J.C. Tara Enterprises, 1993. ISBN 1-883018-03-X.

Coombs, Bernard J. *All Creatures Do Go to Heaven Especially Pets.* Biblio Books, 2004. ISBN 0-9748524-5-7.

Dahm, Paul C. *The Rainbow Bridge.* Running Tide Press, 1997. ISBN 0-9663022-0-6.

Day, Laura. *Practical Intuition—How to Harness the Power of Your Instinct and Make It Work for You.* Villard Books of Random House, Inc., 1996. ISBN 0 679-44932-9.

Dickinson, Hilary. "Safe Home for Life—A local animal sanctuary gives peace of mind to owners and permanent homes to pets." *Star Tribune,* Monday, February 18, 2008.

Donnell, Christina, Ph.D. *Transcendent Dreaming—Stepping Into Our Human Potential.* Wind of Change Books, 2008. ISBN 978-0-9801810-2-9.

Edward, John. *After Life: Answers from the Other Side.* Hay House, Inc. 2004. ISBN-13: 9781932128086.

Edward, John. *Crossing Over: The Stories Behind the Stories.* Hay House, Inc., 2002. ISBN-13: 9-7819-3212-8000.

Fitzpatrick, Sonya with Patricia Burkhart Smith. *What the Animals Tell Me —Developing Your Innate Telepathic Skills to Understand and Communicate with Your Pets.* Hyperion, 1997. ISBN 0-7868-6259-9.

Fox, Dr. Michael W. Animal Doctor Column: "Grief Over Pets Not 'Psychotic,' Needs New Focus." *Star Tribune*, Saturday, October 6, 2007.

Fox, Dr. Michael W. *Dog Body, Dog Mind—Exploring Your Dog's Consciousness and Total Well-Being.* Lyons Press, 2007. ISBN 1599210452.

Harris, Eleanor L. *Pet Loss—A Spiritual Guide.* Llewellyn Publications, 1997. ISBN 1-56718-347-6.

Katcher, Aaron H. and Alan M. Beck, editors. *New Perspectives on Our Lives with Companion Animals.* University of Pennsylvania Press, 1983. ISBN 0-8122-7877-1.

Kowalski, Gary. *Goodbye, Friend: Healing Wisdom for Anyone Who Has Ever Lost a Pet.* New World Library, 1997. ISBN 1-8834-782-2-7.

Milani, Myrna, D.V.M. *Preparing for the Loss of Your Pet.* Prima Publishing, 1998. ISBN 0-7615-1648-4.

MacNamara, Maureen. "Moving On," Pet Central Column, *Star Tribune*, Saturday, August 2, 2008.

Olson, Marsha. *Dogwood and Catnip—Living Tributes to Pets We Have Loved and Lost.* Fairview Press, 2003. ISBN 1-577-4-913-5.

Rosenbloom, Gail. "Before Grief Goes, Grief Grows," *Star Tribune*, Sunday, September 9, 2007.

Sife, Wallace, Ph.D. *The Loss of a Pet—A Guide to Coping with the Grieving Process When a Pet Dies.* 3rd Edition. Howell Book House, Wiley Publishing, Inc. 2005. ISBN 0-7645-7930-4.

Smith, Jacquelin. *Animal Communication—Our Sacred Connection.* Lakeville, Minnesota: Galde Press, Inc., 2005. ISBN 1-931942-24-2.

Strate, Camille Olivia. *Whispers—Gentle Little Nudges.* 2007. e-book available at http://www.joyzachoice.com/Announcements.html.

Tanner, Wilda B. *The Mystical Magical Marvelous World of Dreams.* Sparrow Hawk Press, 1988. ISBN 0-945027-02-8.

Tellington-Jones, Linda. *Getting in T-Touch with Your Dog–A Gentle Approach to Influencing Behavior, Health, and Performance.* North Pomfret, Vermont: Trafalgar Square Publishing, 2001. ISBN 1-57076-206-6.

Van Praagh, James. *Talking to Heaven: A Medium's Message of Life After Death.* Signet Books, New York, 1997. ISBN 0-451-19172-2.

Wills, Jo and Ian Robinson. *Bond for Life—Emotions Shared by People and Their Pets.* Willow Creek Press, Octopus Publishing Group, 2000. ISBN 1-57223-397-4.

Grief Support and Resources

Pet Loss Support Hotlines
(All information accurate as of May 27, 2009)

- Argus Institute: Grief Resources, Colorado State University, 970-491-4143, http://www.argusinstitute.colostate.edu/grief.htm

- ASPCA Pet Loss Hotline (24 hours a day/seven days a week), 877-474-3310. The next available counselor will return your call. www.aspca.org

- Chicago VMA, 630-325-1600. Leave voice-mail message and vets and/or staff will return calls between 7 & 9 p.m. Central Standard Time. Long-distance calls will be returned collect. http://www.chicagovma.org/petlosssupport

- Cornell University, 607-253-3932. Pet Loss Support Hotline staffed by veterinary students Tuesdays–Thursdays, 6–9 p.m. Eastern Standard Time. Messages returned. http://www.vet.cornell.edu/public/PetLoss

- Dove Lewis Emergency Animal Hospital Pet Loss Support Services, twenty-four-hour message line, 503-234-2061. Long distance calls will be returned collect. Send emails to grief counselor, Director of Pet Loss Support Services, Enid Traisman, MSW, at etjournl@teleport.com or visit www.dovelewis.org

- FAHF—Florida Animal Health Foundation's Pet Grief Support Hotline, 1-800-789-6196. Veterinary student volunteers from the University of Florida and members of the FAHF board of directors and volunteers will return calls every evening between 7 and 9 p.m. EST, seven days a week. http://www.flahf.org/html/grief_support.htm

- Iams Pet Loss Support Center, toll-free 888-332-7738. Monday–Friday, 8 a.m.–5 p.m. http://www.iams.com/iams/pet-health/pet-loss-support.jsp

- Idaho area—Sandra Brackenridge, MSW, BCD,LSW-P. Former counselor for Louisiana State University School of Veterinary Medicine and current consultant for Idaho Veterinary Medical Association, email: bracsand@isu.edu. Phone 209-282-2546 for pet loss and grief support. No charge except the phone call.

- Iowa State University College of Veterinary Medicine, 888-478-7574. September–April, seven days a week, 6–9 p.m. Central Standard Time. Calls returned by volunteers. http://cvmweb2.cvm.iastate.edu/animal_owners/petloss/default.asp

- Louisiana State University Best Friend Gone Project. To reach a counselor, call Stephanie Johnson at 225-578-9547. http://www.vetmed.lsu.edu/best_friend_gone.htm

- Michigan State University Veterinary Medicine School, 517-432-2696. Staffed by students Tuesday, Wednesday, & Thursday, 6:30–9:30 p.m. Eastern Time. Summer hours Tuesday & Thursday, 6:30–9:30 p.m. http://cvm.msu.edu/alumni-friends/information-for-animal-owners/pet-loss-support

- National Association of Pet Funeral Directors http://www.petresource.com/NAPFD/napfd_member_directory.htm

- Ohio State University Veterinary School Pet Loss and Bereavement Education Program, 614-292-1823. Veterinary students will return calls Mondays, Wednesdays and Fridays, 6:30–9:30 p.m. & Saturdays and Sundays 10 a.m.–4 p.m.Eastern Time. Voice-mail messages will be returned, collect, during operating hours.

- (The) Rainbow Passage—Pet Loss Support and Bereavement Center, Grafton, Wisconsin, 262-376-0340, http://members.tripod.com/~Cheyene/rainbow.html

- Social Work Services at the University of Minnesota's Veterinary Medical Center, 612-624-9372. Open Monday–Friday, 8:00 a.m.–4:30 p.m.

- Tufts University, 508-839-7966. Monday through Friday, 6–9 p.m. Eastern Time. Veterinary students will return voice-mail messages daily, collect, outside Massachusetts. http://www.tufts.edu/vet/petloss

- University of California-Davis, 800-565-1526. Staffed by veterinary students, 6:30–9:30 p.m. Pacific Time. http://www.vetmed.ucdavis.edu/ccah/petloss.cfm

- University of Florida at Gainsville, 352-392-2235, then dial 1 and 5268. Staffed by Florida community volunteers, weekdays, 7–9 p.m. Eastern Time. http://www.vetmed.ufl.edu/patientcare/petlosssupport

- University of Illinois, 877-394-2273 (toll-free). Staffed by veterinary students, Sundays, Tuesdays, and Thursdays, 7–9 p.m. Central Standard Time. http://www.cvm.uiuc.edu/CARE/

- Virginia-Maryland Regional College of Veterinary Medicine, 540-231-8038. Tuesday & Thursday, 6–9 p.m. Eastern Standard Time.

- Washington State University, 1-866-266-8635 or 509-335-5704. email: plhl@vetmed.wsu.edu. Staffed during the semester on Mondays–Thursdays, 7–9 p.m. and Saturdays 1–3 p.m. Pacific Standard Time. http://www.vetmed.wsu.edu/PLHL

No-Kill Animal Shelters

A Comprehensive List
www.saveourstrays.com/no-kill.htm

Animal Ark No-Kill Shelter
www.animalarkshelter.org

Best Friends Animal Society
www.bestfriends.org

Happy Endings
www.happyendings.us/

Hearts United for Animals
www.hua.org

Home for Life Sanctuary
www.homeforlife.org/angelcare.htm

Kitty Angels Cat Shelter
www.kittyangels.org/

No-Kill Advocacy
www.nokilladvocacycenter.org

No-Kill Animal Shelter
www.fluffynet.com/no-kill-shelters/

Operation Kindness
www.operationkindness.org

Purrfect Pals
www.purrfectpals.org

Pets Alive Animal Sanctuary
www.petsalive.com

Save-a-Life No-Kill Shelter
www.save-a-life.org

Other Pet Loss Support Sites

Association for Pet Loss & Bereavement
www.aplb.org

Candle Lighting Ceremony
www.griefonline.com

Chance's Spot
www.chancesspot.org

Honoring the Animals
http://www.honoringtheanimals.org

Horse-Loss Support
www.hoofbeats-in-heaven.com

Pet Loss Phone Support
http://www.petloss.com/phones.htm

Pet Loss Support Page
www.pet-loss.net

Sappy Pet Loss Support Group
sappypetloss@sbcglobal.net

Self-Healing Expressions
www.selfhealingexpressions.com

Purebred Animal Rescue Sites

Cats   purebredcats.org/

Dogs   www.netpets.org/dogs/dogresc/doggrp.html

About the Author

**Author Sid Korpi (right) is shown with her husband
Anthony Kaczor and their trio of West Highland
white terriers (L–R) Keely, Blanche, & Mortimer (now passed).**

Sid Korpi has combined decades of varied professional experience—as an editor, writer, journalist, English teacher, actor, and ordained minister/animal chaplain—with her lifelong devotion to the animal companions who have blessed and shared her life in creating *Good Grief: Finding Peace After Pet Loss.* Surviving a "tsunami of loss" in her own life led to her discovery of spiritual truths that brought her strength and facilitated her heart's healing. She felt compelled to share these things with others who suffer—often in isolation—from the passing on of their very dearest nonhuman friends, their pets.

She lives in Minneapolis, Minnesota, with her husband Anthony Kaczor and their six animal family members: Blanche and Keely (Westies); Giles and Xander (cats); and Atticus and Scout (finches).